Jeff Miller

Florida-Florida State-Miami
Sunshine Shootouts

Jeff Miller

Florida-Florida State-Miami

Sunshine Shootouts

LONGSTREET PRESS
Atlanta, Georgia

Published by
LONGSTREET PRESS, INC.,
a subsidiary of COX NEWSPAPERS, INC.
2140 Newmarket Parkway
Suite 118
Marietta, GA 30067

Printed in the United States of America

1st printing, 1992

Library of Congress Catalog Number: 92-71793

ISBN: 1-56352-043-5

This book was printed by Horowitz/Rae Book Manufacturers, Inc., Fairfield, New Jersey
The type was set in Stone Serif.

Book design by Rhino Graphics
Jacket design by Lee Holbrook

To Frances, who makes it all worthwhile.

A c k n o w l e d g m e n t s

I am indebted to the following sources of information on Florida, Florida State and Miami football: *The Gators* by Tom McEwen (Strode); *Seminoles! The First Forty Years* by Bill McGrotha (Tallahassee Democrat); *Hurricane Watch: University of Miami Football* by Jim Martz (Strode); Gainesville *Sun*; Tallahassee *Democrat*; Miami *Herald*; Tampa *Tribune*; Florida *Times-Union*; and Dallas *Morning News*.

Many thanks to those who helped in research: Bob Pulley, Frank Frangie, Vaughn Mancha, Terry Mamalis, Tom Piero, Wendy Ledis, Mark Wallheiser, and the sports information staffs at Florida, Miami and Florida State.

Table of Contents

F o r e w o r d

I grew up in western Georgia, near Carrollton. Farm kid. Rode a horse to high school. Being a Georgia boy, I always had the feeling that University of Florida folks sort of fancied themselves as the aristocracy. Miami had a hard time establishing its ultimate purpose in athletics for a good long time. And Florida State was a Johnny-Come-Lately, of course.

Not long ago I was sitting here musing through some national rankings and could not find any one of the three Florida schools in the national rankings at the end of a season until 1950. And it kind of surprised me that Miami was the one to show up. They even got as high as No. 11 in '54, and then in '56 they finished sixth. You don't find Florida in the final national polls until '52. And you don't find Florida State until '77.

To me the most significant thing that happened to football in Florida—and I think it was stimulated by Florida State—they had those two huge Gator Bowl wins. They beat Oklahoma in 1964 and they tied Penn State, a game I did, in 1967. Those were two Bill Peterson teams. In those games, Florida State said to the nation, "Hey, we're here."

Then you hit the '80s with Miami and Schnellenberger. In '81, they beat the hell out of Notre Dame, and that was on television—another game I did. That was with Jim Kelly. The best thing that happened to Miami, when Howard decided that he couldn't get along with the way things were going, was Sam Jankovich. Nobody thinks about little Sam. I've known him over a quarter of a century, and everywhere he's gone there's been success in his wake.

Now they've got a guy your Yalie can live with in Dave Maggard. But on the other hand, Maggard's an old shot putter and he loves to win, so I think Miami's going to stay where they are for a long time. I think winning the national championship last year was a surprise. At least it was to me.

As for Florida, there was never a true declaration in Gainesville from the leadership of the university that they felt football was all that important. But I think Florida's best days are immediately in front of them because Spurrier may turn out to be quite a special guy. Winning that first SEC championship will in some ways help them, and I think going back to playing on grass will help them.

But they've got to quit playing Montana State and Indiana State. Too bad Florida and Miami are no longer playing annually, but Florida has, at the moment, a defensible position considering its SEC demands; that's pretty heady stuff. The SEC is full of snake pits. Otherwise, I think there might have been enough pressure put on 'em that they would have had to keep Miami on the schedule.

The damnedest game I ever saw was the Florida-Florida State game in Tallahassee (in 1986, a 17-13 Florida victory). Tim Brant was standing on the sidelines next to a drain, and the water was above his knees. We called it the "bateau bowl."

Last year's Miami-Florida State game has to go in your Top 10. It's a hard sell to your average guy walking the streets because defense played just a major role in it. See, they'll remember the Boston College-Miami game (the "Hail Flutie" game of '84) because of all the scoring. They don't tend to remember a game like last year's. There were times when the defenses were just purely brilliant. They were playing by instinct, not a coached thing. There was a blending of people for a little while that was remarkable.

In the three coaches, you've got three very, very different personalities.

Bobby Bowden—I call him the preacher. He is as good as anybody at recruiting. If he gets Momma in the kitchen, forget it. He is a personality. He accepts the fact that he is a personality and he uses it. He knows he can entertain people, and so he does. But he does it in such a kind and gentle way that it's a pleasure to spend an afternoon with him.

At the same time, he can be a bitch kitty when it comes to kicking a football team into shape and getting them ready to play a ball game. He's a tough little guy. But I think he keeps his young people interested by doing funky things in practice and letting them have a play that they can play with during the week and then using it during the game. A lot of that goofy stuff is going to hurt you more than it's going to help you, but it keeps the kids interested.

Steve Spurrier, on the other hand—let me give you an example from the USFL. This is sort of a second-hand story but not totally. His daddy's a preacher up in Tennessee, and "dadgum it" is about as tough as he's ever going to get. Once in a while, he'll get a little stronger when he gets completely frustrated. But he's a straight-up kind of guy. Anyway, he suggested to his USFL coaching staff that they don't get too involved in this cursing business. Somebody told me, "You've got to go down to the Bandits' locker room. Just go in there, and you'll be startled." So I go in there and the music's playing and the guys are laughing, but I didn't hear one person swear. This is the very quiet, positive influence of this guy. He's a presence.

I've known Dennis Erickson all of his life. His daddy, Pinky, was a high school coach for 31 years in Everett, Washington. He came from Montana State, which made him tough. He coached at my alma mater, Washington State, which is why we threatened to send Jankovich back to Serbia.

I think Dennis has found himself. He is more separate from his people than the other two, maybe because of having been a coach's son. He wants his team's attention, and that's how he gets it. When Paul Bryant used to walk in the room, everybody held their breath. When Frank Leahy walked in, it was the same way. Bud Wilkinson. Darrell Royal. It goes on and on, where guys have kept themselves just a little bit apart. When they do speak to a player, the player feels like he's been anointed. And I think Dennis has sort of taken that position. He's not as buddy-buddy as the other two. But when Dennis walks over to a kid, I bet he gets his full attention.

The one caution I would lay on the Florida schools is don't become too insulated. If you get all satisfied with your situation, it doesn't take much to get you out of sync.

— Keith Jackson, June 1992

It's getting to be commonplace for the three NCAA Division I-A football programs in the state of Florida to make history.

It happened on November 16, 1991, when the top-ranked Florida State Seminoles entertained the second-ranked Miami Hurricanes at Doak Campbell Stadium in Tallahassee. It's rare enough that the top two teams in college football meet during the course of a season, but it had never before happened when both teams came from the same state.

History was again made on January 1, 1992, when Florida, FSU and Miami appeared in three of college football's so-called major bowls—Florida State in the Cotton Bowl, Florida in the Sugar Bowl and Miami in the Orange Bowl. Were it not for Notre Dame's second-half rally against the Gators, the three schools would have added an unprecedented three-game sweep.

The end result of the '91 season was Miami winning its fourth national championship in nine years, Florida State finishing fourth and Florida seventh. Never before had three teams from the same state landed in the top seven in a final poll. In fact, only one other time since the AP poll was begun in 1936 did three teams from the same state finish in the Top 10—1967, with No. 4 Indiana, No. 5 Notre Dame and No. 9 Purdue.

Of course, landmark achievements for this group aren't anything new. In 1987, Miami and Florida State became the first duo from the same state to finish one-two in the final poll. Miami and FSU finished second and third in '88, then

first and third in '89. Looking for the most recent year in which a team from Florida wasn't present in the final Top 10? Go back to 1982.

Florida teams were collectively considered a dormant power for many years but have been awakened. Now, many college football experts go into each season figuring the Gators, Hurricanes and Seminoles to contend for the national championship. Consider that FSU was unbeaten and ranked No. 1 in the nation last year from the preseason until November 16, only to lose to both Miami and Florida. In 1983, Miami opened the season with a 20-3 loss to Florida yet won the rest of its games to win its first national championship. The following year, Florida opened with a 32-20 loss to the 'Canes en route to a 9-1-1 finish that earned the No. 3 ranking in the final poll. The '89 Hurricanes won the national title with one loss, to Florida State.

Florida, a charter member of the Southeastern Conference when the league was formed in 1933, had never finished in first place in the league until 1984 (though the SEC later voted to strip the Gators of their title for breaking NCAA rules). Miami, whose football program began on a "cardboard" campus in the late '20s, was in such pitiful condition on the field and at the ticket office in 1970 that the school considered dropping the sport. The Seminoles, who started playing football only in 1947, soon after the school had gone coeducational, were among the worst college teams in the nation in the early '70s. The FSU program was in such financial disarray that athletic director Clay Stapleton scheduled as many big-name opponents on the road as possible for the purpose of bringing huge checks back to Tallahassee.

Part of the growth of college football in Florida can be traced to the overall growth of the state. It is the fastest growing state in the country and is projected to soon catch Texas as the third most populous state behind California and New York. The combination of population and good weather makes it a fertile ground for developing quality college football prospects. And when all three schools broke the college football color line in the late '60s and early '70s, it allowed a great percentage of the best players in the state to remain at home.

The state also benefited indirectly from one of its mortal enemies, Alabama coach Paul Bryant. How, you may ask, could a coach who compiled a 20-1-1 record against Floridian teams during his 25 seasons at Alabama mean so much to Florida, FSU and Miami? Well, the three breakthrough coaches of college football in the state—Charley Pell at Florida, Bobby Bowden at FSU and Howard Schnellenberger of Miami—all cut their college football teeth under the Bear in some fashion.

Schnellenberger played two years under Bryant at Kentucky and served as a Bryant assistant for five years at Alabama. One of the players that Schnellenberger coached at Alabama was Pell, a lineman who went virtually ignored by college coaches until Bryant found him on Sand Mountain in northeast Alabama. Bowden, while not technically included among "Bear's boys"—the group of coaches that played for or coached under Bryant—was influenced greatly by Bryant. He was reared in Birmingham, about 60 miles from the Alabama campus in Tuscaloosa and began his college football career at Alabama before dropping out to marry his high school sweetheart, Ann Estock. He finished his playing career in Birmingham at Howard College (now Samford University) and began his coaching career at his alma mater. He often traveled to Tuscaloosa and picked up coaching tips from Bryant. The Bear also often steered players who weren't quite good enough to make it with the Tide to Bowden.

Pell's ability to rally fan support and motivate players helped Florida become a Top-10 team. Some critics will say illegal recruiting that took place while Pell was coach made Florida a top

team, but it's impossible to say how far the Gators might have come had no violations occurred.

Bowden, in 1976, took over a downtrodden FSU program that was sadly lacking in funds and facilities. His enthusiasm, down-home charm and innovative offensive strategies built Florida State into one of the nation's best and most entertaining teams. That led to more funding and capital improvements, which in turn brought Florida State up to par with its rivals.

Miami wasn't an entirely broken-down program when Schnellenberger moved across town in 1979 after serving as an assistant coach for the NFL's Miami Dolphins. But his tireless efforts to pump money into the program, bring top talent from across South Florida to Coral Gables and emphasize a pro-style offense made Miami the national power it has continued to be under Jimmy Johnson and Dennis Erickson. By winning four national titles during the past nine seasons, Miami can argue that it has built the premier program in college football.

Granted, each school had some great coaches before Pell, Bowden and Schnellenberger—Dutch Stanley, Bob Woodruff, Ray Graves and Doug Dickey at Florida; Tom Nugent and Bill Peterson at Florida State; Jack Harding, Andy Gustafson and the irrepressible Walt Kichefski at Miami. But Pell, Bowden and Schnellenberger took what others had developed to a higher level.

The most unfortunate aspect of this three-way rivalry is that the Florida-Miami series now lies dormant. UF stopped playing Miami annually after the 1987 season when its yearly Southeastern Conference schedule increased from six to seven games. The schools planned to continue playing on a limited basis—and had scheduled a game for 1992. But when the SEC added Arkansas and South Carolina in 1990, conference scheduling needs were expanded again, and Miami agreed to let Florida out of its commitment. Two of the best teams in the country, rivals for decades, must find a way to get back together even on a limited scale.

What lies ahead in that regard only time will tell. But in the meantime, let's look back at some of the great games and great names that have made football history when Florida, Florida State and Miami have met on the gridiron. Let's recall a few of the most memorable of the Sunshine Shootouts.

J e f f   M i l l e r

Florida-Florida State-Miami

Sunshine Shootouts

Miami vs. Florida
First Bowl Bid for the Gators

The state of football at the University of Florida entering the 1950s is illustrated by an exchange between Coach Bob Woodruff and tackle Curtis King during drills before Woodruff's first season. Woodruff was lecturing on how games were won and lost on the line of scrimmage when he noticed King daydreaming, watching an airplane overhead. Woodruff barked out: "King, where are most football games lost?"

To which the clever King immediately replied, "Why, right here at Florida, Coach."

Right there at Florida, indeed. Oh, there had been some good years early on. In 1911 Florida was undefeated, with a 5-0-1 record, and Coach Charles Bachman compiled a spectacular 16-3 record during the '28 and '29 seasons. But when Raymond "Bear" Wolf departed after the 1949 season, the Gators had compiled only one winning record in the past 14 seasons. And the Gators continued to wallow in mediocrity in Woodruff's early years. They finished 5-5 in 1950, the highlight being a midseason 31-27 victory over previously unbeaten Vanderbilt in Nashville. UF finished with the same break-even record in 1951, ending the year by snapping a three-game losing streak with a 30-21 win at Alabama.

Woodruff, bolstered by the security of five years still remaining on his contract, prepared for the '52 season. He returned starters like fullback Rick Casares, lineman Charlie LaPradd and running backs Buford Long and John "Papa" Hall.

LaPradd returned for his senior season in the best physical condition of his life. He had worked the previous summer in his hometown of St. Augustine and ran on the beach going to and from work every day. One of his summer tasks was to work on a crew clearing five acres of snake-infested palmettos. It took only about five snakes to convince the rest of the crew there were better ways to spend the summer; only LaPradd continued.

The quarterback was expected to be senior Haywood Sullivan, an Alabamian who chose to come to Gainesville because he didn't want to anger factions from Alabama or Auburn by choosing the other school. In addition to being an exceptional quarterback, Sullivan was an accomplished catcher and in the spring played baseball for UF. His future figured to be in baseball rather than football.

The man who provided Miami football with a solid foundation was coach Jack Harding (far right), shown here in a 1952 photo with assistant coach Walt Kichefski and All-American guard Nick Chickillo. (UNIVERSITY OF MIAMI)

With that in mind, a change in major league rules in 1952 had a major effect on Sullivan—and the Gator football team. The major leagues determined that 1952 would be the last year that a young prospect could receive significant bonus money without the team committing to keep that player on the big-league roster for a minimum of two seasons. Without a draft, the richer teams like the New York Yankees and Brooklyn Dodgers were able to sign much of the young talent and stash the excess away in their minor-league systems.

There was also the matter of Sullivan's military obligation. He was advanced in Florida's ROTC program and would be committed to serving a two-year obligation. By the time he got out, the bonus money would go to only the chosen few that teams could commit to their big-league rosters.

Sullivan was offered $75,000 to sign with the Boston Red Sox, only a few years removed from pennant contention in 1948 and '49. He discussed the offer with Woodruff, who drove him to Jacksonville, where they sought input from baseball Hall of Famer Bill Terry. Terry told them it was the chance of a lifetime. Soon after, Sullivan drove home to Dothan, Alabama, and—after narrowing his choices to the Red Sox and Yankees—signed with Boston. A major player on the '52 Gator football team had been removed.

Woodruff decided to move Casares from running back to quarterback, a position he really never felt comfortable playing. Another possibility at the position was junior Doug Dickey, a hometown kid on the UF basketball team who joined the football team at the urging of assistant coach Dave Fuller. Dickey was a safety but had played quarterback in high school. Even without Sullivan, there was enough veteran talent to spark talk of Florida at least challenging for the Southeastern Conference championship. In the 12-team conference only Florida, Auburn and Vanderbilt had not won the title.

The season began with a 33-6 victory over Stetson; Casares threw two touchdown passes, and Dickey returned a punt 43 yards for a touchdown. Then the Gators traveled to Atlanta to face powerful Georgia Tech, coached by Bobby Dodd. Tech's Pepper Rodgers kicked a 17-yard field goal in the closing minutes to beat UF, 17-14.

Woodruff opted to return Casares to his natural position, fullback, and split the quarterbacking chores between Dickey and sophomore Fred Robinson. Florida rebounded by beating The Citadel and Clemson at home before again losing on the road, at Vanderbilt, 20-13. That gave Florida an 0-2 record in SEC games and muted talk of the conference championship finally coming to Gainesville.

The Gators then headed for Jacksonville and their annual meeting with Georgia. Woodruff scored his first victory over the Bulldogs in three tries, 30-0, then beat Auburn in Gainesville, 31-21, to run Florida's record to 5-2. The win over the Tigers had UF contemplating its first winning season since 1944. With it came bowl talk, but the Gators' trip to Tennessee ended the discussions. The Volunteers beat Florida, 26-12, in Knoxville. That left home games against Miami and Kentucky on the schedule.

The University of Miami had already been to bowl games. The Hurricanes had played four times

Rick Casares was Florida's rushing star, carrying for 127 yards on 29 attempts. (UF ARCHIVES)

in Miami at the Palm Festival and the Orange Bowl and made one visit to the Gator Bowl. But in 1952, there was no bowl talk in Coral Gables. Andy Gustafson's team was 4-4, having been held to seven points or less in four games to date. The 'Canes' top player was senior Nick Chickillo, a 220-pound two-way lineman.

With a crowd of 35,000 filling Florida Field, the Gators got the first break of the game in the first quarter when a mishandled snap on a UM punt gave Florida possession at Miami's 44-yard line. The drive culminated in a touchdown when Dickey took the ball into the end zone on a one-yard quarterback sneak. The subsequent PAT kick failed, leaving Florida with a 6-0 lead.

The UF lead increased to 13-0 early in the second quarter when Hall scored on a six-yard run. The drive was kept alive by a fake punt pulled off by Reed Quinn. Casares added a 27-yard field goal to send the Gators to the locker room at halftime with a 16-0 lead.

Florida took the second-half kick-off and moved 82 yards for another touchdown, Long scoring on a five-yard run to increase the UF lead to 23-0. The next Florida score came after Miami quarterback Don James missed Bob Schneidenbach on a pitchout and the Gators' Bull York fell on the fumble at the Miami five. Casares scored from there for a 30-0 lead through three quarters.

Florida's onslaught continued in the fourth quarter. Miami gambled by going on fourth down at its 48-yard line only to have running back Harry Mallios tackled for a one-yard loss by linebacker Steve DeLaTorre. Long

Florida's Kent Stevens (22) is about to be dragged down just short of the goal line. (UF ARCHIVES)

scored on a 13-yard run that, after a failed kick, left the Gators leading 36-0. At that point, the Hurricanes' rushing total was minus-one yard. UM avoided a shutout when James threw a seven-yard touchdown pass to Frank McDonald. This marked the first time Miami had crossed Florida's 40-yard line. But another interception of a UM pass by Arlen Jumper led to Florida's final score, a four-yard run by Sammy Oosterhaudt.

The 'Canes finished with only 17 rushing yards compared to 255 for the Gators. Casares was the rushing star, gaining 129 yards on a school-record 27 carries. Miami mistakes led to four of the Florida touchdowns and the field goal. The 37-point margin of defeat was the worst suffered by a Gustafson team. As the coaches met at midfield after the final gun, Gustafson told Woodruff that the UF players were "hungry."

"I expected to get beat," Gustafson said after the game, "but I didn't think anybody could whip us by such a score."

Miami was on its way to its first losing season since 1948. The Hurricanes returned home, only to lose to North Carolina (34-7) and Georgia (35-13). With eight completions against the Gators, Miami quarterback Don James had moved within one of Jack Hackett's school record of 52 in a season. Recalls James, now a successful coach who guided Washington to a share of the 1991 national championship: "The thing I remember about playing Florida in those years was how big and strong their backs were. Their backs would be considered big even by today's standards."

Florida, on the other hand, was making its first bowl trip ever, to the Gator Bowl to play Tulsa. Such was the rarefied atmosphere in Gainesville over this accomplishment that school president J. Hillis Miller announced that classes would be suspended for the following Wednesday to allow for an extra day of Thanksgiving break.

John "Papa" Hall's six-yard touchdown run gave Florida a 13-0 lead early in the second quarter. (UF ARCHIVES)

"We appreciate the Gator Bowl honoring our team, and we'll try to play a good game," Woodruff said, in officially accepting the invitation. "It will be like a home game, and we are delighted to be playing before homefolk. Our boys worked long and hard and came a long way this year."

The Gators made their first bowl trip a successful one, beating Tulsa, 14-13, to equal the school record for victories with an 8-3 finish.

LaPradd was named All-American, Florida's first since Dale VanSickle in 1928. He recalls Woodruff as a fine coach but very close-mouthed in his days in Gainesville. "I dropped by Tennessee (after Woodruff became the Vols' athletic director) and stopped by and sat down with him and talked in the stadium for about half an hour," LaPradd says. "He talked more with me in that half hour than he did in the four years that I played for him."

Dickey looks back at his contribution as quarterback of the '52 Gators this way: "It was just my job to give it to someone going somewhere. We had a football team that ran the ball, basically. Some days we could really go." The bowl game prevented him from starting the season with Florida's basketball team, and he gave up the sport collegiately.

As for Haywood Sullivan, baseball didn't turn out so bad for him, though he never became a standout pro. He spent seven relatively nondescript seasons with the Boston Red Sox and Kansas City Athletics. Troubled by a bad back, he retired as an active player after the 1963 season. In 1965 at the age of 34, Sullivan was named interim manager of the A's after they got off to a 5-21 start under Mel McGaha. They played little better under Sullivan (54-82) and finished last with an overall record of 59-103. When club owner Charlie Finley was able to land veteran manager Alvin Dark as his next skipper, Sullivan quickly bid farewell to managing and moved into front-office work. He moved on to the Boston Red Sox and at age 35 was named the team's vice-president for player personnel. In 1978 he became a general partner in the ownership of the ball club.

Florida State vs. Miami
The Seminoles Beat Miami For The First Time

The 1905 legislative act that created the all-male University of Florida in Gainesville also created the Florida Female College in Tallahassee. A year later, the school's name was changed to Florida State College for Women. And for close to 40 years, FSCW operated happily within those restrictions.

But an overload of veterans returning from World War II seeking college education created a need for more collegiate opportunities for men in the state. In September 1946, FSCW agreed to accommodate some of the men that UF received. That portion of the school was officially referred to as the Tallahassee Branch of the University of Florida (TBUF).

That prompted a movement that the Tallahassee school go ahead and except applications from males. Despite protests from many connected with the University of Florida, legislation passed on May 7, 1947 created the co-educational Florida State University.

It wasn't long before the subject of athletics, including football, was raised. Florida president John Tigert sent a letter to Florida State president Doak Campbell demanding that: 1. Florida State would agree to compete in only basketball, tennis, swimming, golf and track; 2. all teams would be considered UF junior varsity squads; 3. UF basically had the right to review all Florida State personnel decisions. Florida athletic director Dutch Stanley sent a similar letter to Ed Williamson, the head of Florida State's men's intramurals and the ranking men's athletic official on campus. Campbell and Williamson, the latter a UF grad, refused to acknowledge such concessions, and Florida State continued to work toward fielding a football team in the fall of 1947.

Williamson agreed to coach the team in '47 while still searching for a permanent coach and putting together a schedule. He called one of his old UF colleagues, Stetson coach Don Clemons, and quickly set up home-and-home dates that included FSU's opener on October 18. Suffice it to say the Gators were not prepared to accept Florida State as an equal and would have no part of playing the new team.

* * *

The Seminoles' 1958 season reached landmark status before the first kickoff. A few years earlier, mounting pressure across the state finally forced the University of Florida to add Florida State to its football schedule—though UF made Florida State agree to play the first six games in Gainesville. The series opener was slated as the finale of the '58 season, with the date November 22 circled on many a calendar from Pensacola to Key West.

But Florida State upstaged its own act. It scored its first road victory over a major college football power earlier that season when it returned from Knoxville with a stunning 10-0 win over the tradition-rich Tennessee Vols. FSU took a three-game winning streak to the Orange Bowl on Friday night, November 7, with a chance to earn its first bowl bid against major college competition. Miami was the first so-called "major" college to agree to play the Seminoles. Its agreement with Florida State was made final in November 1950 with the series beginning the following year. In UM's five meetings against Florida State going into the '58 season, the Hurricanes were 5-0. Miami's schedule was top-heavy with late-season games, and the Hurricanes carried a record of 1-4 into the Florida State game.

Miami coach Andy Gustafson tried to shake up

his beleaguered Hurricanes by inserting Bonnie Yarbrough, a fan favorite, in at quarterback. The home crowd cheered wildly when the usually conservative UM team opened up with Yarbrough throwing a 13-yard pass to Joe Plevel. The 'Canes' first possession featured eight passes and four runs. Miami reached the Florida State 27-yard line, where four consecutive incompletions ended the drive.

Gustafson brought George MacIntyre, his former starting quarterback, into the game midway through the first quarter only to have the move backfire. Florida State's Joe Majors intercepted a pass thrown by MacIntyre intended for end Jon Mirilovich and raced 45 yards for a touchdown.

The Hurricanes charged back with Yarbrough again at quarterback, the drive highlighted by a 26-yard run by fullback Harry Deiderich that gave Miami a first down at the FSU 7. Three plays later, Plevel followed the blocking of lineman Byron Blasko to score with 2:18 to play in the first quarter to pull Miami within 7-6. Gustafson then decided to go for two points and the lead, but

While Florida State's Joe Majors passed for 27 yards while splitting the quarterbacking chores with Vic Prinzi, his biggest contribution to the Seminoles' win over Miami probably was the interception he returned for a 45-yard touchdown. (FLORIDA STATE UNIVERSITY)

fullback Frank Bouffard fumbled when he tried to jam through the left side of the line.

The Seminoles' precision worked against them with a fake that was so good an official called back what would have been another first-half touchdown. On the play, quarterback Vic Prinzi faked a hand-off to the tailback into the line and hid the ball on his hip for a quarterback keeper. So while Prinzi scampered untouched into the end zone and stood there holding the ball over his head, the play had been whistled dead by official Pete Williams.

"Williams called time and came over to the sidelines," recalls Tom Nugent, coach of Florida State at the time. "The crowd was screaming and yelling. He said to me, 'I've never had this happen. I've always lived in fear that it would happen. I lost the ball. I blew the ball dead, and according to the rules that fine touchdown you got has got to come back.'"

Nugent says his reply to Williams was, "They all think I'm screaming at you, but all I have to say is this: I've made a lot of mistakes in my life, and I've always asked people to forgive me. You just made a hell of a mistake, and I forgive you."

Florida State punted the ball back to Miami but quickly regained possession when Deiderich fumbled at the 'Canes' 13-yard line. Three plays later with the ball at the eight, Prinzi faked a hand-off to running back Fred Pickard and dropped back, looking for receiver Tony Romeo in the end zone. Romeo got his hands on the pass but couldn't make the catch when he was sandwiched by a pair of Miami defenders. But Pickard, following the fake into the line, ran out his pattern by jogging into the end zone. Romeo's deflection landed right in Pickard's hands for a touchdown. With 9:53 to play in the half, John Sheppard kicked Florida State to a 14-6 lead.

Again, Miami mounted a furious counterattack. Again, the 'Canes came up short. Behind the running of second-teamers Theron Mitchell and Neil Fleming, UM reached Florida State's 12 with a first down. Fleming bulled his way to the six, but a 15-yard penalty for illegal use of hands forced the Hurricanes into second-and-19 at the Florida State 24. On fourth down, a Yarbrough pass was intercepted by Seminoles linebacker Ramon Rogers.

Gustafson continued to try to coach his team out of its malaise. He began the second half with his third-string unit, quarterbacked by junior Fran Curci. This group used a ground attack to reach Florida State's 19, whereupon Gustafson left in Curci but replaced the rest of the offense with his first-teamers. The Orange Bowl crowd responded with cries of disapproval. Miami pushed forward to the FSU four, but Curci was forced into making a bad pitch because of pressure from Florida State defensive end Pete Fleming. The ball, instead of heading into the hands of Miami's Plevel, fell to the ground and was recovered by the Seminoles' Bobby Renn.

A subsequent fumble by Pickard, recovered by UM tackle Charlie Diamond, gave the Hurricanes another chance to score. But after reaching the Seminoles' six, Curci was sacked for a five-yard loss before throwing an interception. Florida State began pushing downfield as the quarter ended, and in the fourth quarter converted the UM turnover into a 22-yard field goal by Sheppard for a 17-6 lead.

Gustafson continued his shuffling, sending Yarbrough back in. This time, Miami's frustrations reached new levels. The 'Canes were stopped at the Florida State one, where Deiderich was tackled on fourth down. Later in the period, the Hurricanes advanced to FSU's 28 but could move no farther, and time ran out to give FSU its first win over Miami.

The final statistics were confounding for Miami and its fans. The Hurricanes had outgained the Seminoles in rushing (192 yards to 133), in passing (117 to 44) and had totaled 20 first downs to Florida State's nine. But Miami had suffered six devastating turnovers; each of UM's three quarterbacks had thrown interceptions.

Gustafson didn't appear to talk to a single soul as he made his way from the field to the

Florida State coach Tom Nugent tried to force the issue of Florida having to play FSU by bringing it up at speaking engagements all across the state. (FLORIDA STATE UNIVERSITY)

locker room. "I felt like the team gave the effort," he told reporters afterward. "But we just don't do the right things at the right times. We try to throw; it's intercepted. We try to run; we fumble or we just plain don't make the yardage. I just don't know."

Conversely, Nugent received a congratulatory smooch from assistant coach Lee Corso as the clock ran out, then received a ride to midfield courtesy of three Florida State linemen. In the locker room, he told reporters this wasn't FSU's greatest victory—arguably, Tennessee was bigger considering the competition—but it was obvious beating Miami for the first time meant a great deal to Nugent. After finishing with reporters, he hopped from player to player, offering emotional congratulations—and a reminder of what lay ahead.

"We've got one more game to go," he said, not referring to Florida by name. "We're not supposed to win this one, so let's not talk about it."

Many years later, when most people had forgotten the score of the Miami game or that Miami had accomplished so little on its marches deep in Florida State territory, Prinzi—serving as color commentator on the FSU radio network—received a startling reminder of that night in the Orange Bowl.

"I'm sitting in the radio booth down there (in Miami) before kickoff time, and in comes this guy who introduces himself—Pete Williams," Prinzi says. "He came up to apologize. He said, 'You know, it's been almost 30 years.' And I said, 'It's been 30 years exactly.'"

*   *   *

Football under Tom Nugent was part sport, part entertainment. The father of nine, Nugent brought a different perspective to the game.

"He was very interesting and very different for back in that period of time," recalls Prinzi. "Tom was what I would call a psychological coach. He played strictly on your psyche.

"I couldn't wait to get to practice, not so much for the practice but to find out what the hell we were going to talk about during our practice meeting. It would range anywhere from talking about football to talking about show business."

Nugent left Florida State after the '58 season to become coach at Maryland. There, he was tested as a man much more than he was as a coach when he signed the first black to play football for the Terrapins.

The player's name was Darryl Hill, and he grew up only about six miles from the Maryland campus. Nugent saw him as a great wide receiver; many Terrapin fans saw him as an embarrassment to the school. Hill was booed when he ran onto the field for his first game at Maryland. Speaking to a school alumni group the following spring, Nugent was introduced bluntly as "the nigger lover."

"I treated the whole audience as if they were my enemies," Nugent recalls. "They could literally shove the job. I said a lot of things I shouldn't have."

Nugent almost returned to Florida as the coach of the Hurricanes after Gustafson retired following the 1963 season. He says a UM official told him he was the first choice of the school president but that official support had to be extended to longtime assistant Walt Kichefski. As it turned out, UM instead hired Charlie Tate. Nugent got out of coaching and settled in Miami—the site of one of his greatest early victories with the Seminoles.

Florida State vs. Florida
A Rivalry Is Born

For the Florida State Seminoles, the entire 1958 season—even their first victory over the Miami Hurricanes—was simply a prelude to the first meeting ever with the Florida Gators. How much did this game mean to the Seminoles? Florida State quarterback Vic Prinzi received a medical redshirt in 1957 after playing his first three seasons for the Seminoles. His thought at the time was: "Thank God I got hurt because now I'm going to get a chance to play the Gators."

Said FSU's Fred Pickard: "We were above and beyond ready to play. The whole town (Tallahassee) went wild. They carried us off for a couple of days to get away from everything."

The same enthusiasm was not shared by FSU's neighbors to the southeast. As a whole, the Gators really didn't want any part of Florida State. A victory would mean nothing, while a defeat would be the ultimate embarrassment to the program.

Florida coach Bob Woodruff, in fact, was quoted as saying Florida would never play Florida State as long as he was UF's athletic director. This he later denied, claiming that dialogue for beginning the series had begun as early as 1949. He said he actually wanted to play the Seminoles soon after arriving in Gainesville in 1950 but was blocked by school president J. Hillis Miller. It was Woodruff's contention that Miller didn't want to see Florida State placed on the same level as Florida in any area, that he was worried that FSU wanted to challenge Florida in other areas—especially in developing a medical school.

"They had always used as their claim, 'We don't play that sister school up there because they don't always play the same kind of schools consistently,'" FSU coach Tom Nugent recalls. So Nugent added the likes of Miami, Auburn, Georgia, Georgia Tech, Kentucky and Tennessee to FSU schedules. "I went preaching around the state that it (playing Florida) was the only reason I wanted to stay at Florida State. 'I'm going to make sure Florida plays us.' It got us a lot of speaking engagements."

In April 1955, state senator Nick Connor introduced legislation urging the schools to begin playing against each other in football. On April 26, the bill was defeated by a vote of 19 to 15. Years later, it was reported that Governor LeRoy Collins was trying to persuade

Florida State quarterback Vic Prinzi actually rejoiced when an injury forced him to sit out the 1957 season after playing for the previous three years; that meant he would be back for his senior season in 1958, when the Seminoles would get to play the Gators for the first time (FLORIDA STATE UNIVERSITY)

Florida president Wayne Reitz to add Florida State to the Gators' football schedule. Reitz responded to that report in a letter printed by the Gainesville Sun: "Gov. Collins felt this was not an appropriate function of the state legislature. I agree. But he made no request of me." The schools eventually agreed to an annual series starting with the 1958 game at Florida Field.

The '58 season had been a disappointment to Bob Woodruff and the Gators. One of the biggest blows came before the season, when running back Bernie Parrish signed a professional contract with baseball's Cincinnati Reds. After beginning Southeastern Conference play with an opening-day win over Tulane, UF lost to Mississippi State, tied Vanderbilt, then lost to LSU and Auburn. With a 4-3-1 record, Florida somehow earned enough respect to be rated 12th in the country going into the FSU game. They were also talking to representatives of the Orange and Gator bowls. An invitation to play in Miami on New Year's Day would mark Florida's entry into the "major" bowl games. But it would require not only the expected Florida victory over Florida State but also for No. 10 Syracuse (7-1) to lose to West Virginia.

The Gators' top players included All-America tackle Val Heckman and All-SEC end Don Fleming. The backfield was a rather diminutive collection, led by 142-pound senior quarterback Jimmy Dunn from Tampa.

＊　　＊　　＊

Jimmy Dunn had been a quarterback at Hillsborough High School. As a senior in the spring of 1955, he had written a letter to Coach Woodruff, asking for consideration for a scholarship to play for the Gators. But the best offer Dunn had going into the Florida high school all-star game that summer in Gainesville was from the Florida State Seminoles. Dunn had been given a one-year commitment from Coach Nugent.

In the all-star game, Dunn passed for two touchdowns to lead the South to a 14-0 victory. After the game, Woodruff dispatched assistant coach Hank Foldberg to go see Dunn and invite him to play for the Gators. The invitation was offered and accepted only moments before FSU assistant Vaughn Mancha reached Dunn.

"I went across the field to shake his hand and say, 'Boy, am I glad you're coming to Florida State,'" Nugent recalls. "He said, 'Coach, I'm going to Florida.'"

Nugent said he would immediately change his deal to four years, to match UF's offer. Nugent says Dunn responded by saying, "I kind of like Florida now." Woodruff had landed a player whom he later said "is pound for pound the best football player I ever coached." Dunn came off the bench during the third game of his sophomore season in 1956 and earned the starting position for the balance of his UF career.

＊　　＊　　＊

The Florida Field crowd of 43,000 included about 10,000 Florida State faithful. But shortly before kickoff, there was still one thing missing: the Florida State Seminoles.

"We went to a nearby parking lot and did our pregame warmups there," Nugent says. "A rumor went through the stadium like wildfire that we had a bus accident and Florida State wasn't going to show up." When team captains Bobby Renn and Vic Prinzi walked to the center of the field for the coin toss, they were the only FSU players in the stadium.

Once the Seminoles entered Florida Field, it was clear they were keyed up and ready to play the biggest game in school history. Says Prinzi: "We felt pretty optimistic going in. Believe me, our guns were loaded."

Florida State students were more than ready for the Seminoles' first meeting with the Gators in 1958. (FLORIDA STATE UNIVERSITY)

Florida State won the toss and elected to receive. Renn and Jack Espenship jogged out toward the goal line to prepare for Florida's kickoff. The kick came floating down toward Espenship, who caught the football but suddenly handed it off to Renn. The result, with the help of blocking by tackle Bob Swoszowski, was a 78-yard return to Florida's 15-yard line.

The play was more than some spectators could stand. In the press box, St. Petersburg *Times* sports editor Bill Beck yelled, "Stop him!"

Renn was tackled by Jimmy Dunn, who had to skirt through three FSU defenders to get to Renn. Renn later told Bill McGrotha of the Tallahassee *Democrat:* "I had wanted Swoszowski to commit himself—lunge right or left—or fall down. Anything to foul up Dunn."

After waiting so many years to get a shot at the Gators, Florida State prepared for its first play from scrimmage against UF only 15 yards from the Gators' end zone. It took five plays to cover the distance. Fred Pickard pushed over the goal line from the one, and Florida State took a very early 7-0 lead.

The next time FSU got the ball, it stalled and was forced to punt from its 19. On the third-down play, Renn was supposed to execute a quick-kick, but Prinzi noticed that there were two UF defenders unaccounted for in FSU's blocking. Thinking that the formation looked like it could result in a blocked punt, Prinzi took the snap himself, but as he tried to run for the first down, he aggravated an injury to his thigh. He did not return to the game and was replaced at quarterback by Joe Majors. On fourth down, a high snap from center allowed Florida's Dave Hudson enough time to break through the line and block Renn's punt. Hudson picked up the ball

Taking off on possibly the most famous run in Florida State history, Bobby Renn (20) charges down the left sideline on the opening kickoff of the first Florida-Florida State game for 78 yards to the Gators' 15-yard line. Thats UF's Bob Milby in pursuit.
(FLORIDA STATE UNIVERSITY)

Florida's Dave Hudson has position to make the interception in front of the Seminoles' Bobby Renn. (UF ARCHIVES)

at the four and made the short sprint into the end zone. Billy Booker kicked the extra point to tie the score at 7-7 with 6:59 remaining in the first quarter.

Hudson wasn't finished harassing the Seminoles. FSU's third possession of the game began at the Florida 48 following a short punt by the Gators' Bobby Joe Green. The Seminoles faced third-and-15 when Prinzi was intercepted at the three by Hudson. Florida then proceeded on an 89-yard drive that took 16 plays. Dunn scored the go-ahead touchdown by scooting the final nine yards into the end zone on a third-down play. Halfback Doug Partin provided the key block that allowed Dunn to run into the left side of the end zone. With Booker's PAT, the Gators had built a 14-7 lead with 3:35 to play in the first half.

Florida State still couldn't generate any offense. On the Seminoles' second play of their next drive, Florida end Nick Arfaras forced a fumble by Majors and recovered the ball at the Seminoles' 20. Three plays later, the Gators were on FSU's 12 with less than a minute to play in the half. On fourth-and-two, Woodruff elected to try for the touchdown. Dunn rolled out to the right to pass, then ducked back to the left for the touchdown run and—with another PAT—a 21-7 lead.

FSU's offensive woes continued throughout the second half. The Seminoles mounted one charge in the fourth period when they advanced to Florida's 21, but then they lost the ball on downs. That was as close as they would get.

Jimmy Dunn—he who had planned to play his college football at Florida State—was named the most valuable player in the first Florida-FSU game.

The Seminoles actually outgained the Gators in total offense, 286 yards to 238. But Florida State was doomed by mistakes, committing four turnovers.

Was Woodruff relieved to win the game? He downplays the significance of the victory: "Not any more than any other game. All games are very important to Florida."

Nugent was upbeat after the loss. "We have no excuses or alibis," he told reporters at the time. "We played well; Florida played better."

The victory didn't sufficiently impress onlookers from the Orange Bowl Classic, though. With Syracuse beating West Virginia, 15-12, the folks from Miami decided to invite Syracuse to play No. 4 Oklahoma. And Florida actually moved down in the rankings with the victory, dropping to No. 14. One of the teams that passed UF in the ratings (Mississippi) didn't even play a game that weekend. And the Gator Bowl wasn't prepared to commit to Florida. Its adjusted list included UF along with Mississippi, Georgia Tech, Pitt and South Carolina.

UF beat the Miami Hurricanes, 12-9, in Jacksonville to finish the regular season at 6-3-1 and ranked 14th in the final AP poll. That earned Florida a return trip to Jacksonville to play in the Gator Bowl against Mississippi, which held Florida to its lowest point total of the season for a 7-3 victory.

FSU's Carl Meyer dives in vain as Jimmy Dunn scores a Florida touchdown. (UF ARCHIVES)

Jimmy Dunn receives the game's most valuable player award from members of UF's junior class. (UF ARCHIVES)

Florida State (7-3) also landed a bowl bid, to the Bluegrass Bowl to play No. 17 Oklahoma State (7-3). Though this was FSU's third invitation to a bowl, it was the first in which it played major college competition. The result was a 15-6 loss to the Cowboys.

Dunn finished his Florida career with a record of 18-9-3 as a starter. As a senior, he averaged 37.9 yards of total offense, which John Reaves would eventually top by, oh, only about 7 1/2 times that figure. But Dunn will never lose his place in Florida history for what he accomplished in leading the Gators to their first win over the upstart Seminoles.

"When FSU got seven points ahead of us, it kind of woke us up," Dunn says.

What followed was a Florida comeback that constituted the first chapter in a football rivalry so long in the making.

Miami vs. Florida State
Gus

When Jack Harding stepped down as Miami coach following the 1947 season, his hand-picked successor was Andy Gustafson, his old running mate at Pitt. Gustafson weaned Miami off Harding's single-wing offense and introduced what he called the Miami Drive Series. It was an option offense that was a forerunner of the popular Wishbone.

Gustafson's early UM teams were relatively harmless, finishing 4-6 in 1948, 6-3 in 1949. His Hurricanes first gained national attention in 1950 with a 20-14 victory at Purdue. The previous week, the Boilermakers were the toast of the nation for ending Notre Dame's 39-game unbeaten streak and knocking the Fighting Irish from the No. 1 position in the poll. That landed Purdue at No. 9 in the next ranking, with one first-place vote. Then along came the 'Canes and stunned Purdue. They were mobbed when they landed at the airport in Miami. At 3-0, they pushed into the poll the following week at No. 14 with 14 first-place votes. The school's yearbook, the *Ibis,* noted that with the victory over Purdue "the nation finally realized that there is a university down on the tip of Florida."

Miami ran its record to 6-0, reaching No. 9 in the poll, before tying Louisville, 13-13. But subsequent victories over Florida, Iowa and Missouri kept the Hurricanes undefeated with a regular-season record of 9-0-1, the most regular-season wins in school history. This somehow earned Miami only the No. 15 spot in the final AP poll, which at the time was taken at the end of the regular season. Among those rated above the Hurricanes were three Big Ten teams that were trailing league-leader Michigan State—No. 9 Michigan (5-3-1), No. 13 Illinois (7-2) and No. 14 Ohio State (6-3). The irony was that Miami had beaten two Big Ten schools, including the road win over Purdue. The record was good enough, though, to earn the Hurricanes the chance to play in their own stadium on New Year's Day 1951 against Clemson in the Orange Bowl Classic. But Miami's opportunity to show it should be included among the elite teams in the country ended with a 15-14 loss to No. 9 Clemson (which finished 9-0-1).

Gustafson went on to produce other bowl-quality teams in the mid-fifties, but Miami was kept home by NCAA probation. Four games into the 1954 season, the NCAA punished Miami for paying for recruits' campus visits in violation of NCAA rules. The probation was not lifted until January 1957.

*   *   *

In 1959, UM had played only one game before traveling to Tallahassee, opening at home with a 26-7 victory over Tulane of the Southeastern Conference. The Hurricanes were quarterbacked by Fran Curci, a senior nicknamed "The Little General" and an All-America candidate.

"He was like on a pedestal," Curci says of Gustafson. "You did everything to avoid not even seeing him in the office. He was like a general. He had such a commanding voice. But he was like the most friendly guy in the world. He was almost too nice of a guy.

"But, you see, I knew him when he was like that. You can talk to some people before me (who knew Gustafson before he gave up drinking), and they're going to tell you about a different Gus."

With the loss of Tom Nugent to Maryland, the Seminoles brought in Perry Moss as their new coach. FSU was Moss's first trial as a head coach on the college level, having served as an assistant at Illinois, Washington, LSU, Miami and Wisconsin. In putting

G U S

*

20   *Andy Gustafson compiled a 93-65-3 record in 16 seasons as Miami coach before resigning after the 1963 season.* (MIAMI HERALD)

Much of Perry Moss's only year as Florida State coach was spent beneath the cloud of a rumor that he would leave at year's end to coach in the Canadian Football League, which is exactly what happened.
(FLORIDA STATE UNIVERSITY)

Fred Pickard was stopped just short of the goal line on a two-point attempt that would have given Florida State a one-point win over Miami.
(FLORIDA STATE)

over The Citadel. Next would be a visit from the Miami Hurricanes.

*   *   *

Twice during the first half the Hurricanes bungled what appeared to be excellent chances to score, fumbling the ball away at Florida State's 14- and 25-yard lines. But Miami finally put the first points on the board with 7:27 to play in the first half. Curci threw nine yards to Bob Rosbaugh for a touchdown, followed by Al Dangel's PAT for a 7-0 lead. Miami never crossed Florida State's 35 the rest of the evening.

The third quarter ended up being a battle of field position, with neither team making a serious bid to score. This tug o' war continued well on into the fourth quarter. With eight minutes to play, Florida State embarked on a 52-yard drive. Quarterback Joe Majors passed to Fred Pickard for 14 yards to the UM 38, then seven yards to Bud White-head. Jack Espenship ran for four yards and a first down at the 27.

Facing a critical fourth-and-four at the 21, Majors found Jim Daniel for an eight-yard pass to the 13. Espenship carried for four yards on first down to the nine and picked up another yard on the next play. On third-and-five at the eight, Pickard ran off left tackle into the end zone with 2:56 to play. Moss elected to go for two, as many of the 18,600 in attendance at Doak Campbell Stadium yelled, "Two! Two!"

Pickard lined up on the right side and went in motion to the left. He took a pitchout from Majors and charged into the line. He was hit first by tackle Jim Crawford, then by defensive backs Fran Curci and Rosbaugh. Curci was knocked out on the play and left the game. The officials spotted Pickard down

together his staff, he hired Don James, the former Miami quarterback.

The Seminoles opened the season under Moss with a 22-20 loss to Wake Forest, with Norm Snead rallying the Demon Deacons from behind in the second half. In the next game, Florida State cruised to a 47-6 victory six inches short of the goal line. Miami still held a one-point lead and needed to kill fewer than three minutes to win.

FSU almost recovered Bill Brown's onside kick. But the Hurricanes couldn't maintain possession and punted with 29 seconds to play. FSU took over at its 36 and moved to the Miami 46 with two seconds left. On the final play, Majors set sail a long pass intended for Tony Romeo, but UM's Theron Mitchell intercepted the ball at Miami's five to end the game.

"Six inches," Moss told reporters after the game. "Sometimes that's a long, long way. If I had it to do over again, I'd try for two again." In the other dressing room, Gustafson was terse in victory: "No, I'm not satisfied with our performance. But it's still a win."

Curci, who finished with a team-high 61 rushing yards to go with his 54 passing yards, recalls his contribution in what proved to be the game-saving tackle: "Probably the reason I played was because I could play offense and defense. I wasn't big enough to tackle anybody, but I could throw my body at somebody. It was a sweep play. I had a feeling they were going to cut up into the hole. So once he (Pickard) cut up, I just threw my body in front of his legs. He hit me in the head, and he went down about the six-inch line. He knew I got him."

Says Pickard: "I don't want to talk about that one. A lot of other people did (think he scored), but the officials didn't. Fell right on top of the line. I didn't think there was any question about it. Everytime I ran the football after that, in my mind, I hit the goalposts in the back of the end zone. It really cost us a lot that year."

Pickard notes that Moss took the UM win exceptionally hard because he had coached there. "It just killed him because he hated Miami," Pickard says.

The following day, Moss declared that after watching the game films he thought Pickard had made it into the end zone. "It was close enough that it was a judgment call," he said. Response from Coral Gables was predictable, with Gustafson maintaining that the officials' call was the correct one. "We've got the same movies as FSU," he said gruffly.

Moss later told the Tallahassee *Democrat's* Bill McGrotha: "We should have—and could have—won it. And it would have put a different outlook on everything."

During the season, Moss accepted an offer to leave at year's end to coach the Montreal Alouettes of the Canadian Football League. This was decades before the advent of cable or the use of the CFL as a bargaining chip by NFL players. The CFL was not the place to be in 1959. The gamble for Moss, who tripled his $14,000 FSU salary, was that a modicum of success could propel him back to the United States into a much higher paying job than the one he left behind at FSU.

The Tallahassee *Democrat* reported Moss's intentions the day before Florida State, at 3-4, met William & Mary in its Homecoming game. In one of the stranger Homecoming sights you'll want to see, the head coach was hanged in effigy as the Seminoles lethargically lost, 9-0. FSU went on to lose in their return to Gainesville, 18-8, and finished with a 33-0 drubbing of Tampa at home.

"I thought Moss was a great guy," Pickard says, "other than he was really, really emotional. He had a tough, tough time handling people. He was extremely hard on me to start with. But then he treated me unbelievably good. I thought he was one of the smartest football people I'd ever been around."

Moss did slingshot back to the United States, landing an assistant's job with the Green Bay Packers. But what followed was a series of pit stops in which Moss apparently never found what he was looking for as he crisscrossed the various levels of football—the NFL, college, CFL, World Football League, United States Football League, Arena Football League.

As for leaving Florida State as quickly as he did, Moss later said, "I should have stayed. I believe we could have had great success. FSU was on the verge. I regret leaving. Fate, or whatever, changes your whole life."

＊　＊　＊

The Hurricanes moved on to Baton Rouge and a date with the LSU Tigers, defending national champions and ranked No. 1 in the country. It would take a lot more than stopping a two-point run six inches short of the goal line to beat the Bengals. A lot more the Hurricanes didn't have; they failed to reach the end zone and lost, 27-3. Miami then set sail on a choppy season. A victory over South Carolina in early November vaulted the 'Canes into the Top 20 at No. 18. Miami then met Michigan State, ranked 11th with one of the AP poll's first-place votes, and outlasted the Spartans, 18-13. That pushed Miami to No. 12 in the poll—with five first-place votes of its own—and a 6-3 record going into the final regular-season game against the Florida Gators in Jacksonville. A victory would clinch a bid in the Orange Bowl Classic. Instead, the Hurricanes lost, 23-14, and sat home during the holiday season.

But the 6-4 season still managed to wash away the taste of the previous year's 2-8 finish. There was renewed hope with the signing of a highly-touted quarterback prospect from Key West named George Mira, who would become eligible to play for the varsity in 1961.

Gustafson, beginning with Mira's sophomore year, landed consecutive bowl bids the next two seasons. The '61 Hurricanes finished 7-3 and went to Philadelphia to play in the Liberty Bowl, where they lost to Syracuse, 15-14. In '62, Miami again finished 7-3, sweeping Florida State and Florida, and was invited to play in New York's Gotham Bowl against the Nebraska Cornhuskers. Under horrifically cold conditions, Miami fell, 36-34.

During the season, Gustafson made the commitment to remain on as coach for one more year—through Mira's senior season. But a year that expected to bring such promise, with Mira predicting a national championship, instead only brought the curtain down on Gustafson's storied career with the blight of a 3-7 finish. UM was caught flatfooted in the opener and was drubbed by FSU, 24-0. And after recovering with consecutive shutouts of Purdue and Tulane, Miami plummeted with six losses over the final seven

games. The finale was against No. 7 Alabama, coming into the Orange Bowl with a 7-1 record. The 'Canes fought gamely, only to lose, 17-12.

Gustafson remained on as athletic director through 1968. His 93 victories as UM coach through 16 seasons remains the most for a Hurricanes coach. He died in 1975 at the age of 79 and was inducted into the College Football Hall of Fame 10 years later.

Miami vs. Florida
Woodruff's Parting Shot

Bob Woodruff looks back on the day that he walked to the center of the Gator Bowl turf in Jacksonville after his Gators stunned Miami, a tear in his eye according to eyewitnesses, and insists he wasn't certain that would be his final game as head coach at Florida. "You never know in advance what some board's going to do," he says.

But everyone in and around the Florida football program as the 1959 season drew to a close was sure. Bob Woodruff was out as coach of the Gators after 10 seasons. All that remained was the technicality of the Board of Regents making it official following the season.

The Miami Hurricanes could have cared less. Coming in with a 6-3 record, they knew that a victory over the Gators would earn UM its first crosstown trip to the Orange Bowl in nine seasons. It would mean the Hurricanes' first bowl trip, period, since the '51 team beat Clemson at the Gator Bowl. The '59 team, dominated by underclassmen and guided by senior quarterback Fran Curci, was playing surprisingly well. Georgia had been considered the favorite to play Missouri in the Orange Bowl until the 'Canes upset Michigan State the previous week. Suddenly, it was

Miami's bid to lose, and Coach Andy Gustafson was being mentioned as a viable candidate for national Coach of the Year.

Miami, a three-point favorite and out to end a two-game losing streak in the series, had everything to gain; Florida had virtually nothing to gain. But the 25,000 people who watched the game (about 4,000 Hurricanes fans made the trip from Miami) saw the Hurricanes' season go up in flames. Georgia accepted the $175,000 Orange Bowl bid; Miami went nowhere. And it was Woodruff, who had flung his hat down the sideline as time expired, who was triumphantly carried to midfield by his players.

*   *   *

Woodruff was an assistant under Gustafson, though only on a temporary basis, when the saga of his tenure at Florida began to unfold. This was December 1949, when Woodruff was the 34-year-old coach of the Baylor Bears. A Tennessee graduate, he had been an assistant at Army and Georgia Tech before trying to rebuild the Bears in Waco. He was assisting Gustafson, who was coaching the

South team at the North-South Shrine Game in Miami, when he received a call from Florida people, asking him to come up to Gainesville and interview. The Gators were looking for a successor to the retiring "Bear" Wolf.

Florida had not compiled a winning season in 14 years of Southeastern Conference play. Wolf's four seasons had seen Florida go 2-17-2 in the SEC and finish no higher than 10th place in the 12-team conference. Woodruff realized some changes would have to take place to transform the Gators into a team that could compete with Tennessee, Georgia Tech and the SEC's other upper-division schools. UF simply didn't have the facilities or the financial commitment. That began to change quickly, in part because of a meeting on M. M. Parrish's back porch in Gainesville. A group of influential businessmen who were Florida fans established Gator Boosters. The organization helped Florida improve its fortunes throughout the '50s, '60s and '70s and— infused with the enthusiasm brought about by Charley Pell's hiring in 1978—propelled the leap into the top five of the nation in the early '80s. Woodruff also decided the Gators didn't need to be playing home games everywhere from Miami to Jacksonville. He anchored home games in Gainesville, a move that brought about the expansion of Florida Field. "Our student body would get the team

for a normal number of games," Woodruff says. "It paid off because more and more seats have been added."

With more seats came better players and the '52 team that earned UF's first bowl bid by going to the Gator Bowl. But Florida never finished any higher than third in the conference throughout the mid '50s. The '58 team was a disappointment despite earning the school's second bowl trip, a return to Jacksonville to face Johnny Vaught's Ole Miss Rebels. The '58 Gators gave up an average of only 9.1 points during the regular season— never more than 14 in any game—yet were never in the SEC race. Consider a four-game conference stretch during which Florida tied

Bob Woodruff went into the final game of the 1959 season needing a victory over Miami at the Gator Bowl to clinch a fourth consecutive winning season for Florida. (UF ARCHIVES)

Florida running back Jon MacBeth (left) evades Miami's Jack Novak (55). (UF ARCHIVES)

Dave Hudson (87) leaps above Miami's Doug Davis (45) to make a catch. (UF ARCHIVES)

Vanderbilt, 6-6, then lost to LSU, 10-7, to Auburn, 6-5, and edged Georgia, 7-6.

The '59 season got off to a good start with consecutive victories over Tulane, Mississippi State and Virginia. Next came Rice; Woodruff played for the tie . . . and got one, 13-13. After the game, he was quoted as saying words that may have contributed to his downfall in

Gainesville: "I gamble to win, but I'll never gamble to lose." A loss the following week to an 0-2-1 Vanderbilt team started Florida on a four-game losing streak (all SEC games) in which the Gators were outscored by a combined 49-16. An 18-8 victory over Florida State in the second year of the schools' rivalry did little to appease Gator fans heading into the season finale against Miami.

*　　*　　*

It didn't take the Miami Hurricanes long to realize something was wrong when they trotted onto the field to play the Gators on a 52-degree day in Jacksonville. The Hurricanes had brought their white road uniforms, but the Gators, too, were wearing white. Recalls Miami quarterback Fran Curci: "I went to Andy Gustafson and said that since we were kind of a passing team, we should go out and get some high school jerseys, go down and buy some at a sporting goods store. He said, 'Forget it. Just concentrate on the game.' He was so pissed."

Florida was quarterbacked by Dick Allen, a 26-year-old former GI whom Woodruff had convinced to return to the team. Allen was the No. 1 quarterback in 1956, before he went into the service, though his 56 attempts that season had resulted in 17 completions and 10 interceptions. He came into the '59 Miami game having a nondescript season, hitting only 22 of 52 passes for 411 yards. It was apparent on Florida's first drive, though, that Allen had the touch. His passing moved the Gators to Miami's 18-yard line, but his field goal attempt fell short of the goalposts.

Miami took over, and a dismal afternoon for the 'Canes quarterback was about to begin. Curci led UM to Florida's 31, the last 25 yards coming on a lateral to right halfback Jim Vollenweider. Forced into a fourth-down situation, Curci's pass intended for Vollenweider was intercepted by Doug Partin, who raced 58 yards to the Miami 32 before he was tackled by Frank Bouffard and Bob Eggert. Allen threw 29 yards to Dave Hudson, and

ran for a three-yard score on third down. Allen added the extra point with 2:05 to play in the first quarter.

Curci's two second-quarter interceptions didn't produce any Florida points, but each cut off a Miami scoring threat. The 'Canes reached Florida's 15 early in the quarter before Billy Hood returned an interception to Miami 47. Not long after, Gene Page picked off a Curci pass at Florida's 48 and returned it 20 yards.

Miami wasted little time getting even after receiving the second-half kickoff. The six-play touchdown drive took only 2:47, capped by Bouffard's one-yard plunge. Curci set up the touchdown with a 40-yard run two plays earlier, starting right and breaking back to the left before Florida's Jack Westbrook, a Miamian, and Hood temporarily prevented the touchdown. Curci was also the catalyst behind the drive that put Miami ahead, 14-7, later in the quarter. At Miami's 40, Curci rolled left only to discover both short-range receivers to that side were covered. He stopped, twisted around and threw deep for sophomore end Larry Wilson, who was waving madly behind the secondary. Wilson's catch gave the Hurricanes a first down at Florida's 12. After gaining a first down at the two, fullback Stan Markowski burrowed into the end zone from about six inches out. With less than three minutes left in the third quarter, Al Dangel kicked Miami to a seven-point lead.

At this point, Florida boosters must have figured they were making the right move in sacking Woodruff; the Orange Bowl's Van Kussrow was preparing his invitation speech for the Miami locker room; and Gator Bowl executive director George Olsen was set to invite Georgia—the Orange Bowl's safety valve—as long as the Bulldogs disposed of Georgia Tech that afternoon at Tech's Grant Field in Atlanta. But a native Atlantan, Florida's Allen, would literally throw all of these plans into disarray.

Florida opened its next possession with Allen passing 24 yards to Perry McGriff to the

Gators' 47. On third-and-10, Allen completed a 53-yard touchdown pass to halfback Don Deal, who caught the ball on the dead run to pull Florida within 14-13 before the conversion attempt. But Allen missed the kick and left the Gators trailing by a point.

Where Allen's kicking failed, Florida's defense shut down the Hurricanes for the rest

down pass at the Hurricanes' four. Miami's defense held, and Allen—still looking for his first successful field goal as a collegian—kicked a 30-yarder that put Florida ahead, 16-14, with 7:22 to play.

Curci's desperate attempt to push the 'Canes downfield immediately backfired. He was intercepted at the Miami 38 by

Perry McGriff (left) holds onto a pass while falling. (UF ARCHIVES)

of the game. The Gators got the ball back, and Allen hit three passes worth 40 yards to put Florida in a fourth-and-10 situation at Miami's 22. Woodruff sent in backup quarterback Jack Jones, who hit McGriff with a first-

Westbrook, who returned the ball to the UM four. The Gators were pushed back to the nine before Allen pitched to Hudson, who beat Miami's Bob Rosbaugh to the end zone. Allen kicked Florida to a nine-point lead with 5:22 to play. Two of the four interceptions to this point had resulted in 10 points. There was one more interception left in Curci's arm. This one went to Partin at midfield and ended Miami's hopes of regaining the lead.

Woodruff burst into tears before his players lowered him to the turf at midfield after the game. Gustafson, too, was emotional . . . at the opposite end of the spectrum. Coming out of the locker room after 15 minutes to meet with reporters, he was hit in the face by a pile of wood shavings that floated down from the stands. He began his summation of the game by saying, "Let's bury the dead." His analysis included the revelation that he wished Allen had successfully kicked the extra point that would have tied the score at 14-14 late in the third quarter, thinking that Woodruff would have played more conservatively in the fourth quarter knowing that he was assured of no worse than a tie.

Miami outgained Florida 344 yards to 276. Curci ran for 43 yards and passed for 152, giving him a school-record 1,068 passing yards for the season. Curci, who went on to become a successful coach at Tampa, Miami and Kentucky, never forgot the loss to Florida in '59. He claimed the similar jerseys made it difficult for him to pick out his receivers.

"I hadn't thrown five interceptions all year. It wasn't so much that I couldn't distinguish," he says. "It made me hesitate. It cost us the game, cost us the Orange Bowl. I think Woodruff did it as a ploy. Since that time, whenever I coached, it taught me that I always brought alternating color jerseys."

If Hurricanes fans thought that Miami would simply replace Georgia as a Gator Bowl selection, they were sadly mistaken. The Gator Bowl invited Georgia Tech, another team with four losses, to play Arkansas in a game that would match Tech coach Bobby Dodd against one of his former players, Razorbacks coach Frank Broyles. Eight years separated from its most recent bowl appear-

ance, Miami would wait another two years before receiving a bowl bid.

* * *

Woodruff would wait a few weeks before learning that he indeed had coached his final game for the Gators. He returned to Tennessee, where he became athletic director and hired one of his former UF players, Doug Dickey, as coach in 1964. Together, they accomplished at Knoxville what neither would do as coach at Florida—winning the SEC football championship (the Volunteers did it twice under Dickey, in 1967 and '69). Ironically, during Woodruff's final year as AD, Tennessee led the move to have the conference officially strip Florida of its first SEC football championship (won in 1984) because of the NCAA probation that the Gators were hit with the following January. Woodruff retired as athletic director in 1985 and brought back Dickey—by then out of football and working in private business in Lakeland—to succeed him.

Woodruff compiled a 53-42-6 record at Florida and left behind the core of a team that nearly won the SEC in 1960 under Ray Graves. His tenure at Gainesville had seen Florida make its first bowl trip and begin, despite Woodruff's initial objections, what would become a thriving rivalry with Florida State. "It was great years down there at Florida," Woodruff says. "I'm very proud of the progress they've made in all sports. That's my ambition and what I worked for."

Florida State vs. Florida

MacBeth's Option Play: Take the $1,500 to Run?

James Taylor was a likable sort. A janitor at the University of Florida's athletic department, Taylor was the kind of guy that many of the athletes got to know and talk with freely.

Fate had it that James Taylor was the first person that Florida senior fullback Jon Mac-Beth ran into after walking over from the Pi Lambda Phi fraternity house on the night of August 22, 1960. MacBeth was used to being in sticky situations, often the result of his desire to be the life of the party. But MacBeth had not sought to be the center of attention at the frat house that night, where he was an associate member and visited only three or four times a semester. And what had happened on a night when he simply was looking to show his brother Dan around the Lambda house had disturbed him enough that the first person he ran into—Taylor—became a worthy audience.

MacBeth asked Taylor to sit down. Then MacBeth pleaded, "What are these people going to think of me walking into the coach's office and saying these guys are trying to bribe me?"

Only a few hours earlier, life had seemed incredibly simpler. He was looking to com-plete his football career at Florida as a regular fullback—certainly not one of the stars for new coach Ray Graves, but at least someone who expected to see plenty of playing time. Now, as he sat on a stairwell in the athletic department, he played over again in his mind the fact that he was just offered $1,500 to shave points when the Gators played Florida State in September.

MacBeth, 21, the third of six children from Pensacola, originally planned to play at Georgia Tech. He was told he needed to take an additional geometry course the summer before coming to Atlanta to meet Tech's entrance requirements, but never took the course and never enrolled at Tech. He instead agreed to sign with Florida.

"He had nothing," recalls Harry Philpott, a vice president at UF. "I mean, he had a scholarship and room and board and so forth. But he had nothing extra." He was, said Philpott, a likely target for gamblers.

On August 22, one of the Lambda brothers, 19-year-old junior Phil Silber of New York, had introduced MacBeth to Aaron Wagman, a 27-year-old New Yorker who said he was a vendor at Yankee Stadium. Wagman, it turned out, had been arrested in New York in 1954 for burglary and in 1956 for felonious assault. Later investigations revealed that Wagman apparently was part of a syndicate, telling FBI officers about bets of up to $10,000 made in Las Vegas. One Miami bookie told police that Wagman by himself "couldn't offer my grandmother anything to throw a point in a tiddledy wink match." The investigations also showed that the bribery plot was hatched the previous spring in Miami by Wagman, who had then asked Silber to introduce him to some Gator football players.

Even with MacBeth's brother in the room, Wagman and Silber broached the subject of MacBeth's helping to shave points in the Florida-FSU game. The Gators would go into the game as 13-point favorites, after having beaten the Seminoles the previous two meetings.

"It really made me mad," MacBeth recalls of the bribery offer. "I was so young—I hate to say crazy, mixed-up, whatever. I was gung-ho, fearless. I was more upset because regardless of what you are, you are a team member. It went against my loyalty." And did the offer

frighten him? He laughs and says: "If you knew some of the kinds of bars I went in . . ."

This was not the kind of news that Graves expected as he prepared for the Seminoles. "I didn't know what to think," Graves says. He informed Philpott, and they huddled with authorities. A plan was set: MacBeth would tell no one else of the bribe, go along with the gamblers and hope that police could nab them before the game.

MacBeth arranged to meet with Wagman and Silber the night before the game in Wagman's car. The car was parked on SE 7th Street, where MacBeth was paid in advance with 15 $100 bills. Wagman told MacBeth that he could earn an additional $3,000 by shaving points in November—and there was a possible "bonus" of another $1,000 if both the FSU and Georgia scams worked out. The gamblers suggested that MacBeth return the original $1,500 so that they could increase his return by betting it for him. MacBeth declined, telling them he wanted the "cold cash."

All the while, MacBeth was anticipating that police would arrive, make the arrests and

Jon MacBeth, only hours after turning gamblers over to police, watches from the sidelines. (UF ARCHIVES)

end this real-life drama. But the officers lost Wagman's car in traffic and failed to make any arrests that night. MacBeth, somewhat shaken that things had gone awry, spent the night at Philpott's home. Silber returned to the Lambda house and, according to later police reports, slept off a drunk.

On the morning of the game, police still couldn't locate Wagman or Silber. University police officer J.S. Tillotson decided to check

Only minutes before kickoff, the Florida team was told of the bribery attempt, of MacBeth's role and how he had worked with police toward the arrests of Wagman and Silber. Recalls placekicker Billy Cash: "As I remember, word started getting around about it (before the team was told). The real story had not come out yet. Unless there were one or two exceptions, none of the players knew what was going on. (MacBeth)

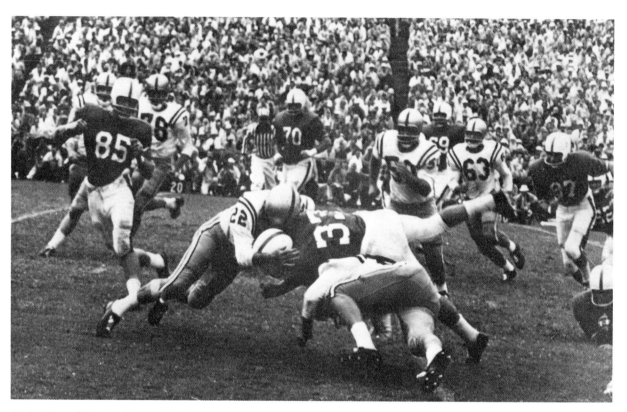

Lindy Infante (33) gains five yards for the Gators. (UF ARCHIVES)

out the Lambda house, where students informed him that Silber had spent the night before leaving the next morning for his apartment on SE 6th Terrace. Tillotson went to the apartment and arrested Silber at 11:15 a.m. Wagman was arrested at 12:30 p.m. at Jacksonville's Imeson Airport, where he had booked a flight for New York. Wagman was charged with attempted bribery with bond set at $10,000. Silber was charged with conspiracy to bribe with bond set at $5,000.

made the right decision; he was a pretty tough character."

MacBeth said he was worried how his teammates would react to the news that one of the Gators had agreed—though as part of a setup—to shave points. "It had been emotional to try to keep it secret and go on," he says. "Dr. Philpott took me in (to the locker room just before the game) and announced to the team what was going on. I kind of looked around, and they all listened. Several

Florida State's Tony Romeo (80) lunges at UF's Larry Libertore (14) on a second-quarter pass.
(UF ARCHIVES)

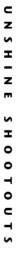

of them just walked up and patted me on the butt and said, 'Way to go, Jon. Let's go.' They took it the right way."

On the field, Florida was troubled by the innovative platooning system that Coach Bill Peterson had brought to FSU, patterned after the one that he had seen at LSU under Paul Dietzel. Peterson employed an overall first team called the Renegades, a No. 2 offensive platoon called the Chiefs and a No. 2 defensive unit called the Warriors. (The counterparts at LSU, which used them to win the national title in 1958, were the White team, the Go team and the Chinese Bandits.)

But as it turned out, the Gators scored the game's only points on a 25-yard field goal by Cash with 6:31 to play in the first half.

The Seminoles nearly took the lead late in the half when quarterback Eddie Feely, who had played at Gainesville High School, drove FSU to the Florida 28. But on fourth-and-one, Feely was stopped for no gain by Pat Patchen. Florida State threatened to tie the score in the fourth quarter, but a 39-yard field goal attempt by Ken Kestner was deflected by Nick Arfaras and caught by Lindy Infante, who returned the ball to FSU's 27. The Seminoles had one last gasp with a fourth-and-five play at Florida's 45 with 2:56 to play, but Feely was intercepted by Bobby Dodd, Jr.

Being unaware of the MacBeth drama, the Florida Field crowd of 45,000 was consumed by the fact that Florida State had nearly pulled off its biggest victory ever. While the Seminoles' two previous losses to the Gators were hardly routs—21-7 in 1958 and 18-8 in 1959—this game proved FSU was on par with Florida. Peterson was bitterly hurt by the loss, having come so close to doing what so many Gators believed was impossible. "Keep your heads high, boys," Peterson told his players after the game. He shook his head and added, "It's a darn shame to lose one when you play like that."

MacBeth's contribution to the game was neither spectacular nor suspicious. He played 31 minutes on offense and defense, carrying five times for 20 yards at fullback and making

three tackles as a linebacker. "Those guys kept telling me how easy it would be to fumble or miss a tackle now and then," he told reporters after the game. "I guess I just feel complimented that anyone would think I'm that good a player."

The bribery episode soon would be forgotten. Graves' first Gator team finished the regular season 8-2, equaling the school record. A 13-12 Gator Bowl victory over Baylor added the unprecedented ninth victory. Florida State's close call against a solid Florida team was a false indication of the quality of the Seminoles. They struggled to a 3-6-1 finish, including losses of 23-0 at Miami and 57-21 at Auburn.

Wagman was convicted of paying MacBeth $1,500 and Silber $1,250 in the point-shaving scam and served 23 months in Florida prisons. He later was also found guilty in connection with a probe of illegal activities involving college basketball games at New York's Madison Square Garden and was given a sentence of three to five years in prison. Silber was expelled from Florida by university president J. Wayne Reitz.

MacBeth tried to go on with his life but found it difficult. He never knew the whereabouts of Wagman and Silber and years later still received anonymous phone calls in the middle of the night. He could only wonder.

"Time heals all, they say," MacBeth says, "but I'm stuck with this for life. When everyone else forgets, I'm going to have to live with it."

Florida State vs. Florida
FSU Wins, 3-3

Ray Graves was coaching under Bobby Dodd at Georgia Tech in 1959 when he received an inquiry from a school in Florida. Dodd had often fished down that way and told Graves it would be a good place to coach—nice area, up-and-coming program. A dean at the school called Graves and they met in Jacksonville to discuss the job. But Graves decided not to pursue the job at Florida State.

"I almost took it," Graves recalls.

As it turned out, Ray Graves did come south from Atlanta. But it was in 1960, to Gainesville, to replace Bob Woodruff. Dodd's son, Bobby Jr., was playing for the Gators. So when Florida president Wayne Reitz was hunting for a successor to Woodruff, he called Dodd and asked for a recommendation. Graves came to Gainesville for an interview and immediately put in a good word for one of his competitors, young Ara Parseghian of Delaware. "We were playing in the Gator Bowl, and I hadn't even thought about the job," Graves says. "The president of the Florida alumni association, Dick Stratton, called me out of a meeting and said, 'Why don't you apply for the job?' I said I hadn't even thought about it; that's where it

started. I think the committee couldn't even pronounce Parseghian."

Reitz and Graves came to an agreement, and Florida had itself a new football coach—with Dodd's blessing. Says Graves: "I think Bobby said, 'All right, go down and coach at Florida and find us some new lakes to fish.'"

His primary mission, though, was to find ways for Florida to begin competing with the nation's elite. The state was beginning to grow by leaps and bounds, yet the Gators still had not won a Southeastern Conference championship. Of course, there was also the matter of UF holding strictly to academic guidelines that made it tougher to recruit in the SEC.

Graves met with immediate success, which later in his career fueled higher expectations. He equaled the school record for regular-season victories in 1960 with an 8-2 finish that led to a Gator Bowl invitation. For the 1961 season, the Associated Press reduced its weekly poll from 20 rated teams to 10, with others listed that received votes. Florida was listed among the vote-getters in the preseason poll. The Gators opened the season against a Clemson team that also appeared in

A high point of Ray Graves' early days at UF was the 1963 win over Alabama that marked "Bear" Bryant's first loss as Tide coach in Tuscaloosa. Bryant would go on to compile a record of 71-2 at Denny Stadium. (UF SPORTS INFORMATION)

that category and came away with a 21-7 victory at Florida Field.

Florida State was coming off a 3-6-1 finish in Bill Peterson's first year as coach. Seminole fans weren't pleased when the '61 team opened the season by struggling to beat George Washington, 15-7. Such a victory would have been acceptable 10 years earlier when the FSU program was still getting its feet wet. But having defeated the likes of Tennessee and Miami in recent years, Florida State no longer received polite applause for disposing of the smaller schools.

"I don't think there's any question about FSU being good enough to beat us this year," Graves said during the week before the game.

"I believe that FSU this year has as much depth overall as we have. I didn't think that last year."

UF assistant Jimmy Dunn, speaking to the Tallahassee Quarterback Club, said that there was more pressure on Florida to maintain its winning streak over Florida State than on the Seminoles to end the streak. "This game won't make our season, but it sure could break it," he said. "And it won't break FSU's season, but it sure could make it."

Jacksonville *Journal* sports editor Jack Hairston expressed similar sentiments in print: "This is still not THE game for Florida players and fans, while it is THE game for the FSU side. Eventually, Florida State will beat the Gators, and thereafter it will be THE game for Florida, too, and the Gators and their supporters will never again be bored over the prospect of beating FSU."

＊　　＊　　＊

A sellout crowd of 44,200 jammed into Florida Field to see if the Gators could make good on the pregame line that established them as two-touchdown favorites.

The game's first score was set up by FSU's Roy Bickford. He blocked a Don Ringgold punt, then fell on the loose ball at the Florida 17. Florida's defense prevented Florida State from picking up a first down, but sophomore John Harllee came in and kicked a 29-yard field goal with only 5:48 gone in the game to give the Seminoles a 3-0 lead.

Bickford proved to be an FSU hero again in the second quarter. With Florida pushing toward the Seminoles' goal line, UF quarterback Larry Libertore looked for Lindy Infante inside FSU's 10. The pass was batted by Infante right into the arms of Bickford at the six.

Facing into the wind, Florida State played it safe and punted on third down. Sophomore Charley Calhoun's kick traveled only 23 yards, giving UF possession at the Seminoles' 33. On Florida's second play, Libertore raced 15 yards to the 15. But the Gators were betrayed by another penalty and instead found themselves back at the 44. Graves sent

The Gators' Mike McCann (89) provides a block for Larry Rentz (10). (UF ARCHIVES)

in Bobby Dodd, Jr., to replace Libertore, and Dodd threw a 34-yard pass to Paul White. Don Goodman picked up a yard on first down, and Infante followed with a four-yard gain to the five. On third down, Florida State's Fred Grimes, who was playing despite a broken hand, broke through the line and tackled Ron Stoner for a six-yard loss back to the 11. Florida was forced to send in kicker Billy Cash, whose field goal was the only scoring in the Gators' 1960 victory. He made a 28-yarder to tie the score with 3:23 to play in the first half. The Gators gained more momentum when FSU's Keith Kinderman stumbled at the goal line on the kickoff and was ruled down at the one. Florida State was forced to punt deep in its own territory, but UF gra-

ciously let Florida State off the hook. Libertore called for a fair catch around FSU's 35 but fumbled, with the Seminoles' John Levings making the recovery.

The Seminoles had reached UF's 23 with 17 seconds left in the half when Peterson sent in the field goal unit. Going into the wind, Peterson had planned a fake all the way. Eddie Feely raced toward the goal line but was stopped well short, at the 16, to end the half.

Neither team showed much offense in the second half. Late in the game, Bickford intercepted a pass thrown by Dodd and rambled 28 yards to set up Florida State with a first down at UF's 28. But then Florida State was penalized 15 yards for an illegal substitution. Peterson eventually sent in Harllee with 1:06

Bob Hoover (34) dives over the Seminoles' line for short yardage. (UF ARCHIVES)

to play to attempt a 51-yard field goal with the wind, but the attempt fell way short.

Florida State fans raced onto the field after the game and tried to pull down the goalposts. One set had been dismantled before UF fans responded to defend, which led to a brawl on the field that continued for 30 minutes. It even included some of the Florida players who were ineligible at the time. Graves recalls: "It was an exciting fifth quarter; I have some film of that fight. It was a pretty good little brawl."

Graves was not in such a lighthearted mood after the game, though. His assessment of the first Florida effort that did not lead to victory over the Seminoles: "It was like a death in the family."

Peterson, conversely, saw only the silver lining in the tie. He attended church services the following morning in Tallahassee, and the day's first hymn was "Blest Be The Tie That Binds." Florida had outgained Florida State 291 yards to 58, collecting 15 first downs to FSU's five. But the Gators committed five damning turnovers to only one for the Seminoles. Florida end Sam Holland said, "We ought to be shot for this performance."

✳   ✳   ✳

Graves' stint as Florida coach became known as the Silver Sixties. In his 10 seasons, the Gators made five bowl trips, including the Orange and Sugar bowls during the Heisman Trophy-winning career of quarterback Steve Spurrier. A milestone victory came in 1963

when the Gators traveled to Tuscaloosa and handed "Bear" Bryant his first loss at Denny Stadium, 10-6.

Graves had taken on the chores of athletic director, and before the 1969 season, he met with Reitz and discussed giving up the coaching job. "It got to where athletic director and coach were two jobs," Graves says. "It got to where I was really concerned about it." The

Gator braintrust of the early '60s (from left): offensive coach Pepper Rodgers, coach Ray Graves and defensive coach Gene Ellenson. (UF ARCHIVES)

decision was made to start looking for a new coach without making any formal announcement of a vacancy. Players eventually got wind that Graves probably wouldn't return as

Gators quarterback Larry Libertore (14) gets some help from Sam Holland (80). (UF ARCHIVES)

coach. The informal search included former Florida quarterback Doug Dickey, who was in the process of winning his second SEC title in the past three seasons as coach at Tennessee.

Tennessee was scheduled to play Florida in the Gator Bowl. "Doug had come over and visited while they were training for the Gator Bowl," Graves recalls. "There was so much written and talked about at that time. I told the players that I'd certainly let them know, but right now I was still planning on being head coach and they'd be the first ones to know if I decided to step down."

That didn't prevent the Dickey-to-Florida rumor from spreading. This was not a popular choice with the players. If Graves were to step down, most of them wanted assistant coach Gene Ellenson promoted to head coach. "Then the (Gator Bowl) game came along, and it was a weird game," Graves says of Florida's 14-13 upset of the Vols. "We shouldn't have won, but we won." The fact that Dickey couldn't beat the Gators with what was considered a superior team didn't sit well with the Ellenson supporters.

One of the all-time confusing Gator scenarios was about to get even more complicated. Almost immediately after the game, a UF board of trustees meeting was called at the team's hotel in Jacksonville. Graves told the members that in view of everything that had happened in recent weeks, he thought Dickey would turn them down and that he should stay on as coach in 1970. He left the meeting having

Ecstatic Florida State fans tear down one of the goalposts at Florida Field, which prompts action by Florida faithful. (UF ARCHIVES)

43

talked the board into that course of action.

But he soon learned that some of his assistant coaches were weighing job offers, under the impression that a new staff was on its way in to Gainesville. Graves decided he couldn't leave loyal assistants stuck in a job that he knew they probably would lose within a year. He arranged another meeting with Reitz and told him it was time to make the change.

"He said, 'You won't believe this,'" Graves says. "'Doug has just gotten back to Tennessee and wanted to know if the job is still open.'" It was. Amid such shifting winds did Doug Dickey succeed Ray Graves as coach of the Gators.

Graves, like many UF coaches before and after him, lamented the failure to bring an SEC championship to Gainesville. But Graves was prouder of his style of coaching than he was of the net results. "These boys you're playing with are going to be the best friends you'll have the rest of your life, whether you realize it or not," he says. "Coaches all thought I had my door open too much and let them come in with their problems. But I always thought that was important."

The result is that Graves and his players have become probably the most close-knit group in UF football history; the Silver Sixties group still gets together every summer to catch up on old times and new.

"His role was basically to keep everybody in harmony, in good spirits," recalls Spurrier, now quite familiar with the role of the Florida head coach. "The atmosphere in practice was such that we enjoyed going out every day. He pretty much let his (assistant) coaches coach, and he would make the big decisions—go for it, punt, go for two."

Says John Reaves, who played his first two UF seasons under Graves: "The thing about Coach Graves is he's always there. When I needed a scholarship, he was there. When I threw nine interceptions, he was there. When I got arrested for possession (of drugs), he was there. He came over on a cane to a fund-raising that we had. He's always been a friend."

Miami vs. Florida
The Matador's Amazing Left-Handed Pass

Being from Key West meant there was something a little different about George Mira.

It meant that he thought the winters on the University of Miami campus were too cold. It meant that he was an unbelievable hypochondriac, always fretting over his health and consequently staying so nervous he would chew his fingernails until his fingers would bleed. It meant that he was afraid to fly on airplanes, so the team trainer gave him sugar pills under the guise of sleeping pills.

There was, of course, much more to George Mira. In particular, there was a gifted right arm that may have never seen its equal on the Coral Gables campus, even with the arrival of the likes of Kelly and Kosar and Testaverde and the rest. It was a right arm that almost steered him toward becoming a professional baseball pitcher. He chose instead to play college football and brought theretofore unequaled national attention to the Miami Hurricanes.

But for all the great feats George Mira performed with that talented right arm, perhaps his most memorable accomplish-ment as a Hurricane occurred thanks to his left arm.

*   *   *

It seemed like everyone in Key West had heard of George Ignacio Mira and felt pride in his accomplishments. At Key West High School, he was a quality boxer, following in the footsteps of his father, Jimmy. As a pitcher, George compiled a record of 31-2, leading Key West to a pair of state Class 2A championships. Of course, having a powerful hitter like John "Boog" Powell on the team didn't hurt. And in football, Mira was not only a magnificent quarterback but also the team's best defensive back.

Mira was offered $13,000 to sign a contract with baseball's Baltimore Orioles, who had signed Powell a year earlier. Mira and the family, though, had their hearts set on George going to college. Jimmy Mira had labored long and hard running an ice plant, and he told his son that while $13,000 looked good in the short run, he had a better investment in a college scholarship. He visited UM, Florida and Florida State along with one out-of-state school (Georgia). George, who spoke mostly Spanish at home, signed with Miami to play football.

Mira wasted little time showing just what he was capable of on a football field. In his first spring scrimmage before his sophomore season, Mira threw a 15-yard pass so hard that it not only was not caught, it bounced all the way back to the line of scrimmage. He

incumbent Eddie Johns to running back, as Miami hoped to improve on the 6-4 record of the 1960 season.

Mira and UM nearly beat Pitt in their opener at the Orange Bowl before losing, 10-7. While Mira impressed many with his passing, it was the great fake that he pulled off during the game that convinced many that this kid had everything to be a standout quar-

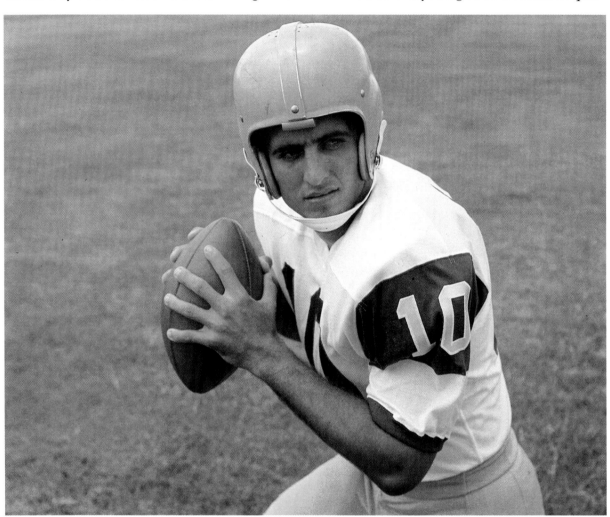

George Mira gave up the opportunity to sign with the Baltimore Orioles to play football at Miami. (UNIVERSITY OF MIAMI)

would later throw a pass that would break a finger of teammate Ben Rizzo. Combined with his Latin good looks, this powerful arm earned Mira the nickname of "The Matador" from Miami sports publicist George Gallet. Coach Andy Gustafson named this sophomore as the starting quarterback, moving

terback. And after the Hurricanes beat Kentucky on the road and Penn State at home, they were already receiving votes for the Associated Press Top 10.

Miami wound its way through the year to arrive at the last game of the season with a record of 6-3 and a berth in the Liberty Bowl in Philadelphia. Along the way, UM was beset by injuries and internal strife. Mira missed parts of three games because of rib injuries. Gustafson was coming down toward the end of his career, his contract extending through the 1962 season. But it was reported in mid-November that some of the school's trustees wanted him fired at season's end and kicked upstairs to replace Jack Harding as athletic director. They reportedly wanted to bring back former UM assistant Hank Stram, who was coaching the Dallas Texans of the American Football League.

The Hurricanes' final game was against Florida. The Gators, likewise, were a middle-of-the-road team that lacked consistency. From a record of 4-4-1, the 3-3 tie against Florida State was clearly the blackest mark on the season. Florida needed a win to avoid its first losing finish since 1955.

*   *   *

A raucous crowd of 42,000 showed up at Florida Field for UF's fourth game on campus that year. The two teams battled through a scoreless first quarter as the fans settled in for what looked to be a nail-biter.

In the second quarter, Miami junior halfback John Bahen fumbled a fair catch at the UM 25, with Florida's Jack Thompson making the recovery at the 26. A similar fumble by Bahen against nationally-ranked Colorado in mid-season led to Colorado's game-winning field goal. After three plays yielded only three yards, Billy Cash came in to attempt a field goal. Gustafson was on the press-box phone when the ball was hiked. But it was a fake, with holder Bobby Dodd passing to Lindy Infante at the UM 4. Three plays later, fullback Don Goodman scored to give Florida a 6-0 lead.

Miami tied the score on the subsequent kickoff by Bruce Culpepper when Bahen returned it 93 yards for a touchdown on a play designed especially for this game. All season long, Miami ran its kickoff returns up the middle. This time, the play was designed to break

to the sideline. Bahen stumbled at the UM 20, broke to the outside, got a block around the 30 and was gone. Bobby Wilson missed the extra point, leaving the score tied, 6-6.

In the closing minutes of the half, the Gators lost Infante because of a head injury. He was blocked hard by a Miami player on a run by Nick Spinelli, suffered a concussion and was taken to the university medical center.

Miami moved ahead in the third quarter, which wasn't so unbelievable in itself. It was the method, though, that had the Florida Field crowd numb.

UM started on its 42 with a four-yard run by Jim Vollenweider. Mira then pitched to Bill Miller, who took the ball 40 yards to the UF 14. Sam Fernandez carried seven yards to the seven. From there, Mira rolled out as if following blocking for a sweep around left end. But he was hemmed in by Florida defenders and switched the ball to his left hand after having his right shoulder grabbed by UF defensive end Sam Holland, who played with Mira at Key West High. Mira pushed a soft, basketball-like pass with his left hand toward the end zone. Spinelli leaped to catch the ball for the touchdown that put Miami ahead, 12-6.

Florida threatened twice afterward but couldn't score. Miami added a fourth-quarter field goal, a 19-yarder by Wilson and the game's first successful kick, to make the final score 15-6.

Soon after the Hurricanes' victory, joyous Miami fans made their way to the north end of the stadium and proceeded to dismantle the goalposts. This was more than Gator fans could bear, especially after watching FSU fans do the same thing earlier in the season. Florida's final defensive stand of the day was played out in the end zone by its fans, who fended off Miami's attack. The UM band helped defuse the situation by breaking into a quick rendition of "The Star Spangled Banner."

The win gave Miami a 12-11 lead in its series with the Gators, meaning UM was again in possession of the Seminole war canoe presented by Governor Farris Bryant.

Mira takes a breather on the sidelines. (Miami Herald)

"It wasn't our best ball club but the most satisfying," Gustafson said afterward. "I got to go see the governor. This hasn't happened in four years."

Bahen's kickoff return was the second-longest in UM history, topped only by Russ Coates' 96-yarder against West Virginia in 1942. "We'd worked on setting up the outside lane for that sideline kickoff return all season," Gustafson said. "We'd been saving this one for the Gators."

Overall, it was not a spectacular game for Mira. He finished 8-of-18 for 112 yards. The main topic of postgame conversation, though, was Mira's amazing left-handed pass. Said Mira: "There was nothing else I could do."

"I didn't think he was going to throw," Spinelli said afterward, "and I certainly didn't dream he was going to throw it lefthanded. After seeing that, I just had to catch the ball."

Graves' succinct comment on the pass was, "He wasn't billed to do that."

Miami went on to lose its Liberty Bowl meeting with Syracuse, 15-14, and close the season at 7-4. Florida, with its 4-5-1 record, could again look to "next year." But as the Gainesville *Sun's* Whitey McMullen quoted UF fan Bill O'Neal following Florida's midseason loss at Georgia Tech, "Wait until last year."

✳   ✳   ✳

During spring practice before his junior season, Mira was tutored by Baltimore Colts star Johnny Unitas. Unitas's tips—moving Mira closer to center, adjusting his crouch—may have helped. As a junior, Mira finished second in the nation in passing with 2,059 yards and fifth in Heisman balloting (the best UM showing since the award was started in 1935) and was a first-team All-American. The 'Canes finished 7-3, scoring their first sweep of Florida State and Florida since 1956, and lost to Nebraska in the frigid, snowy Gotham Bowl. Mira completed 24 passes for 321 yards against the Cornhuskers and was named the game's most valuable player.

Gustafson agreed to give up coaching after the '63 season when Harding died in February 1963. Hialeah Stadium packed in 7,200 fans for the spring game looking ahead to Mira's senior season. Packer Street in Key West was renamed George Mira Street in honor of the favorite son. When Ron Fraser took over the Miami baseball program in 1963, he tried to get Mira, having finished his junior season of football, to come out and play baseball. After word of Fraser's courtship of Mira had made the local paper, Gustafson told Fraser that Mira would not be playing baseball for the Hurricanes.

Gallet prepared a 16-page booklet called *The Amazing George Mira*. But Miami lost the opener to Florida State, 24-0, and amazingly struggled to a 3-7 finish. For Mira's three varsity seasons, the 'Canes compiled a 17-15 record including two bowl trips. He finished with 5,048 yards passing, with 2,155 coming as a senior. He finished 10th in Heisman balloting as a senior. His career passing yardage record held up until Jim Kelly began the parade of great UM quarterbacks with a career total of 5,228 yards in four seasons from 1979 through 1982.

Mira's pro career consisted of a series of frustrations in which he found himself for the most part playing as a backup in San Francisco (behind John Brodie), Philadelphia (Norm Snead), Baltimore (Unitas) and the Miami Dolphins (Bob Griese). He headed to Canada in the early '70s, then returned south to play for the Birmingham Americans of the new World Football League in 1974.

The Americans won the World Bowl championship game, and Mira was voted the game's most valuable player. But before Mira could claim the actual MVP trophy, Jefferson County (Alabama) sheriff's officers stormed into the team's locker room and confiscated all of the Americans' tangible possessions. The front office had not kept up with its bills. Mira played in the second WFL in 1975, in Florida for the Jacksonville Express, until that league folded before the end of the season.

Back in Key West, Mira watched his son, George Jr., become a starting linebacker for the Hurricanes as UM became the dominant team of the '80s.

"I feel fantastic," Mira says. "It's kind of a dream."

Florida vs. Florida State
Never, FSU, Never? Not Quite

Florida State's Seminoles reached new heights in 1964. Five weeks into the season, FSU was unbeaten at 5-0 having given up only 20 points total. That propelled them into the Associated Press Top 10 rankings at No. 10—one slot behind a 4-0 Florida team. A midseason loss at Virginia Tech and a 13-13 tie at Houston later in the season left the Seminoles with a record of 7-1-1 with one regular-season game to play.

They had already earned an invitation to play in Jacksonville's Gator Bowl against Oklahoma. But none of that really mattered to FSU fans going into late November.

What mattered to them was that the Florida Gators were coming to Tallahassee and Doak Campbell Stadium for the first time. Ever since UF had begrudgingly agreed to play Florida State in football, beginning in 1958, the games had been held at Florida Field in Gainesville.

And in six games in Gainesville, the Gators had never been beaten, although UF treated the 1961 tie as a moral defeat.

The Gators were not timid in reminding Florida State of this historical fact. They were, in fact, rather blatant about it. Maybe it had something to do with coming off a draining 14-7 loss to Georgia in Jacksonville, which left UF with a 5-2 record with three games to play. Whatever the motivation, some of the Gators wore stickers on their helmets during practice that read "Never, FSU, Never." The Gators' slogan for the week was "Go For Seven" as in go for seven consecutive games against Florida State without a loss.

Not the most prudent behavior for a Florida football team that was about to become a guest in Tallahassee for the first time ever.

*   *   *

The architect of Florida State's best season to date was affable Bill Peterson. He had first been recommended for the FSU coaching job in 1959 while serving on Paul Dietzel's LSU staff that had just won the national championship. He was invited to come to Tallahassee for an interview but told FSU officials that he couldn't at the time because he was recruiting in his native Ohio for the Tigers.

Florida State instead hired Perry Moss, who left after only one season. Peterson again appeared on the Seminoles' new list of

Florida State's Bill Peterson unwittingly entertained fans and journalists with malaprops, such as asking his players to "stand on your helmets with the sideline under your arms." (FLORIDA STATE UNIVERSITY)

"So I get up at six o'clock, had breakfast, was there at seven; nobody came. Eight o'clock—nobody came. Eight-thirty—nobody came. Nine o'clock, and I'd just gone to the telephone to tell the pilot we're going back, that they just called me down here for a courtesy call.

"About that time, Vaughn Mancha (FSU's athletic director) came in and said, 'Are you ready to go for your interview?'"

Peterson actually had a great interview, though he didn't have time to inspect the facilities because he had to get to back to Louisiana to scout a high school playoff game. By the time he got back to Baton Rouge, there was a message waiting for him that the Florida State job was his.

His early days in Tallahassee were actually a struggle, with Florida State continuing to upgrade its schedule. His first Seminole team (1960) finished 3-6-1, the highlight being the 3-0 loss to Florida. It was more of the same in 1961, finishing 4-5-1 including that glorious tie against the Gators. The '63 team managed to attain a winning record at 4-3-3 only thanks to a couple of blowout victories over Furman and The Citadel.

For 1964, Peterson brought in University of Miami defensive coordinator Bill Crutchfield as his offensive coordinator. Crutchfield had coached under Peterson in high school in Ohio but declined an opportunity to join Peterson's first FSU staff. His main task was to refine a passing game that boasted plenty of raw materials, including the senior combination of quarterback Steve Tensi and wide receiver Fred Biletnikoff.

Biletnikoff had already made his mark—perhaps most indelibly against Miami a year earlier. In that game Biletnikoff not only

coaching candidates. But the job was offered to Clemson's Charlie Waller, who turned it down. Peterson then landed an interview, took a flight to Tallahassee and was greeted at the airport by— no one.

"I come to the hotel, and still—nobody," he recalls. "It was about nine o'clock (at night), and a couple of the committeemen came up to my room and talked to me. About eleven o'clock, somebody called me and said, 'We've changed your interview time from nine o'clock (the next morning) to seven o'clock.'

Fred Biletnikoff, shown during pregame introductions at the Gator Bowl game against Oklahoma, became the first Florida State player to be inducted into the Pro Football Hall of Fame. (FLORIDA STATE UNIVERSITY)

The Gator quarterbacks for 1964: sophomore Steve Spurrier (left) and senior Tom Shannon. (UF ARCHIVES)

caught two Tensi passes for touchdowns; he also snagged a George Mira pass for an interception and returned it 99 yards for a touchdown. Despite lacking great speed, Biletnikoff would develop into one of the great wide receivers. In this his senior year, his 57 catches would rank fourth in the nation. He became a consensus All-American and grabbed four touchdown passes in FSU's 36-19 victory over Oklahoma. He became an even bigger name in pro football with the Oakland Raiders, making two AFL all-star teams and playing in four Pro Bowls. Biletnikoff was the most valuable player in the Raiders' Super Bowl win over Minnesota in 1977.

The FSU offense even featured a center—Jack Edwards—who occasionally called signals in Spanish. But it was the Seminole defense that deserved most of the credit, especially early in the season. FSU opened with three consecutive shutouts, over Miami (14-0), Texas Christian (10-0) and New Mexico State (36-0). Florida State's next test came against a Kentucky team that was likewise undefeated, ranked fifth in the nation and included among its victims the pre-season's top-ranked team, Mississippi.

FSU somehow designated Kentucky as its Homecoming opponent—then set out to treat UK like a Homecoming sacrifice by throttling the Wildcats, 48-6. Florida State was recognized among the Associated Press Top 10 after scoring another landmark victory, winning at Georgia, 17-14.

The Seminoles' defense was anchored by five linemen and two linebackers who became known collectively as the "Magnificent Seven," so named after a popular movie at that time. The seven players even had their heads shaved to take on the look of one of the movie's stars, Yul Brynner. The chrome domes belonged to ends George D'Alessandro and Max Wettstein, tackles Frank Pennie and Avery Sumner, linebackers Dick Hermann and Bill McDowell and middle guard Jack Shinholser.

"It (shaving the heads) wasn't my idea," Peterson says. "One day I come in the meeting room, and there they all are sitting up in the front row with all their hair cut off."

Florida State's subsequent loss at Virginia Tech and tie down the stretch at Houston did little to temper the enthusiasm in Tallahassee. FSU athletic administrators worked out a complicated informal deal with Gator Bowl officials by which Florida State would be invited to play in the Jacksonville game if the

The Gators went further than wearing their hearts on their sleeves. They went to the extreme of having "GO FOR SEVEN" –as in seven consecutive games against Florida State without a loss– printed on their game jerseys. (UF ARCHIVES)

'Noles won, tied or lost to the Gators by fewer than 17 points.

FSU folk certainly didn't perceive that as an impossible mission. Rather, they saw the invitation as the ultimate achievement of parity with UF. Jacksonville had long been considered a "Gator" town. Just having the opportunity to make the trip down U.S. 90 was enough to break down a lot of psychological barriers for the Seminoles. Florida still held out hopes of going to a bowl game, possibly the Bluebonnet in Houston.

Florida was established as a slight favorite in the game. UF senior Tom Shannon was returning as the starting quarterback for the first time in four games. Shannon, a left-hander, had lost his position to the sensational sophomore, Steve Spurrier. Senior running back Larry Dupree gained 131 rushing yards the previous year against the Seminoles. He was Florida's best overall threat at running and receiving. UF coach Ray Graves thought his Gators would still be in the bowl hunt, win or lose. He pointed to the difficulty of the Gators' schedule and how it would prepare them for such a big game: "A pressure-packed game like this one lends itself to crucial mistakes," Graves said. "We have proven we have poise in playing big teams like Alabama, Ole Miss, Auburn and Mississippi State."

For Graves, the Florida-FSU rivalry had been costly in odd ways. For instance, he was prepared to hire Don James, the former Miami quarterback, off Peterson's staff. But Peterson challenged the impending hire, stating that Florida State and Florida had agreed that they would not hire off each other's staffs unless a promotion was involved. The James hire was a straight lateral hire and was rejected by the Board of Regents.

A Gator fan from Cocoa Beach took the trouble to send Peterson a wreath with an accompanying card that read: "Give it to those Florida rejects in care of the Florida State dressing room." Two years earlier on a Gainesville television show hosted by Gators assistant coach Pepper Rodgers, Shannon

noted that he chose Florida over FSU because Florida State took Florida's rejects. At a Thursday night pep rally on the FSU campus, Peterson summed up the feelings of virtually every Seminole when he yelled out to no one in particular: "Come and get us!"

*   *   *

What would become the largest crowd to date to watch a Florida State football game in Tallahassee (43,000) got an early start in filling Doak Campbell Stadium. Early as in slightly after midnight, when some students began to occupy their first-come, first-served section. By early afternoon FSU fans rose in unison and yelled at their guests, "Go to hell, Florida." To which the UF supporters waved pieces of yellow paper and asked the question: "What color is FSU?" Graves sampled some of the Florida State taunting before the game and mused: "I think FSU may be overemphasizing football."

And the Gators didn't exactly leave that "Never, FSU, Never" spirit in the locker room. In a blunt display of confidence, Florida players emerged from the locker room wearing blue jerseys that were emblazoned with the words "Go for Seven" across the front. To the Seminoles, it was as if UF was sticking out its collective chin and saying, "Punch me."

Peterson also learned that Gator Bowl officials apparently had backed off of their original agreement with FSU. Forget that business of the Seminoles playing in Jacksonville if they tied or lost by fewer than 17 points. It would take a Florida State win, pure and simple, to deliver a Gator Bowl bid.

Florida State did little more than kill some clock on its first four possessions, with the Gators in turn failing to score despite some good field position. In the second quarter Spurrier looked to have running room for a first down near midfield but dropped the ball. Howard Ehler made the recovery for FSU at the 45.

The Seminoles wasted no time capitalizing. Tensi threw 55 yards to Biletnikoff for a stunning

Bill Peterson made the passing game the focal part of the Florida State offense, much to the delight of quarterback Steve Tensi. Tensi passed for a school-record 3,392 career yards and also broke the FSU record for passing yards in a season with 1,681 as a senior in 1964. (FLORIDA STATE UNIVERSITY)

touchdown that sent the crowd into a frenzy. It would be Biletnikoff's second and last catch of the game. Les Murdock kicked the extra point to give Florida State a 7-0 lead.

The Gators began the second half with another mistake. Marquis Baeszler fumbled the kickoff, with George D'Alessandro recovering at the UF 34. Florida State moved inside Florida's 15 but stalled. This time, Murdock salvaged a 24-yard field goal to increase the Seminoles' lead to 10-0.

Late in the third period, Charley Casey got behind the Florida State secondary for an apparent touchdown. But he dropped the ball in stride. The 'Noles took over, marched

to Florida's 15 and—with three minutes gone in the fourth quarter—tacked on another Murdock field goal from 34 yards to increase their lead to 13-0.

The Gators took over at their 25 with the urgency of knowing their unbeaten record in the series depended on their outscoring the Seminoles by at least 14 points. Mixing runs with Spurrier's passes, Florida finally put together a formidable drive—without a betraying turnover. The final six yards came on a run by Jack Harper, who had just made a 35-yard catch to set up the first-and-goal, with about six minutes to play. Jimmy Hall added the PAT. Trailing 13-7, there was time for Florida to stop Florida State, get the ball back, add a touchdown plus extra point to eke out a victory and make for a successful first trip to Tallahassee after all.

But Graves took the advice of one of his assistants and decided to try to recover an onside kick rather than risk running out the clock trying to stop Florida State. The Seminoles, though, gained possession at the UF 49. On the first play, Tensi threw for 27 yards. A couple more plays netted modest gains, but they were enough to move Florida State into field goal range for Murdock. With a 40-yard effort sailing between the uprights for Murdock's third successful field goal attempt of the game, the Seminoles built their lead to 16-7.

The Gators were left with a series of futile efforts in the closing minutes. The clock wound down toward game's end, with everyone in the stands realizing it also marked the end of an era in the young Florida-FSU rivalry. For all the "Never, FSU, Never" rhetoric and the "Go for Seven" shirts, the Seminoles were about to notch their first victory in the emotional series.

✳   ✳   ✳

The 9-1-1 record in 1964 (including a 36-19 win over Oklahoma in the Gator Bowl) was Bill Peterson's best in 11 seasons at Florida State, but it by no means ended his success in Tallahassee. He delivered three more bowl trips—Sun, Gator and Peach—among his overall seven winning seasons. The Seminoles finished 7-4 in 1970 without landing a bowl bid.

Peterson was frustrated at his failure to increase the football budget, losing assistants every time he turned around because they could earn more money elsewhere. So when Rice—dragging around seven consecutive losing seasons—was seeking a combination football coach and athletic director, Peterson accepted the offer and left Florida State. "I left the best football team I ever had," Peterson says.

In Houston, Peterson's first Rice team finished 3-7-1. And it turned out to be Peter-son's last Rice team. He was subsequently offered the coaching position of the NFL's Houston Oilers. Peterson was unwittingly walking into a disaster area, one that ultimately ended his coaching career. He lasted only two horrific seasons.

But for all his accomplishments, Bill Peterson became better known for his words off the field. He became the master of the malaprop throughout his coaching career, with a knack for saying the wrong thing at the right time. Some examples as collected by Tallahassee *Democrat* sports editor Bill McGrotha: "Fred Biletnikoff's limitations are limitless" . . . "They gave me a standing observation" . . . "I want you men standing on your helmets with the sidelines under your arms."

Says Peterson: "I went to a one-room schoolhouse. It wasn't conducive to a good education. I lived way back in the hills in West Virginia. My dad had a business, a pulp stone quarry corporation. It was just not being corrected when I was a young kid.

"I'm credited with a lot of things I haven't said. They say sticks and stones hurt, but sayings never hurt me. I don't know who can be out of coaching as long as I have and still get their name in the paper. If people think I'm stupid, that's fine."

Florida vs. Miami
Jolly Cholly's Hour of Triumph

The smile was always there on Charlie Tate's face—that and a cigar. But the smile never looked larger than on this night, which featured the second-largest home crowd at a Miami Hurricanes game.

The opposition had been a 10th-ranked Florida which planned to parlay a victory into a bid to play Missouri in the Sugar Bowl. UM, on the other hand, had little prospect of finishing with a winning record. The Hurricanes had come to the game with a 4-4 record, and after Florida there would be a visit from No. 4 Notre Dame. Yet everything seemed to go Miami's way on this Saturday night in the Orange Bowl. Florida junior quarterback Steve Spurrier played what probably would be the worst game of his UF career. Miami, after being outgained 203-65 in the first half, would hold the powerful Florida offense scoreless in the second half and turn an interception into the winning field goal.

Amid the glee of the UM locker room after the game, Tate—who had a winning record for the first time in his two seasons with the 'Canes—was asked about Miami's finale with the Fighting Irish. His quick reply: "Don't ask me about Notre Dame," Jolly

Cholly bellowed. "My heart hasn't stopped pounding from this one."

Miami football would apparently break Jolly Cholly's heart five years later. But on this night at the Orange Bowl, it was a great love affair between Tate and the Hurricanes.

*   *   *

Miami's search for a coach after Andy Gustafson's retirement following the 1963 season had wandered in many directions. There was an attempt to hire a young up-and-comer at Northwestern, Ara Parseghian. Miami's proposal, it turned out, pushed Notre Dame into hiring Parseghian and returning the Irish to glory. There was an attempt to bring back former UM assistant Hank Stram, who by now had coached the AFL's Kansas City Chiefs for four seasons, but that, too, failed.

In the process, UM looked to Bobby Dodd's staff at Georgia Tech and an assistant named Charlie Tate. Tate was an all-Southeastern Conference fullback at Florida and had coached the Gator freshmen in 1956 before joining Dodd in Atlanta. In 1960, Florida had reached into Dodd's staff to hire Ray

Wayne Barfield's 24-yard field goal puts the Gators ahead of the Hurricanes, 10-6. (MIAMI HERALD)

Graves, who brought great success to UF football. Tate brought wife Annie Lee and his family to Miami, and the coach and his new staff moved into the athletic dorm as a sign of commitment to their new players.

The 1964 season began with back-to-back defeats, by Florida State (14-0) and by Dodd and Georgia Tech (20-0). At 0-4-1, Miami then went on a four-game winning streak by beating Detroit, Tulane, Boston College and Vanderbilt. With a chance to finish with a winning record, the 'Canes lost at Florida, 12-10.

What would turn out to be one of the most significant events in UM football history occurred during the fall practice for the 1965 season. The city of Miami, after failing in its bid to gain an NFL expansion franchise, was awarded the AFL's first expansion team on August 16, to begin play in 1966. It's doubtful that Tate or anyone at UM realized what a force the new team—to be nicknamed the Dolphins—would become in South Florida.

The 'Canes opened poorly again in '65, with only a victory over Syracuse to show for its first four games. Again, UM found its footing at midseason and won three of its next four games to reach .500. But two Top-10 teams, Florida and Notre Dame, lay ahead.

* * *

Sugar Bowl officials, who had told Graves during the week that the Gators would be invited to New Orleans, must have rested

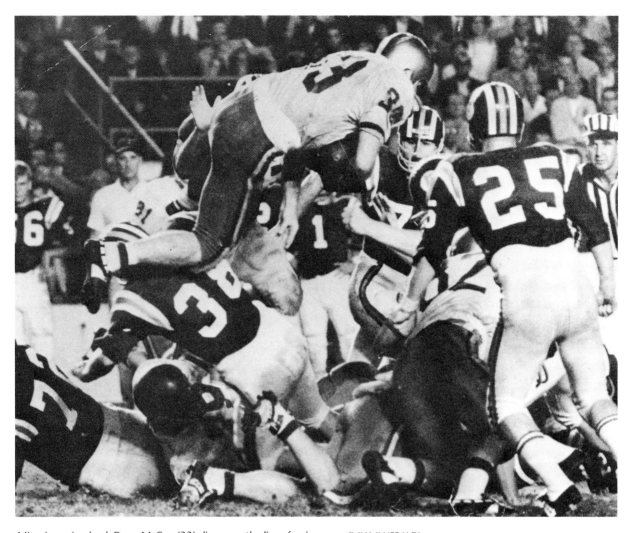

Miami running back Doug McGee (33) dives over the line of scrimmage. (MIAMI HERALD)

more comfortably in their seats when Gator halfback Jack Harper threw a 34-yard pass to wide receiver Charley Casey in the first quarter to give Florida a 7-0 lead. Miami countered later in the period thanks to Gator mistakes. The 'Canes got possession at the Florida 37 when Miami's Bernie Yatta recovered a fumbled punt return by Allen Trammell. A pass interference call against the Gators on fourth-and-two at the Florida 15 kept Miami's drive alive. Tate's game plan was to point senior fullback Pete Banaszak and sophomore halfback Doug McGee, who was subbing for the injured Russ Smith, toward the middle of the UF defense and pound away. Banaszak plunged over from

the one for the touchdown, but the PAT attempt drifted wide to leave Miami behind, 7-6, after one quarter.

Spurrier struggled through the rest of the first half, but Florida salvaged a pair of field goals. Gator kicker Wayne Barfield hit from 24 and 30 yards to give Florida a 13-6 halftime lead.

The Gators would again help Miami back into the game in the second half. A short kick by Miami punter Art Zachary bounded inside the 10, took a side hop and brushed the leg of Gator returner Dick Kirk. Larry LaPointe, who transferred to UM from Florida, recovered for the 'Canes at the UF eight. Miami sophomore quarterback Bill Miller ran around left end for an eight-yard touchdown and the PAT kick gave the Hurricanes a 13-13 tie in the third quarter.

UM punter Zachary, forced into service in the secondary when regular defensive back Jim Wahnee went out with an injury, slipped in front of Florida receiver Barry Brown to intercept Spurrier at the Miami 47. What followed was one of Miami's most important drives of Tate's tenure.

McGee ran off right guard for four yards to the Florida 49. He gained another seven yards off right guard for a first down at the UF 42. Banaszak bulled up the middle for seven more to the Florida 35, and McGee got a first down at the 30 with a five-yard gain off right guard. On first down at the 25, Florida was penalized for being offside, then Miller tossed an 11-yard pass to wingback Jerry Daanen for a first down at the 14.

Banaszak gained four off right guard, and Miller sprinted to his left before flipping to wide receiver Jim Cox for a seven-yard gain and a first down at the three. Here, the Florida defense stiffened. Banaszak found no running room on first down, and McGee was limited to a one-yard gain to the two on second down. Miller tried a rollout pass on third-and-goal, but was sacked at the 10 by Lynn Matthews. Don Curtwright came in to kick a 25-yard field goal to give Miami its first lead of the game, 16-13, with 12:35 to play.

Midway through the fourth quarter, Spurrier moved the Gators to Miami's 15. But a torrid rush from Ken Corbin and Rex Wilson forced Spurrier into an intentional grounding call on second down and pushed Florida back to the 31. On third down, Spurrier was sacked by Gene Trosch for a five-yard loss. Spurrier went for Harper and the touchdown on fourth down but threw the ball beyond the end zone. It would be Florida's last scoring threat. Spurrier recalls: "I think

that was probably one of the worst games I called. They let me call the plays down near the 10-, five-yard line."

Spurrier's night was a minor disaster: 8-for-22 for a season-low 79 yards with two interceptions. The Sugar Bowl representatives sheepishly extended their invitation to the Gators after the game. Graves found it difficult to think in terms of an overall season that led to such a bid while absorbed in losing to the 'Canes. "Gene Ellenson (longtime assistant to Graves at Florida) said don't ever underestimate Miami when they play Florida," Graves says. "They always believe they're better than Florida. They can always get ready for Florida, and they did."

The Gators completed the season with Spurrier playing one of his finest

Florida's Steve Spurrier outdueled Purdue quarterback Bob Griese to win the 1966 Heisman Trophy. (UNIVERSITY OF FLORIDA)

games in a 30-17 victory over Florida State and a 20-18 loss to Missouri in the Sugar Bowl. The

Tigers led 20-0 with 10:32 to play before Spurrier began a frenzied comeback. But after the first UF touchdown, assistant Ed Kensler elected to go for two points—later saying he thought losing 20-8 would look better than losing 20-7—and the miss left the Gators in the unenviable position of having to go for two on each subsequent touchdown. Going 0-for-3 on two-pointers left Florida as a loser despite matching Missouri in touchdowns.

For Miami, there would be another massive crowd (68,077) coming to the Orange Bowl to watch the 'Canes battle to a 0-0 tie with the Irish, rated sixth. The tie clinched a winning season, and Tate had Miami pointed in the right direction.

The '66 'Canes went 7-2-1—beating Spurrier and the Gators again, this time in Gainesville, 21-16—and beat Virginia Tech in the Liberty Bowl. Tate broke college football's color line in the Deep South with the signing of lineman Ray Bellamy of nearby Palmetto (who also was being recruited by Florida and FSU) in December 1966. The '67 team made it three consecutive over Florida and advanced to the Bluebonnet Bowl, losing to Colorado to finish the year 7-4.

That was Miami's final bowl trip under Tate. The '68 team opened 4-1 but collapsed to a 5-5 finish. The '69 team lost to Florida State and Florida in its first and last games and finished 4-6. And somewhere along the line, the smile was fading from Jolly Cholly's face.

*　　*　　*

Tate entered the 1970 season with one year remaining on his contract. He was spending more on recruiting than Florida or FSU, in part because he wasn't convinced that he could win with primarily in-state talent. "I just don't believe that year-in, year-out, there are enough blue-chippers in Florida or any state where there are three schools the size of Florida State, Florida and Miami," he was quoted as saying. The 'Canes opened the season with a 36-14 victory over little William & Mary before a crowd of 27,286, UM's smallest

opening game gathering since 1953. The same weekend saw the Dolphins, playing their first home game as a member of the NFL and with Don Shula as coach, draw 57,140 to the Orange Bowl. Miami traveled the following Saturday to Atlanta to play Georgia Tech, where Dodd still served as athletic director, and lost to the Yellow Jackets, 31-21.

The following Tuesday, with Miami scheduled to play Maryland, Tate called school president Henry King Stanford and told him of his intention to resign, effective immediately. Stanford, according to published reports, asked Tate to reconsider but was rebuffed. Stanford then asked Miami assistant Walt Kichefski, who had been turned down for the job when Tate was hired in 1964, to serve as interim coach, which he did for the remainder of the season. Tate, who didn't attend the Wednesday news conference to announce his departure, was interviewed by the Miami *Herald* five days later at his brother's home in Jacksonville. He said he simply was tired of the job. In a subsequent interview with the *Herald,* printed November 7, Tate explained that in Miami, his family had been harassed and his property vandalized. He also cited poor communication between the athletic director and overall university administration, the social climate on campuses, the increased use of drugs by college students and the intrusion of pro football on the college game.

Tate declined opportunities to be interviewed for this book. Friends and colleagues offer varying views on why Tate suddenly quit. Former assistant Fran Curci says: "You get yourself tied up in so many things—all the things you have to do as a head coach beside coaching—that pretty soon you begin to rely more on your assistants. And pretty soon your assistants begin to undermine you. I think in Charlie's case, he had a really severe problem on his staff, and he didn't even know about it. Charlie began to rely on people he didn't know or they didn't know him. All of a sudden, he looks up one day, and kids are drinking; they're falling apart. I guess it was more than he could handle, and he said the heck with it and gave it up. He was too good a coach to just give up."

Bill Peterson remembers Tate as someone who wanted to talk football no matter the time or place. Peterson said Tate called him after the resignation to inquire about a position on Peterson's staff at Rice, but there were no openings. "I think he got disgusted at not being able to discipline the guys at that time," Peterson says.

The coach who perceived pro ball as something of an intruder ironically became a pro coach in 1975, in the second season of the World Football League, with the Jacksonville Express.

But the way to remember Tate's coaching days are on the collegiate level, and with a smile on his face, even if there were times when Tate didn't want to let it show. Former UM assistant George MacIntyre recalls one such occasion when Tate's assistants couldn't understand why Tate was more than 45 minutes late one morning for the regular staff meeting.

"We're sitting talking about what we're doing, but the head coach isn't there," MacIntyre recalls. "It's early in the week, and we haven't got the game plan yet. And all of a sudden he comes in. He's got this yellow pad; he worked football all weekend on the yellow pad. Threw his yellow pad on the desk. He's kind of heavyset, and he's got these squinty little eyes. He looks at us and says, 'Anybody who says they run their own household . . . will lie about other things!' I thought I would just die because Annie Lee had him doing something and he couldn't get away when he was trying to get a game plan done."

Florida vs. Florida State
Lane Fenner's Catch

There have been more important Florida-Florida State games than the one at Doak Campbell Stadium in 1966. But this game will forever hold its place in history, possibly the most memorable of the series.

And it can all be boiled down to two words: Lane Fenner.

A gangly junior receiver from Evansville, Indiana, Fenner had never played a down of football previously for the Florida State Seminoles. But he was about to become synonymous with this hard-fought series.

There was another reason to remember the '66 game. It would be the last appearance in the series of Florida quarterback Steve Spurrier, arguably the best player to ever put on a Gator uniform, arguably the best college football player from the state of Florida.

Spurrier, in his senior season, was playing with receivers Richard Trapp and Paul Ewaldsen and sophomore running back Larry Smith. The glittery UF offense had made the quarterback a Heisman Trophy candidate.

And there might not have been a better year to be the Heisman winner than in 1966. The bidding war between the established National Football League and the upstart American Football League was continuing to escalate. Assuming that the NFL didn't give in to a merger, Spurrier might have been in position to command a million-dollar salary from the pro football team that won his services.

With a record Doak Campbell crowd of 46,698 on hand, Florida wasted little time getting its first touchdown out of the way. Spurrier directed UF 73 yards in 10 plays, capping the game's first possession with a 35-yard touchdown pass to Trapp, who was backpedaling into the end zone behind Florida State's Butch Riser.

The Seminoles replied on their first play from scrimmage when Gary Pajcic turned a quarterback sneak into a 27-yard run. A 42-yard pass to Ron Sellers gave Florida State the ball at Florida's one-yard line, where fullback Jim Mankins carried over for the tying score.

(The catch by sophomore Sellers, by the way, was a taste of things to come. His junior year he would catch an FSU record 70 passes, and the following year he set an NCAA record with 86 receptions. He became the first FSU player to be selected in the first round of the NFL draft when the Boston Patriots signed him in 1969.)

UF coach Ray Graves (right) was urged by his brother, the postmaster in Knoxville, Tennessee, to look at a fabulous quarterback from nearby Johnson City named Steve Spurrier. (UF ARCHIVES)

FSU took a 10-7 lead about six minutes into the second quarter on a 26-yard field goal by Pete Roberts. But Spurrier quickly brought Florida back. In 12 plays, the Gators covered 70 yards. Of the 12 plays, nine were passes—seven caught by Trapp. The last one was a six-yarder that provided the go-ahead touchdown with 48 seconds to play in the half.

The second half began with Florida State's John Hurst fielding the kickoff at FSU's 15 and racing 58 yards before being halted at the Florida 27. Four plays later, Mankins bulled over from the one as the Seminoles regained the lead, 16-14. Later in the third quarter, Roberts added a 37-yard field goal to increase Florida State's lead to 19-14.

In the fourth quarter, Spurrier covered 61 yards in only two plays—a 20-yard pass to Ewaldsen and a 41-yard touchdown pass to Smith with 10:44 to play. The touchdown gave UF a 20-19 lead, a two-point conversion—Spurrier to Trapp—increasing the Gators' lead to 22-19.

With the ball on Florida's 45 with 17 seconds to play, six-foot-five Lane Fenner was sent in for his first play from scrimmage as a Seminole. He ran a fly pattern down the right sideline toward Doak Campbell Stadium's north end zone, chased by UF defensive backs Larry Rentz and Bobby Downs. Pajcic tried to get the ball to him, with Fenner turning to the inside to check for the ball over his left shoulder. Neither Rentz nor Downs was in good position to break up the play; Rentz, in fact, all but screened Downs out of the play.

Fenner appeared to grab the ball with his fingertips and lodge it against his shoulder pads while falling across the goal line with neither foot anywhere near the sideline. According to college rules—control of the ball with at least one foot in bounds—Fenner appeared to have scored a touchdown. Field judge Doug Moseley thrust an arm in a gesture that some later interpreted to mean he was signaling that Fenner made the catch in bounds. But after Fenner rolled out of bounds, Moseley made his first definitive motion—signaling emphatically that the play was an incompletion. With three seconds to play, Roberts attempted a field goal that would have earned the Seminoles a 22-22 tie. But the kick was wide and short.

"I'm sure I was in bounds," Fenner said after the game. "I know I was in bounds until Larry Rentz hit me. If he hit me after I got the pass it should have been a touchdown. If he hit me before, it was pass interference. I was sure I had it."

Seminoles coach Bill Peterson wasn't quite as controlled in his disappointment. He pulled his keys out of one of his pockets and threw them at the carpet in his office. Then he picked them up and threw them at the wall. Next came another bashing into the carpet. "Tell me," he said. "What does it take to beat Florida?"

Peterson was asked, of course, about the Fenner play. "I wasn't in position to see," he said. "All I know is 40 people came up to me and said he was in bounds when he caught it. Fenner said he thought he was in bounds. He said he was concentrating on the ball and couldn't be sure where he was when he caught it. The official made a good call. He was in position to see the play and called it the way he saw it. The overflow crowd down there confused things, too."

FSU partisans weren't the only ones who thought Fenner made the catch in bounds. Joe Halberstein, sports editor of the Gainesville *Sun,* began his Sunday-morning column: "It looked good to me."

That night, Peterson got his first glimpse of still photographs of the play, from the St. Petersburg *Times.* The photos appeared to show Fenner at least two feet within the end zone with possession. "I'm going back and tell the boys they've won it, and we're going on from there," Peterson said. At a Sunday night student rally, Peterson declared FSU the winner of the game.

Such "evidence" as the St. Petersburg photographs evoked a volley of verbal and printed punching and counter-punching. Tallahassee *Democrat* sports editor Bill McGrotha wrote for the Monday paper that "It should have been ruled a touchdown. There is no longer any reasonable question about it." He pointed not only to the photos but to game films. And, contrary to Peterson's postgame statement, McGrotha said Moseley was not in good position to make the call.

McGrotha speculated that Florida State would be receiving an official apology from Moseley's supervisor, George Gardner of the Southeastern Conference. In fact, Peterson was scheduled to speak to the Atlanta Touchdown Club that Monday, and he spoke with Gardner before making his public appearance. When he spoke to the Touchdown Club, Peterson advocated the use of electronic devices to help officials determine such con-

troversial calls. Back in Tallahassee, FSU athletic director Vaughn Mancha said he wished Florida coach Ray Graves would acknowledge Moseley's error considering what could be seen in the photos.

On that Monday in Gainesville, Graves broke his silence regarding the play and supported Moseley. "I had not planned to make any further statements . . . But due to the continued one-sided version of the call by FSU officials, and the resulting castigation of an honest official, I feel it necessary for me to make a statement for the students, alumni and fans of the University of Florida . . . I honestly believe the call which was made

Florida State coach Bill Peterson didn't have a scholarship form available when he wanted to sign Jacksonville's Ron Sellers so he had an assistant coach deliver a mimeographed copy.
(FLORIDA STATE UNIVERSITY)

Florida State quarterback Gary Pajcic, shown against Florida in 1968, passed for 208 yards and rushed for 11 in the Seminoles' controversial 22-19 loss to the Gators in 1966. (FLORIDA STATE UNIVERSITY)

was correct, and support the official's decision that the play was absolutely not good."

That night, the game's referee appeared before a group of more than 100 people in Tallahassee. He noted that he himself made a couple of errors during the game. He also said that Moseley should have positioned himself around the 12-yard line on the play instead of the five-yard line.

Says Spurrier in recalling the play that he watched (sort of) from the UF sideline: "I peeked out. It was down our bench side. I sort of leaned out, sort of watched the guy catch it as he was falling and twisting and going out of bounds. It was definitely—you could have

been called in, could have been called out. It would have been one of those instant-replay shots, and I don't know how the replay would have proved it."

Larry Rentz's memory of the play: "I tipped it on the top of my fingers. Fenner still caught it, and all I really recall is all three of us (Fenner, Rentz and Bobby Downs) landed out of bounds. If he was down or out, I think it will be a topic of conversation as long as Florida and FSU have an athletic program. At the time, there wasn't enough time to analyze it. The referee, I think, immediately signaled him out of bounds. I remember Coach Peterson coming on the field at a ginger trot and having a word or two with the umpire."

Graves has been often reminded of that game and that play on his many business trips to Tallahassee. "'Pete' and I were the best of friends. I always kid him. I tell him he was a better coach than he was official," Graves says. "I think that's one that will always be controversial. Even looking at the film we have—most of them were taken from the west side, and he was falling out of bounds toward the east side—there was no way you could tell whether he was juggling the ball or whatever."

Peterson says: "Of course I think Ray thinks he was in."

The FSU coach says that even though he wasn't sure what happened, he needed to make a stand in support of his players. "When you're Florida State, you lose to Florida and your season is over. I was trying to make the players think they'd won the football game without losing their morale. I wasn't getting on the official, but I had to, to make the kids think they won that game."

Fenner has remained a veritable recluse since 1968, when his football career ended one year after leaving FSU with a year's duty with the AFL's San Diego Chargers. Tallahassee *Democrat* sports writer Gerald Ensley located Fenner in 1986 while researching a story on the 20th anniversary of the game, and dis-

It appears that Florida State's Lane Fenner (82) makes his infamous catch in bounds in the end zone as Florida's Bobby Downs (12) and Larry Rentz defend; official Doug Moseley ruled no catch. (FLORIDA STATE UNIVERSITY)

Another view of the Fenner catch, showing him with his right knee about to touch the ground in the end zone, well within bounds, as he cradles the ball with his right hand against his left shoulder. (TALLAHASSEE DEMOCRAT)

covered a complex individual who sometimes seemed guarded and hostile about his football past yet other times seemed curious and entertaining. Fenner told Ensley he regretted having been forever linked with this otherwise innocuous moment in his life, though he still maintained he was in bounds with possession of the ball.

* * *

The Fenner controversy overshadowed Spurrier's magnificent performance. He completed 16 of 24 passes for 219 yards, but he always seemed to get the ball to the right per-son at the right time. That was nothing new for the senior from the hills of Tennessee.

Florida coach Ray Graves was from Knoxville, Tennessee, where his brother served as the postmaster. Graves' brother saw Spurrier play as a junior in high school in nearby Johnson City. The son of a Presbyterian minister, Spurrier was born in Miami Beach shortly before the family moved to Tennessee. Spurrier was a three-sport star in high school and intended to get a basketball scholarship from either Tennessee or Kentucky before Graves intervened. He brought Spurrier to Gainesville for a football visit. With football now an option, he narrowed his field to UF, Mississippi and Alabama. Finally, Spurrier picked football and picked Florida.

As a sophomore in 1964, Spurrier's first collegiate pass was good for 54 yards to Jack Harper. Before the year was out, Spurrier had thrown for 943 yards to lead the Gators to a 7-3 finish. In 1965, he led the Southeastern Conference in passing and shattered school records en route to an 1,893-yard season. UF, in the meantime, was invited to the Sugar Bowl, the school's first major bowl appearance. UF lost to Missouri, yet Spurrier set six records for total offense and passing to become the first player in the bowl's history to be named most valuable player after playing for the losing team.

As a senior, Spurrier increased his yardage to 2,012 and increased his touchdown total from 14 to 16. Heisman Trophy ballots went out across the country the week that Florida—6-0 and ranked seventh in the nation—faced Auburn. Not only did Spurrier throw for 349 yards and three touchdowns, he punted seven times for an average of 46.9 yards and kicked the winning field goal from 40 yards out to beat Auburn, 30-27. Spurrier outdistanced Purdue quarterback Bob Griese to win the Heisman, the first ever for a player from a college in Florida. By the time bowl bids were announced, Florida had lost only once, to Georgia. UF was invited to play in its first Orange Bowl Classic, which was a victory over Georgia Tech.

*   *   *

It's interesting to note, though, that Florida lost its regular-season finale, and Spurrier's last home game, to Miami. The Hurricanes, led by Ted "the Mad Stork" Hendricks, only a sophomore at the time, held the high-scoring Gators to 16 points and forced Spurrier into two interceptions. Hendricks would go on to become a two-time All-American and a star with the Baltimore Colts and the Oakland Raiders.

Hendricks was a bright kid from Hialeah and said one of the reasons he chose Miami

was for its math honors program. But once on campus, the problem was deciding which part of the football coaching staff would get a chance to mold this mass of raw talent in the fall of 1965. Assistant coach Walt Kichefski, who coached offensive and defensive ends, told freshman coach Fran Curci never to even put the Hendricks kid on defense. That kind of talent in that kind of body would make for an unstoppable receiver, Kichefski said. Sure enough, Hendricks caught 12 passes in the game against the Florida freshmen and looked like the weapon of the future.

But going into the '66 season, Coach Charlie Tate planned some staff changes and asked Kichefski about coaching strictly defense. Kichefski said he would consider the move but complained that Miami didn't have enough talent on defense and that he wanted to "draft" a couple of players from the offensive platoon. The first choice was Phil Smith, whom Kichefski wanted as middle guard. The second was Hendricks, which prompted a distressed cry of "Ted Hendricks?" from backfield coach Ken Shipp.

When Miami opened the season at Colorado, ABC broadcaster Bud Wilkinson got his first glimpse of Hendricks and asked Kichefski, "My God. Where did this kid come from?"

Hendricks was named to one All-America team as a sophomore, quite a feat considering there were a couple of senior defensive ends out there named Alan Page of Notre Dame and Bubba Smith of Michigan State. He not only repeated as an All-American as a junior and senior but finished fifth in the Heisman balloting that was won by Southern Cal's O.J. Simpson.

*   *   *

Still, 1966 was Steve Spurrier's year.

"More people, alumni around the state, still talk about the years that Steve was quarterback, that they were the most exciting in the football annals of Florida," Graves says.

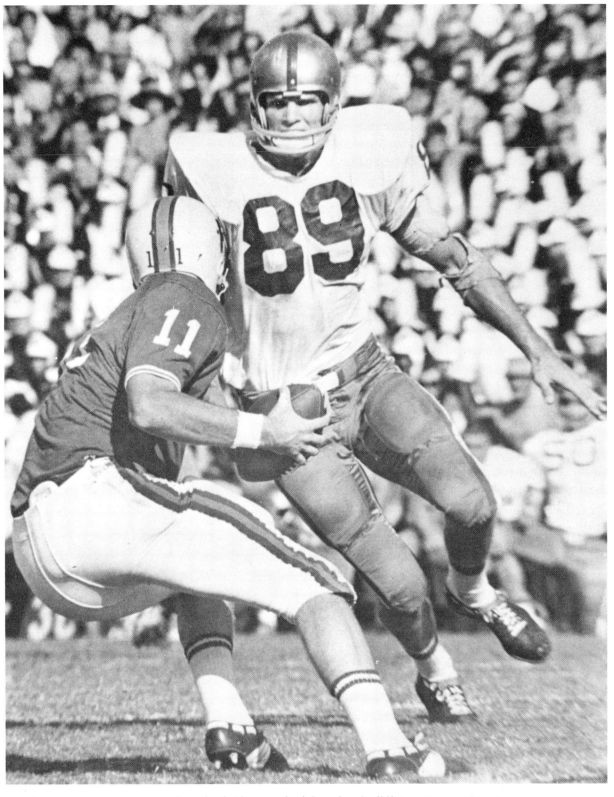

Ted Hendricks presents an imposing figure for Florida quarterback Steve Spurrier (11). (UNIVERSITY OF MIAMI)

"They (fans) used to be able to leave in the middle of the fourth quarter and get started home, but Steve kept 'em there until the end of the game."

Says Spurrier: "I was very fortunate (regarding the Heisman voting) in that most of the Southern writers got behind me. As far as the votes, I had 1600 and something and Griese was second, and he had 800 and some. So I don't know if any one game made an 800-vote difference."

Spurrier did not experience the same level of success in pro football after being picked in the first round by the San Francisco 49ers. There were a few seasons in which he jostled for a starting role with incumbent John Brodie. He eventually played nine years in the NFL with the 49ers and later the expansion Tampa Bay Buccaneers before going into coaching at Florida during Doug Dickey's last season in 1978. He then latched on with former UF assistant Pepper Rodgers at Georgia Tech for a year before becoming offensive coordinator at Duke.

His first well-known project was Duke quarterback Ben Bennett, who finished his career as the NCAA's all-time leading passer with 9,614 yards. Spurrier then landed his first job as a head coach by taking the position with the Tampa Bay Bandits of the new United States Football League. In Tampa, he displayed the wide-open style that was marketed as "BanditBall." It wasn't long after the demise of that league that Spurrier was in demand as a head coach. Back at Duke in 1987, he again attracted national attention by taking an otherwise dormant program and not only delivering impressive offensive numbers but victories as well. His '89 team won the school's first Atlantic Coast Conference title in 27 years, a sure sign that he would be coaching at a higher-profile program very soon. That turned out to be his alma mater, the following season.

✳

Florida vs. Miami
The Cuban Comet Takes Miami

The joy being more than he could hold inside of him, Florida assistant coach Lindy Infante threw off his head set, burst out of the visitors' coaches booth at the Orange Bowl and raced for the field. As he ran, hundreds of Cubans—many of them watching their first American football game in person—stood in the west end zone, dancing and cheering.

The object of their affection was a 5-11, 180-pound sophomore wide receiver for the Gators named Carlos Alvarez. Though only completing his first season of varsity ball, the North Miami resident by way of Cuba had dazzled the Orange Bowl crowd of 70,934 by tying a Southeastern Conference single-game record with 15 catches for an SEC-record 237 yards as UF closed its regular season at 8-1-1 with a 35-16 victory over the Miami Hurricanes. This finish gave Alvarez, nicknamed the Cuban Comet, 88 catches during the season for 1,329 yards and 12 touchdowns, all SEC records.

While Alvarez's feats delighted every Gator in attendance, it was a particular point of pride to Infante—a native Miami-an who had signed Alvarez to a UF scholarship—and the Cuban contingent that traveled to the Orange Bowl hoping to cheer on one of its own.

"You talk about putting on a show," recalls Florida coach Ray Graves, who, though few at the time knew it, was coaching his last regular-season game for the Gators. "With all those Cubans in the south stands, it was a great exhibition."

* * *

Ten-year-old Carlos Alvarez Vasquez Rodriguez Ubieta sat in St. James Catholic School in North Miami. Paul Armstrong sat in front of him, and for a month Alvarez copied everything off Paul Armstrong's paper . . . including his name. You see, Carlos Alvarez came to St. James Catholic School knowing almost no English. Only a few weeks earlier he had lived in Havana, where his father, Licinio, was an attorney. But Fidel Castro had come into power and Licinio Alvarez feared for his family. Leaving Cuba had become increasingly difficult, so Licinio decided the time had come to take the ferry to America, to Miami. The ferry that the Alvarez family boarded was one of the last to leave Cuba before Castro cut off relations with the United States.

Licinio didn't know much English himself when the family arrived in the U.S. At the time, most Spanish-speaking people coming to Miami settled on the city's south side. But Licinio purposely decided to make a home in North Miami, where few residents spoke anything other than English. While young Carlos was forced to copy off Paul Armstrong's papers for weeks, it wasn't long before he learned the new language and became comfortable with his new home.

By the time Alvarez reached North Miami High School, he was a fleet-footed wide receiver who also played basketball and ran track. He had hurt his right knee playing basketball, but that didn't discourage Coach Graves from wanting Alvarez to come to Gainesville. He made his wishes clear to Infante: Bring back Alvarez. Says Alvarez: "Lindy said to my mother that he was Cuban, then my mom really pushed to go there." Of course,

Miami coach Charlie Tate wasn't pleased by what he saw of Florida's Reaves-to-Alvarez passing combination.
(MIAMI HERALD)

Alvarez already had pretty much made up his mind to go to Florida since he had two brothers—Cesar and Arthur—already attending UF and because he liked the Gators' commitment to the passing game. Meeting academic requirements wasn't a problem; Alvarez scored 491 out of a possible 495 on the state placement test.

*   *   *

Alvarez had never won a game at the Orange Bowl when he stepped out on the field this night in 1969. Twice, while playing for North Miami High, he had lost there, and the Gator freshmen had lost there the previous year. For all the offense that Florida would put on display, the Gators' first points were scored by their defense. Miami quarterback Kelly Cochrane was drifting across his own end zone midway through the first quarter, looking for a target for a screen pass, when he was tackled for a safety by Florida linebacker David Ghesquiere. Florida soon added to the lead with a 16-play, 80-yard drive that ended when running back Tommy Durrance scored on a three-yard run during the opening minute

Florida coach Ray Graves rejoices as the Gators score again. (MIAMI HERALD)

❈

of the second quarter. The most important play of the possession came on a third-and-26 call at Florida's 43-yard line. Alvarez made a diving catch on a John Reaves pass between two Miami defenders for a 36-yard gain to Miami's 21.

Florida linebacker Tom Abdelnour quickly set up UF's next score with an interception that gave the Gators possession at the Miami 35. Alvarez caught a 12-yard touchdown pass that, after a failed point-after kick, left Florida with a 15-0 lead only three minutes into the second quarter. The Gators held Miami and took over at their seven. Reaves heaved the ball downfield for Alvarez, who strained to make the catch, lost his balance and fell out of bounds untouched following a 41-yard gain. Florida fumbled two plays later; had Alvarez not lost his balance, his night would have featured one more touchdown catch and an additional 52 yards.

Miami closed Florida's lead to 15-7 with five minutes to play in the first half on a 32-yard touchdown run by running back Tom Sullivan.

The Hurricanes returned to the field in the second half, showing no signs of quitting. Miami pushed to Florida's 19 midway through the third quarter, but had to settle for Jim Huff's 33-yard field goal to cut the Gators' lead to 15-10 with 8:23 to play in the third quarter. But this Florida team could virtually score at will and calmly pieced together a 12-play, 63-yard scoring drive. Durrance scored from four yards out with 4:25 left in the third quarter to put the Gators ahead, 22-10. Miami scored in the opening minute of the fourth quarter when Cochrane passed 25 yards to Kevin Griffin. The subsequent two-point attempt failed, leaving UM behind, 22-16.

But Florida's big-play capabilities simply were too much for the Hurricanes. Durrance bolted for a 62-yard touchdown run with 5:44 to play (giving him 110 points that season, breaking a school record that stood since 1928) to give Florida a 29-16 lead. A Gator interception late allowed Reaves to throw one more touchdown pass to Alvarez, a 33-yarder with 3:36 to play. This was when Infante left the press box in joy, and the two UM fans who carried the sign that read, "THE CUBAN COMET WILL BE HIGHJACKED TONIGHT," must have realized that their cause was a lost one.

*   *   *

Alvarez, Reaves, Durrance and the rest of Florida's talented sophomore class—to be known collectively as the Super Sophs—reported to Gainesville in August 1969 shouldering a heavy load. Florida football had been thrown for a loss following the graduation of Heisman Trophy winner Steve Spurrier after the '66 season. While Spurrier had closed his career by helping Florida make trips to the Sugar Bowl and Orange Bowl, UF failed to go to a bowl in 1967 or 1968. Of the combined 12-7-1 record, the most painful blow was the 51-0 loss to Georgia in '68.

Graves was going to go with youth in '69, making Reaves the No. 1 quarterback and Alvarez a starting wide receiver, among other changes. The Gators opened on September 20 against Houston at Florida Field. The Cougars couldn't have been expecting much of a passing attack; the Gators threw two touchdown passes during all of 1968. It was doubtful that Houston was very familiar with Reaves or Alvarez. Surely, Houston wasn't aware that a UF scrimmage that week saw Alvarez, Reaves and the first-team offense win, 93-0.

Alvarez recalls: "Our offensive coordinator, Fred Pancoast, was, in my mind, the best. Right before the (Houston) game started, he told John and me that on the third play of the game we were going long. And we did, and it clicked." Clicked, as in a 70-yard touchdown pass on Reaves' first collegiate attempt and Alvarez's first real pass route. Reaves threw for 342 yards and five touchdowns as the UF Super Sophs made

Carlos Alvarez, the youngest member of Kodak's 1969 All-American team when he was named as a sophomore, talks with Kodak's Dr. Norwood Simmons during the festivities in New York. (UNIVERSITY OF FLORIDA)

their debut with a 59-34 victory over the stunned Cougars. Recalls Reaves: "Coach Graves said they sold 5,000 seats at halftime (with Florida ahead, 38-6). The whole student body came out of the stands and made a big tunnel for us to run out of at halftime."

* * *

The knee that Alvarez had hurt in high school didn't give him any trouble during his first two years at Gainesville. But the injury was aggravated during the spring of 1970 while he was running track. "There was no injury per se," he recalls. "My right knee just started to swell." After many diagnoses, it was Auburn's team physician—Dr. Jack Hughston of Columbus, Georgia—who determined that the end of Alvarez's bone was beginning to wear out. There was no way Alvarez could continue to practice every day and play normally during his final two years at UF. This all happened at the time that Doug Dickey came in from Tennessee to replace the popular Ray Graves, and the passing game —with Pancoast moving on to Georgia—no longer was emphasized. While no longer as effective on the field, Alvarez continued to work in campus awareness movements and was a force behind a group called the Florida League of Athletes. Many people believed the group was meant to be a type of union for players, meant to make bold demands of coaches and administrators.

"That was probably the most misunderstood group that ever got together on a college campus," Alvarez says. "All it was ever meant to do was to apprise people that athletes were students, too, and that we could participate in campus activities whether they were controversial or not. They took it as a radical organization perhaps because of the times—the campus demonstrations and the Viet Nam War. Certainly, there were some active students in that organization that went to rallies, and I was one of them. And I was proud of

that. You should participate in things that you have a deep sense of feeling for."

As a junior, Alvarez's numbers dropped to 44 catches (half his '69 total) for 717 yards and five touchdowns. As a senior, he caught 40 passes for 517 yards and two touchdowns. Hence, his junior-senior totals for catches, yardage and touchdowns didn't equal what he produced as one of the Super Sophs. For the record, his final two games against Miami produced nine total catches for 95 yards.

But that didn't diminish his overall achievement or his academic pursuits; he went to law school and now is a practicing attorney in Tallahassee. And no subsequent disappointment on the field could mute the joy that the Cuban Comet felt that night at the Orange Bowl in 1969 when he thrilled his countrymen.

"I knew in the beginning when we were warming up that something was going to happen in that game," Alvarez recalls. "Then the whole evening: we just couldn't miss. Having all your relatives there, a lot of Cubans up in the stands. It was pretty magical."

Miami vs. Florida
Coach Kichefski Gets "The Gator"

Walt Kichefski dedicated most of his adult life to the University of Miami football program. It was a love affair that went unrequited in only one respect; while various university officials down through the years recognized his ability as a coach and his devotion to UM, they never entrusted the Hurricanes' football team to him on a permanent basis.

And if Kichefski's love for Miami was boundless, it was almost equaled by his contempt for the University of Florida. He was standing on the UM sidelines the first time Miami faced Florida in football in 1938 and faced the Gators as a UM player and coach for the better part of five decades.

Kichefski defined the bitter rivalry in his own, unique terms. He made it a point for years to refer to the Gators only in the singular, as if they were some sort of evil force.

The Gator.

In 1970, Kichefski got a shot at "The Gator" as a head coach. Charlie Tate's shocking resignation as UM coach two games into the season prompted the Miami hierarchy to turn the program over temporarily to Kichefski, who had sought the position six years earlier when Tate was hired to succeed Andy

Gustafson. Kichefski accepted the offer, hopeful that he could convince those in power that he indeed was the man to lead the Hurricanes.

However, beginning with a 1-1 record, Kichefski's 'Canes were a disappointment. After beating Maryland, they suffered an embarrassing loss against the University of Tampa, coached by former UM quarterback Fran Curci. The losses continued to mount— Pittsburgh, Florida State (extending UM's losing streak against the Seminoles to five games), Tulane, Alabama and Syracuse. The loss to the Orangemen extended Miami's road losing streak to 11 games.

"Syracuse butchered us pretty good," Kichefski recalled. "It was cold, and it was rainy. After the game in the dressing room, I said, 'Well, men. We have to play Florida. Tell you what I'm going to do. I'm going to burn these movies because whoever comes in as the next coach, I wouldn't want him to look at this. We're gonna whip that damn Gator in Gainesville.' "

Kichefski said he tried to hold down his emotions during game week, though the players elected to work out in pads Wednesday when Kichefski wanted them to taper

Walt Kichefski, shown during a UM workout at the Orange Bowl, said Miami could upset Florida if the Hurricanes could grab an early lead. (MIAMI HERALD)

down. Then again, he brought in Eddie Dunn one afternoon to tell the '70 Hurricanes about the '38 Hurricanes who rode the train up to Gainesville and scored the monumental victory in the first game of the series.

"If our ballplayers get a gnaw of Gator meat early in the game, it'll excite them," Kichefski said. "They'll want more."

The Gators had gone through something of a disappointing season themselves. Big things were expected of a team dominated by juniors that made up the core of the 9-1-1 Super Sophs team of 1969. But the Gators floundered against the Southeastern Conference. After opening with wins over Duke and Mississippi State, Florida was crushed, 46-15, by an Alabama team that ended up 6-5. At Knoxville, Florida was humbled by Tennessee, 38-7. A subsequent 63-14 drubbing by Auburn—with Pat Sullivan outdueling John Reaves in a match-up of the nation's premier junior quarterbacks—left UF with a 5-3 record.

An upset of Georgia followed by a victory over Kentucky rekindled bowl interest. If Florida beat Miami, it probably would be invited to play in the Liberty Bowl against Colorado, although Liberty Bowl officials politely said no invitation would be issued until its other contender, Tulane, completed its Saturday night game against LSU.

Going into the Miami game as a favorite of between 21 and 24 points, the Gators still had a chance to win nine games and build momentum for the 1971 senior season of Reaves, Carlos Alvarez and Co.

* * *

The University of Miami's football program had operated for 12 seasons before getting the chance to play the University of Florida. The opportunity first arose in 1938, when the 'Canes were in their second season under coach Jack Harding. About 3,500 UM fans made the trip to Gainesville to watch the 'Canes (2-0) face the Gators (1-2). Miami was led by Eddie Dunn and an end from Wisconsin named Walt Kichefski. Dunn scored three

touchdowns, and the Hurricanes left town that day—fighting their way to the train station—with a glorious 19-7 victory.

Kichefski had come to UM in 1936, didn't letter and returned home after the season. He boarded a train for Wisconsin with about fifteen cents to his name and ate nothing but a couple of candy bars for the duration of the trip. He was determined to leave his frustrations far behind in South Florida and continue his college football career at the University of Wisconsin.

But when he arrived back in Rhinelander, Wisconsin, the temperature was in the neighborhood of thirty below zero. That in itself was a convincing argument for making another go of it back in Coral Gables.

Kichefski earned two football letters, the latter coming in 1939 when he served as a team captain. After a brief fling in pro football, Kichefski was drawn back to UM and began a long term as Miami assistant coach under Harding, Dunn, Gustafson and Tate.

* * *

Miami took the opening kickoff of the 1970 game and silenced the better part of a Florida Field gathering of 50,149 by moving down the field for a touchdown. The 'Canes were aided by a pass interference penalty called against UF's Harvin Clark, a 35-yard mark-off that gave Miami a first down at the Florida 14-yard line. Tom Sullivan scored on a one-yard run with 11:30 to play in the first quarter. Mike Cummins added the extra point for a 7-0 UM lead. The 'Canes had their first taste of Gator meat; they wanted more.

The Hurricanes had two more good chances to score in the first half but came away empty. Punting from his own end zone, UF's John James boomed a kick out to the UF 47, but Miami return man Burgess Owens brought the ball back to the Gators' seven. Miami quarterback Kelly Cochrane's pass on first-and-goal bounced off the back of a Miami receiver and was intercepted by Florida's Robert Harrell.

UF's Robert Harrell (77) tries to cut off the corner on a sweep by Miami quarterback Kelly Cochrane. (UF ARCHIVES)

What followed was similar frustration for the Hurricanes. Miami's Larry Lancaster fielded a James punt at the Florida 40 and returned it to the 15. UM earned first-and-goal at the five then settled for a short field goal attempt by Cummins in the final minute of the half. It was blocked by Alan Cole.

At halftime, the Hurricanes headed to the locker room with a seven-point lead they must have thought could have been 21. UM senior tackle Bubba Chauvet asked Kichefski to leave the room, that he and junior tackle Dickie Trower had something to say to the rest of the players. The message was simple: Coach Kichefski might not be back after the current season, and it was up to the Hurricanes to get him some more points.

Miami responded by increasing its lead to 14-0 on a two-yard touchdown run by sophomore Scott Mundrick. The key play of the drive came when UM converted a fourth-and-

two at Florida's 20 with Cochrane passing to Steve Gaunt for the first down. Cummins added his second PAT of the game.

When Miami stopped Florida on its next possession, it looked like the Hurricanes actually could take control of the game. But Florida's John Clifford, a sophomore from Coral Gables, intercepted a Cochrane pass at midfield and went back 50 yards for a touchdown. UF kicker Jim Getzen, a sophomore from Miami's Newberry High School who had become the starter two games earlier following the suspension of first-stringer Richard Franco, added the extra point to pull the Gators within 14-7.

In the fourth quarter, a string of five consecutive Reaves completions—none of them to Alvarez—got the Gators back in the end zone. The last pass was a 41-yarder to Terry Ash. But Getzen's kick faded to the left of the uprights and left Florida trailing, 14-13.

Miami's last threat came after Chauvet blocked a punt by James and recovered it at the Florida 27. But the Gators held, and Cummins tried a 43-yard field goal attempt that fell short.

UF had 2:37 left to make something happen. Facing fourth-and-two at their 28, coach Doug Dickey had no choice but to go for the first down. Reaves hit Jim Yancey for

Miami quarterback Kelly Cochrane (16) gets a pass off over the middle just beyond the reach of the Gators' Eddy Moore (75)
(UF ARCHIVES)

John Clifford makes an interception for the Gators. (UF ARCHIVES)

an 18-yard gain to give the Florida Field crowd renewed hope with only a couple of minutes to play.

Reaves then threw 17 yards to Willie Jackson for a first down at the Miami 37. Dur-

rance ran for nine yards to the 28. Duane Doel followed by gaining three to the 25 for another UF first down. Reaves dropped back to pass again and Miami defensive back Chuck Foreman was called for pass interference at the UM 12 with 1:18 to play. It appeared the Gators were certainly within the field goal range of Getzen.

On first down, Durrance rumbled around right end for seven yards to the five. Dickey called Durrance's number again, but this time he was stopped for a three-yard loss back to the eight. Facing third-and-six, Reaves lofted a pass out in the flat to Durrance, who was standing at the three, but he dropped the ball.

That left Florida with fourth-and-six at the Miami eight, trailing by one point with 29 seconds to play. Dickey sent in Getzen for the game-winner from 25 yards.

Getzen's kick sailed left, as did his last PAT attempt, and was so low that it almost grazed one of Trower's upraised arms. No matter; the kick left Miami to kill off only the final 23 seconds.

Jim Getzen sat in front of his locker and wiped tears from his eyes. "I guess I'd better

go back to playing the guitar," he said. "I'm not as good a kicker as I thought I was.

"I had plenty of time both times. I wasn't nervous. I should have been able to kick there (the 25-yard field-goal attempt) with my eyes closed."

Tommy Durrance walked out of the shower and received an affectionate pat from his father, Leonard, who told him: "You've caught a lot of passes, and you'll catch a lot more."

"I wanted that pass in the worst way," Tommy lamented. "I had it. It was there. Then it wasn't."

In the visitors' dressing room, Walt Kichefski was presented with the game ball. The hugs included one from none other than Eddie Dunn, he of the three touchdowns scored against the Gators in '38.

"If we could only win one game this year, this is the one we wanted," Kichefski said.

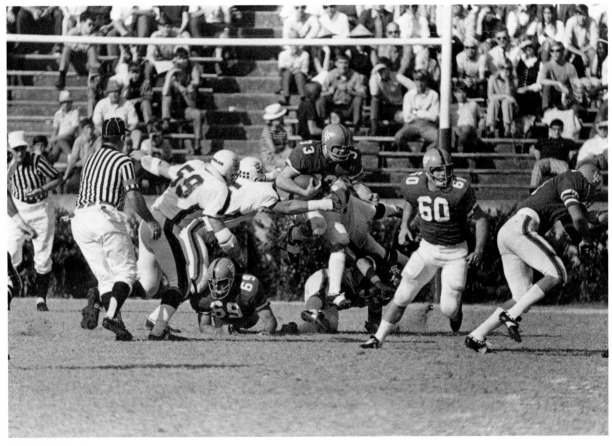

Florida running back Tommy Durrance follows his blocking up the middle. (UF ARCHIVES)

Walt Kichefski gets a victory ride from his players after the Hurricanes upset "The Gator" in his only head coaching confrontation against Florida. (MIAMI HERALD: BOB EAST)

"We kind of felt like we were playing for an undefeated season today.

"I feel that it was one of the greatest efforts ever put forth by a Miami ballclub."

* * *

The victory at Florida Field was Walt Kichefski's last as a college football coach. UM closed the season at the Orange Bowl with a 36-3 loss to Houston. That left the Hurricanes with a 3-8 record, 2-7 under Kichefski.

As the university continued its search for a coach, Kichefski was convinced he would not be the man. "When you're around for thirty years, they figure somebody new is going to do a better job," Kichefski said. "I even had a meeting with all the recruits in the area and told them not to run off and sign with somebody else."

On December 19, Miami announced the hiring of Fran Curci, the former UM quarterback who had coached Tampa's Spartans to victory over the 'Canes in October. Not only was Kichefski passed over for the head coaching position; he was overlooked when UM went looking for a new athletic director. Kichefski stayed on at the university in a newly created job running the Athletic Federation —fund-raising— until he retired in 1978.

He remained a revered figure in UM athletics, granting interview requests annually from across the state when it came time for Miami to renew its rivalry with "The Gator." Kichefski suffered a heart attack in November 1991 and died of inoperable stomach cancer on January 9, 1992 at the age of 75.

While he had many Miami victories to savor and many Miami defeats to endure from the '30s on, it's doubtful he was as emotional about any game played by the Hurricanes as the one in which he was the head coach of a team that beat The Gator.

No, not the Gators. To Kichefski, it was always The Gator.

Florida State vs. Florida
Winless UF Beats Unbeaten FSU

Was Bill Peterson out in Houston second-guessing his decision to leave Florida State to become football coach and athletic director at Rice? Back in Tallahassee, Larry Jones was still undefeated five weeks into his career as Florida State football coach. Southern Mississippi, Miami, Kansas, Virginia Tech and Mississippi State had been dispatched, and the Associated Press recognized FSU in its Top-20 rankings for the first time all season (at No. 19). In Tallahassee, there already was talk of the bowl season.

Jones couldn't have imagined it would be this easy. Florida State was his first collegiate head coaching position. He had played at LSU in that school's glory days of the late '50s, when Peterson was an assistant to Paul Dietzel. Jones later joined Dietzel's LSU staff and remained with him during subsequent stops at Army and South Carolina before coming to Tallahassee.

Jones inherited a potent passing game featuring junior quarterback Gary Huff, senior wide receiver Rhett Dawson and junior Barry Smith. The program was coming off five consecutive winning seasons under Peterson, who cited the school's lack of financial commitment when he left. Maybe in spite of those problems, Florida State was bound for

big things under Jones. The outlook in Gainesville, though, was decidedly gloomy. While Florida State had yet to be beaten, Florida had yet to win. This was a crushing development considering the individual talent that the Gators boasted. The vaunted "Super Sophs" of 1969 were seniors. Quarterback John Reaves was among the best in the nation. Wide receiver Carlos Alvarez was no longer the threat he was earlier in his career because of knee problems but could not be overlooked. In the backfield, Tommy Durrance was a dangerous runner.

With all of this, the Gators had somehow gotten off to an 0-5 start, winless through five games for the first time since they went 0-9 in 1946.

The day before the Florida State game, coach Doug Dickey announced that Florida's "first" season was over and the "second" was about to begin. The players decided something a little more drastic was necessary. A group of seniors called a team meeting for 11 p.m. that night at the 50-yard line at Florida Field. Recalls UF's John Clifford: "There was still a lot of resentment between the players and the coaches. I think the team just made a commit-

Larry Jones began his Florida State coaching career with five consecutive victories—until running into the previously winless Gators.
(FLORIDA STATE UNIVERSITY)

ment to play for themselves." Some of the more inspiring words came from Gene Conrad, a reserve guard. Conrad's greatest contributions to the UF program to date were his unusual acts at the annual football variety show—eating three pounds of Crisco as a sophomore and trying to top that a year later by munching on 56 live minnows and an earthworm.

There was another factor, more tangible than a coach's speech or a players' meeting, that had a bearing on the game. Huff, it turned out, had injured his passing arm in the victory over Mississippi State. Jones succeeded in keeping word of this out of the press during the week even though Huff didn't practice much of the week. Little did anyone

UF's acclaimed "Super Sophs" were finally seniors, but Doug Dickey's 1971 Gators lost their first five games while scoring only 36 total points. (UF SPORTS INFORMATION)

know that Jones planned to come to Gainesville and concentrate on the running game because his quarterback was wounded. But running back Art Munroe was also hurt, planning to play despite having an injured shoulder and a fractured wrist. Florida State was established as a 10-point favorite.

Likewise, Dickey had decided that week that he would use Florida's feared passing game basically as a decoy. The Gators would run until the Seminoles proved they could stop them.

* * *

With a record Florida Field gathering of 65,109 in attendance, Florida lost the coin toss for the first time all season—which they hoped was a good omen considering their results to date.

Florida State's first possession ended in a 48-yard field goal attempt by barefoot kicker Frank Fontes, whose effort fell short. Florida took over and, to the astonishment of the crowd, came out running. Mike Rich ran four consecutive plays. Reaves' first pass came on a third-and-seven. It fell incomplete. After forcing FSU to punt late in the first quarter, Florida remained on the ground for what would become a 14-point blitz early in the second quarter.

Florida's Tommy Durrance (33) cuts inside, trying to avoid FSU's Robert Ashmore (28). (UF ARCHIVES)

Florida's Willie Jackson tries to hold onto the ball despite pressure from FSU's Eddie McMillan. (UF ARCHIVES)

The Gators opened the second quarter in the middle of a 75-yard drive that culminated in a one-yard touchdown run by Rich—Florida's first rushing touchdown of the season. The PAT attempt failed when center Mark King's snap sailed over the head of holder John Schnebly, leaving Florida ahead, 6-0. On FSU's first play after the following kickoff, Munroe fumbled at the 26-yard line just before he was hit by UF's Robert Harrell. The ball fell right into the waiting hands of Jimmy Barr, who raced for the end zone to give the Gators another touchdown. Trying to make up for the missed PAT, Dickey decided to go for two points. Reaves found Durrance in the end zone, and the Florida lead increased to 14-0. The Gators had scored more points in 20 seconds than they had in any of their previous five games. Neither team mounted much of a threat for the remainder of the half, or in the third quarter.

Early in the fourth period, Florida State got on the scoreboard thanks to a 73-yard drive that ended with a three-yard touchdown run by Paul Magalski. Having cut the UF lead to 14-7, Florida State then forced the Gators to punt, but Huff had a pass intercepted by John Faix at the FSU 33. The Gators converted that into a 42-yard field goal by Richard Franco to take a 17-7 lead.

The combination of Huff to Dawson clicked for a six-yard touchdown pass with 3:02 to play, pulling the Seminoles within 17-13, and FSU added two points after on a Huff-to-Dawson pass.

The Gators recovered FSU's onside kickoff but were held to one yard on three plays and punted. The Seminoles took over at their 27

Richard Franco's 52-yard field goal attempt is blocked at the line of scrimmage by Florida State's Richard Amman.
(UF INFORMATION SERVICES)

with 2:10 to play. Huff's first pass of the series fell incomplete, intended for Dawson and broken up by Doug Sorenson. Huff then threw to Munroe for six yards and to Dawson for 13 yards and a first down at the FSU 45.

There was little more than a minute to play, and the Seminoles kept passing. Huff threw to Gary Parris for six yards, then was sacked for a 10-yard loss. On third down with 49 seconds to play, Dawson appeared to make a diving catch at the Florida 28. But the field judge ruled that he lost possession when he slammed into Florida Field's artificial turf. Now there was only one chance for Florida State to keep the drive alive and hope to bring in Fontes for a game-winning field goal attempt. Instead, Huff overthrew Smith near the right sideline to give the ball over to the elated Gators with only seconds to play. Only one plunge into the line by Rich was required to run out the clock.

For those used to UF's incredible passing numbers during the Reaves era, the postgame statistics looked like a cruel joke. Eleven passes attempted, only three in the first half, for a total of 44 yards. Reaves resorted to exaggeration in his postgame comments: "As long as we win, I don't care if I never complete another pass." The Gators rushed for 152 yards, 18 short of FSU's total. Durrance came into the game having rushed for 50 yards over five games in Florida's pass-oriented offense but led the way against Florida State with 60.

Huff didn't play like a quarterback who couldn't throw. He completed 22 of 40 passes for 198 yards. Dawson caught six for 71 yards. But Florida State's final totals included four lost fumbles (three by Munroe) and an interception. Said Jones afterward: "It just wasn't our day."

Looking back, Dickey puts it succinctly: "It was a game that, gee, we had to win."

*　　*　　*

The dramatic victory didn't change the course of Florida's already floundering season too much. After edging Maryland to improve to 2-5, the Gators were plastered by Auburn

(40-7, behind the passing of eventual Heisman Trophy winner Pat Sullivan) and Georgia (49-7). Subsequent wins over Kentucky and Miami only slightly eased the pain.

Florida State went on to an 8-3 finish and was invited to play in the new Fiesta Bowl on the Arizona State campus outside of Phoenix. The Seminoles' opponent was host Arizona State, with coach Frank Kush and its wide-open passing attack. Florida State couldn't keep up with the Sun Devils and lost, 45-38.

Jones put together another impressive season in 1972, though the year finished on a disappointing note. The Seminoles won their first four games to rise to No. 13 in the AP poll—before being brought back to earth again by Florida, 42-13. FSU took a 7-3 record into its season finale at South Carolina. A victory would send Florida State to the Peach Bowl. Instead, the Seminoles lost and stayed home despite their 7-4 mark.

That loss—and the subsequent loss of a bowl bid and the financial rewards that go with it—did immeasurable harm to the program, Jones says. Unlike most schools that had wealthy donors to help fill the athletic coffers, Florida State had been coed only since the late '40s. "The money (in the athletic department) was really tight," he recalls. "We just didn't have the funds to go out on the road recruiting. It was just a matter of time to just survive with all the other things happening until FSU had some graduates that were getting older and getting established in their profession. We had a small group of people fighting hard to help FSU, but it just wasn't enough."

Particularly damaging to Jones, more so than lack of money, was the St. Petersburg *Times'* revelation that Jones used an off-season conditioning drill in which players wrestled on a mat beneath a 4-foot-high sheet of chicken wire. The intent was for players to learn to keep low; the result was that Florida State's program was criticized nationwide for this dehumanizing tactic. The NCAA investigated FSU and penalized the school—not for the tactics of the workout program but because the drills were mandatory. In NCAA terms, the subsequent probation was virtually a warning—one year with no sanctions, meaning the Seminoles were free to play in a bowl and on national television. But the negative publicity to Jones and the program couldn't be measured.

With Huff and Smith gone and no running game yet in place, Jones says Florida State entered the '73 season "with no players." That certainly appeared to be the case. The Seminoles finished 0-11, with only a couple of close games to point to. They ended the year at Gainesville with a 49-0 loss that extended their losing streak against the Gators to six games. Many in and around Tallahassee were calling for Jones' dismissal, discounting what he had accomplished in his first two seasons at FSU. Jones, it turned out, was more than willing to comply with the wishes of those who wanted a new coach. He submitted his resignation four days before Christmas 1973.

"I felt like it was best for the university to go," he says. "I never complained that we never had the facilities and we never had the money. The thing to do was give them a chance. Go ahead and make it good and clean for them."

The NCAA investigation of the chicken wire episode also hurt Jones. "It took its toll on the coaches," he says. "If the NCAA stuff hadn't come along and added to it—you can only do so much. You can only put your family and your coaching staff through so much."

Jones became an assistant at Tennessee under Bill Battle and eventually made it back to LSU as an athletic administrator. "A lot of people who supported the program have told me, 'You were just there at the wrong time.' It was the time of investigative reporting, and everybody was upset on the college campuses. But I don't regret anything about FSU."

Florida vs. Miami
The Florida Flop

Even John Reaves admitted that setting the NCAA career passing record in Florida's season finale against the Miami Hurricanes was a long shot. Reaves would need to pass for 344 yards to equal the record set the previous year by Jim Plunkett at Stanford. But after Reaves threw for 162 yards in the first half, Gators coach Doug Dickey decided—with his team comfortably ahead, 17-0—to alter his game plan and allow his senior quarterback to take dead aim at the record book.

It appeared Reaves would get his chance when Florida forced Miami to punt with about eight minutes to play and Reaves needing 35 yards to break the record. But Florida's Harvin Clark fielded the punt at the Gators' 18-yard line and proceeded to make one of the greatest runs of his career, hurdling defenders and returning the punt for a touchdown—and giving the ball back to Miami. It's possible no one in college football history was more distraught over scoring a touchdown for his own team. Clark raced from the end zone to the UF sideline and apologized to Reaves for scoring. It indeed appeared Clark had cost Reaves a shot at the record when Reaves was intercepted 14 yards short of the record with about five minutes to play. Miami,

though trailing 45-8, was content to use a controlled running game to eat away at the clock. With less than two minutes to play, Clark, who also played linebacker, called timeout and asked Dickey to do the unthinkable.

Let's let Miami score, and get the ball back for Reaves. An astonished Dickey refused the request. The Hurricanes continued to move downfield. Clark called another timeout and pleaded again with Dickey. After a third request Dickey relented.

What followed was one of the strangest plays in college history. Clark, upon returning to the huddle, not only told his fellow defenders to let Miami score, he told them to go so far as to drop to the Orange Bowl Poly Turf. Fall on the ground and let the 'Canes walk into the end zone untouched. And that's exactly what happened.

❋   ❋   ❋

John Reaves became Florida's starting quarterback as a sophomore in 1969 after the Gators had thrown all of two touchdown passes in 1968. But with Reaves and wide receiver Carlos Alvarez, a fellow sophomore, Gators coach Ray

Graves knew he possessed a stellar passing combination. The previous year, Graves recalls, "We couldn't stop the freshman team. It was demoralizing. If they had been eligible (to play varsity ball as freshmen, a rule that was passed by the NCAA in the early '70s), we might have won the conference championship."

The '69 Gators finished the regular season 8-1-1, losing only when Reaves and Alvarez were outdueled by Auburn's own sophomore passing combination of Pat Sullivan and Terry Beasley, 38-12. Reaves threw for 2,896 yards and 24 touchdowns, but the season ended with a bittersweet Gator Bowl victory over Southeastern Conference champion Tennessee, 14-13, with rumors flying that Graves would announce his retirement after the game and be replaced by Tennessee coach Doug Dickey, a Florida grad. The players wanted defensive coordinator Gene Ellenson to take over if Graves indeed was going to step down, or at least be given some say in the matter. Instead, they learned that Dickey had become their new coach via telegrams while they were home between semesters.

Injuries and an awkward transition blunted the Gators' accomplishments during Reaves' junior and senior seasons. In 1970, the machine that had averaged 31.2 points in 1969 was limited to an average of 20.4, with receivers Alvarez and Andy Chaney both hampered by injuries, not to mention the loss of much of the '70 offensive line to graduation. Also, Dickey didn't consider Reaves a complete quarterback. "He could make the ball go down the field extremely well," Dickey recalls, "but he was an awkward athlete. He couldn't do much more than drop back and throw, but he was very good at that. We tried to do a few other things and realized we just couldn't get anything else done." Reaves threw for 2,549 yards and 13 touchdowns as a junior. Florida's scoring average was whittled to 10.4 in nine games through the 1971 season, and the final game against Miami—which allowed an average of 99 yards passing—didn't mean much . . .

Having set the NCAA passing record, John Reaves (7) is mobbed by his Gator teammates. (UF ARCHIVES)

Fran Curci returned to Miami as coach in part because of his impressive victory over the Hurricanes while coaching the University of Tampa in 1970. (UNIVERSITY OF MIAMI)

unless Reaves could somehow, incredibly, break Plunkett's passing record.

❉   ❉   ❉

Fran Curci could barely control his enthusiasm when he was hired by his alma mater in December 1970 and entrusted with the mission to turn the Miami Hurricanes' football program around. Wanting to eat and breathe UM football, he actually moved his family into the players' dorm.

Curci played three varsity seasons with Miami, his best being the 6-4 campaign of 1959, in which Florida stole an Orange Bowl bid from the 'Canes in the final game with a 23-14 upset in Jacksonville. After a stint of benchwarming with the American Football League's Dallas Texans, Gustafson asked Curci to return to Miami as an assistant coach. Six years later, he accepted the job as head coach at Tampa, where he produced a 25-6 record over three seasons. His '70 Spartans finished 10-1, including a surprisingly easy victory over Miami in Kichefski's second game as interim coach.

When Miami approached Curci after the season about its coaching vacancy, he was more than eager to listen. But he was also realistic about the state of Hurricanes football. "Miami was really in bad shape," he says. "There was talk that they were dropping basketball. . . . I said, 'If you guys drop basketball, then you're going to get the reputation that football's going to be next.' Also, I wanted a five-year renewable contract."

Curci got his contract and was told basketball was safe. It was, for about two weeks.

After two losing seasons (4-7 in 1971 and 5-6 in '72), and disillusioned by a recruiting budget of less than $40,000, Curci was attentive when Kentucky governor John Y. Brown asked him to consider the head coaching job at the University of Kentucky. He flew to Lexington, and UK subsequently offered him the job. Curci says he was given the important points he asked for, including a competitive recruiting allowance, so he accepted the new challenge. Kichefski, that longtime UM loyalist, was enraged. "This was his alma mater," Kichefski said. "I could have killed the little booger when he left."

＊　＊　＊

Miami went into the Florida game as a solid favorite, but Curci used the previous off week to install a Wishbone offense. Coincidentally, in Gainesville, Dickey was disappointed in his defense and switched from a 5-2 alignment to a wide-tackle six—perfect for stopping such an option attack. (Some newspaper stories after the game questioned whether Florida had spied on UM's practices and switched defenses to contend with the Wishbone.)

Actually, it took Reaves and Florida almost a quarter to get warmed up. The Gators didn't score their first touchdown of the game until only four seconds remained in the first quarter,

Reaves tossing a 10-yard touchdown pass to senior running back Tommy Durrance for a 7-0 lead. Florida got the ball back early in the second quarter on an interception by cornerback Doug Sorenson, and Reaves lofted a pass over UM linebacker Al Palewicz to Durrance for a nine-yard touchdown with 10:11 left in the first half. Miami made its first serious trip into Florida territory late in the half, but quarterback John Hornibrook was stopped short of the first down on fourth-and-two at the Florida 30-yard line by safety Jim Revels. The Gators were able to tack on three more points when kicker Richard Franco made a 47-yard field goal with one second left before halftime. In the first half, Reaves completed 18 of 26 passes for 162 yards. Dickey, apprised that Reaves now was 182 yards short of the record, allowed his offense to concentrate on passing in the second half.

When Reaves threw 12 yards to Durrance for a third touchdown early in the third quarter, that tied him with Auburn's Sullivan with an SEC-record 53 career touchdown passes—and provided a 24-0 Florida lead, for anyone who still was interested in the game's outcome. Florida's Chris McCoun recovered a fumble by UM's Tom Smith at the Miami 17 to set up another Reaves touchdown play. But this one saw Reaves *catch* a touchdown pass from Durrance, beating Miami's Daryl Reeh. "We had been working on that for two years, and we finally talked Coach Dickey into using it in a game," Reaves recalls. "I had visions of grandeur; I did my best Terry Beasley act when I crossed the goal line." It was this play, more than the subsequent Flop, that angered Miami *Herald* sports editor Edwin Pope, describing the call as "a little cheesy."

No matter your opinion of the play, Florida was now in command, 31-0, still in the third quarter. When the Hurricanes' Chuck Foreman followed Jack Brasington's block to score a one-yard touchdown and a two-point conversion, Miami at least was within 31-8. The touchdown was set up when Miami's Larry Lancaster returned an interception 53 yards to the Gators' 19. The Gators came right back, thanks to a pass interference call, to go ahead 38-8 when Reaves

Miami quarterback John Hornibrook runs around left end for a touchdown that allowed Reaves to break the NCAA record for career passing yards. (UF INFORMATION SERVICES)

threw his fourth touchdown pass, a one-yarder to Vince Kendrick.

About eight minutes remained as the Gators anticipated getting the ball back for Reaves, when Clark made his dramatic punt return. "I started to the return wall and I saw that Miami had picked up the stunt," Clark says. "I just cut back . . . and left the wall and headed to the corner of the end zone. As soon as I crossed the goal line, I said, 'Good Lord, what have I done?' So I ran over to J.R. and I said, 'John, I'm sorry, buddy!'"

The Gators' defense forced Miami to punt with about six minutes to play, leaving Reaves in good shape to gain the necessary 35 yards. Two

completions cut the magic number to 23, and he appeared to have it on the next pass to Alvarez, but the play was called back by a penalty. Reaves' next pass was intercepted by Gary Altheide, who returned the ball 10 yards to the Florida 23.

❊   ❊   ❊

When Harvin Clark first came over to Doug Dickey to ask about letting Miami score, Dickey could scarcely believe his ears. Well, actually, he had heard the idea before Clark brought it up. It seemed every Florida fan among the 35,000 or so people who paid their way into the Orange Bowl that night had been chanting, "Let 'em score! Let 'em score!" while Miami slowly drove downfield.

It was on Clark's third attempt at getting Dickey to approve the Miami score that Dickey gave in. "I thought I had my sales pitch pretty well down pat," Clark recalls. "He was weakening. By the third time I called time out, he looked at me and said, 'All right, all right. Let 'em score, but block the extra point.' Why he said that, I don't know." (Trailing by 31 points after the touchdown, Miami, of course, went for two points.) Dickey, so often accused of being too mechanical a coach, gave in to emotion. "Ain't gonna hurt nobody," Dickey recalls thinking at the time. "What we want is the ball. Well, I figured we'd practiced all the time full speed with no tackling. So I figured that's what they'd do."

Clark, of course, had other ideas. He returned to the huddle and told his teammates to simply fall on the turf when the ball was hiked to Miami quarterback John Hornibrook. Junior defensive back John Clifford immediately protested. "I've got to play these guys next year!" Clark remembers Clifford saying—but there was little that he could do about it. "I think of the end of that game," Clifford says, "and you could just feel the frustration of what should have been a great team, a great class that started out 9-1-1. I didn't do anything to stop the kid."

With 1:20 to play, Hornibrook took the snap from center on third-and-seven at the Florida eight and began to run a sweep to the left. The Gators, as if ordered by some drill sergeant to "Drop and give me 10!" fell to the turf on their bellies—all except for two. Clifford stood in his place on the far side of the field, and Clark dropped not to his stomach, but onto his back. "Because I wanted to see what happened," he says. The dumbfounded Hurricanes simply trotted into the end zone as the fans began to scream—Gator fans in ecstasy, Hurricane fans in anger. Hornibrook threw to Bill Perkins for the two points, cutting Florida's lead to 45-16.

Miami then tried an onside kick, but Florida's Bill Dowdy recovered the ball with 1:10 to

play. Reaves' first pass was nearly intercepted. The next pass was a 15-yarder to Alvarez—who was barely able to play at that point because of the pain in his knees—to break the record. Says Alvarez: "Both my legs were cramping up. I couldn't have gone out again." In case there had been some mixup in the statistics, Reaves threw another pass for three yards to Hollis Boardman. He finished the game going 33-for-50 for 348 yards, gaining 2,104 for the season and 7,549 career yards to Plunkett's 7,544. By contrast, the Wishbone 'Canes completed one of 14 passes for 19 yards with two interceptions. Running back Chuck Foreman gained 81 of Miami's 191 rushing yards.

After the game, an enraged Curci refused to meet with Dickey, running straight to the locker room. The Gators, meanwhile, added one more bizarre chapter to the evening's events by running to the east end zone and jumping in the pool in which the Miami Dolphins housed their mascot, Flipper, during games. Here was Carlos Alvarez, bad knees and all, climbing up a flagpole that was used to help Flipper perform tricks. "Jumping in the pool and just having a grand time of it is really what sports is all about as far as I'm concerned."

To be sure, Miami didn't share that enthusiasm. There already had been bad blood between the schools after Curci told a Daytona Beach quarterback club the previous year that part of the reason Florida never reached its potential was that the team had a bunch of "crybabies." Curci says: "At that same meeting, I said the University of Miami would win the national championship before Florida wins the SEC, and that's exactly what happened. That was just a smart-ass statement to make, but as it turned out it was the right thing because I always knew they'd find a way to screw it up." Says Reaves, who at the time was angered by the "crybabies" remark: "Probably what he said was true."

Curci tore into Dickey after the game, saying that the UF coach had no class and knew going in that Miami's defense was crippled by injuries. Curci recalls: "I'll never forget; it was like yesterday. We come out and run the snap, and they all fell down. And they were laughing, you know how kids are, and hee-hawing. I remember (Miami) kids coming off the field, and they were crying. I thought it was a tainted record; I was mad as hell. I thought for a coach to let someone do that was crazy." Dickey managed some off-beat humor during post-game interrogation of his decision. "Harvin Clark's punt return killed us," he said.

If Florida wasn't following the letter of the law in college football, then Alvarez contends Miami wasn't either when it stuck to a conservative running game trailing badly in the fourth

quarter. "Miami didn't want John Reaves to break the record," he says. "You ought to try at least some passes."

The Flop didn't end that night for Dickey. He had to appear before college football's ethics committee to explain his actions and continued to receive criticism long after most people had forgotten the score. "Kids are kids, and there's no telling what they're going to do," he says. "What the heck? The game's like 44-16; who gives a damn whether they get a touchdown at the end or not? So we're trying to help this kid get a record that he probably deserved." Nor did the Flop die that night for

Carlos Alvarez (45) gets set to catch the pass from John Reaves (7) that allowed Reaves to break the NCAA record for career passing yards. (UF INFORMATION SERVICES-PHIL BANNISTER)

Curci. During his stint as coach at Kentucky, Curci's Wildcats beat some of Florida's best teams, including the 1974 Sugar Bowl squad. "The Kentucky-Tennessee game is the biggest game because they're big rivals," Curci says, "but for me, it was always the Florida game."

*　　*　　*

Grabbing the career passing record gave Reaves a measure of respect that eluded him through his college career. Consider that despite collecting passing yardage totals of 2,896, 2,549 and 2,104, he never finished in the Top 10 of the Heisman Trophy balloting. Auburn's Sullivan, the '71 Heisman winner, threw for 1,686, 2,586 and 2,012 during his three seasons. As seniors, Sullivan threw 20 touchdown passes to Reaves' 17 and played on a team that was 9-0 when the Heisman ballots were counted, compared to the Gators at 2-7.

Reaves appeared bound for pro stardom after being picked in the first round of the draft by the Philadelphia Eagles and making the NFL All-Rookie team. But he was arrested during the off-season for possession of marijuana, and was relegated to the bench before being traded to Cincinnati. There, he merely sat behind Ken Anderson. There were more trades—to Minnesota and Houston—and more publicity over his problems with drugs and alcohol.

"It was the lowest point of my life," he says. "I had a problem; first it was drinking, which began in high school, then drugs began in college. It progressed to where I became an addict, and I'm not proud to say that. I was probably the first NFL player to admit I had a problem, and my name was really raked over the coals because of it. I came clean in 1980 and have been clean ever since."

Says Alvarez: "He never talked to me about (drugs), but that wasn't John Reaves. It's happened to a lot of other good people, but it doesn't mean it's the end of your life. It just means you need to make some corrections and continue, and I think John made that correction real well."

Reaves finished his pro career in the early '80s with the USFL's Tampa Bay Bandits before going into the real estate business in Lakeland and continuing to do ministry work that he began during his rehabilitation. In 1988, he nearly won a seat in the Florida House of Representatives. He returned to football in 1990 as the tight ends coach on Steve Spurrier's staff at Florida.

Florida State vs. Miami
The Seminoles End the Drought

After years of nurturing the program under Tom Nugent and earning national recognition under Bill Peterson, FSU had attracted the nation's eye for an entirely different reason. The 1973 Seminoles were arguably the worst major college football program in the nation.

The school's administration was not eager to give Larry Jones another chance in '74. Not with an 0-11 record fresh in their minds. And not with the notoriety of the "chicken wire" training scandal still lingering. Athletic director John Bridgers, who had coached alongside Jones as assistant earlier in their careers at South Carolina, tried hard to fend off the critics. But the pressure to make a change only became greater. Jones spared the university the task of firing him by handing in his resignation near the end of 1973.

School president Stanley Marshall sought a successor with a proven record as a winner, but Florida State surprised many people by hiring Darrell Mudra, coach of relatively unknown Western Illinois.

In Tallahassee, Mudra inherited most of the problems that Jones left behind—and

they weren't confined to the football field. The program was in debt by $300,000. The Seminoles' version of weight training would have drawn sneers and laughs from most major colleges.

And there was the schedule, another burden that Mudra had to bear. The product of former athletic director Clay Stapleton, Florida State faced another tortuous gauntlet in 1974 that was pieced together in the name of bringing home big paychecks from large gates on the road. For 1974, this meant traveling to two of the Southeastern Conference's powerhouses—Alabama and Auburn. There would also be a couple of visits to Doak Campbell Stadium by teams fulfilling home-and-home contracts. This meant greeting Pittsburgh, with sensational sophomore running back Tony Dorsett, and Houston, a powerful independent that was in the process of pushing its way into the Southwest Conference.

In the opener against Pitt, Dorsett was nearly outrushed by FSU freshman Larry Key. Dorsett was limited to 81 yards rushing compared to Key's 63, but Pitt broke a halftime tie with a third-quarter field goal and hung on for a 9-6 victory. Florida State followed the loss to

Pitt with seven more defeats. If there was one thing that could be said for the string of futility, it was that the Seminoles were unpredictable. They could play tight with a solid team—losing by four points to a Baylor team that would win the SWC and play in the Cotton Bowl—yet get left in the dust by a struggling program such as Memphis State (42-14).

The epitome of the 'Noles' plight came at Tuscaloosa against the Crimson Tide, which was midway through its effort to complete a second consecutive undefeated regular season. Mudra correctly figured that some sort of gimmick might give Florida State a chance at least to stay on the field with an admittedly superior team. Assistant coach Bob Harbison suggested using an unbalanced line to keep the Tide—well, off balance.

The strategy worked, and Florida State built a 7-0 halftime lead that had the Denny Stadium crowd flustered; Alabama had not lost in its on-campus stadium since 1963, when it was upset by Ray Graves' Gators. In the second half, Alabama cut its deficit to 7-3 on a 44-yard field goal by Bucky Berrey. The Seminoles answered with an impressive drive within two yards of the Tide end zone. But the drive stalled, and a field goal attempt failed. In the closing minutes, Florida State was backed up to its five-yard line and was forced to punt. Mudra feared Alabama would block the kick, so he had the punter down the ball in the end zone for a safety, conceding Alabama the two points. He was willing to take his chances stopping the Tide following the FSU free kick, still ahead by two points.

But the free kick only traveled to the Seminoles' 48. For an Alabama team that had averaged more than 32 points a game in its first four victories, getting back on the scoreboard didn't seem like too great a challenge. And it wasn't. The Tide marched downfield with relative ease, Berrey kicked a 36-yard field goal in the final minute, and Mudra's plan had backfired into an 8-7 loss. That extended the 'Noles' losing streak to 17 games, dating to the 10th game of Jones' 1972 season.

The losses continued to pile up for Florida State—by 10 points at home against Florida, by 32 at Auburn, even by four touchdowns to Memphis State—by the time FSU was scheduled for its annual meeting with the Miami Hurricanes. And the way Pete Elliott's team was playing, there was little reason to believe Florida State could end its horrendous losing streak—which had reached 20 games—on a Friday night at the Orange Bowl.

Miami came into the Florida State game at 5-2, in excellent shape to record its first winning season since 1967 and also with an outside chance of earning its first bowl berth since that same season. The 'Canes opened the season with an impressive 20-3 win at Houston, then barely got past Tampa by two points.

The same Auburn team that would dominate Florida State only escaped the Orange Bowl with a 3-0 victory. Miami's other loss going into the FSU game was 28-7 decision at Notre Dame, a far cry from the 44-0 blasting that UM absorbed from the Fighting Irish in Miami the previous year to close Elliott's first season with the Hurricanes.

Mudra had the curious habit of coaching his team from the press box instead of the standard vantage point along the sideline. He said he could better understand the game with the improved view of the entire field. He didn't even call plays, he just relayed advice to his assistants.

About the only things working in Florida State's favor were its surprising legacy of success at the Orange Bowl and a glaring vacancy on the Miami defense. The 'Noles were carrying in a seven-game winning streak on the road against Miami. Plus, UM's superb middle guard, Rubin Carter, had been lost at midseason because of an ankle injury.

*　　*　　*

The Seminoles suffered through the first half, as FSU running back Larry Key left the game in the first quarter with a sprained ankle and a similar injury sidelined starting offen-

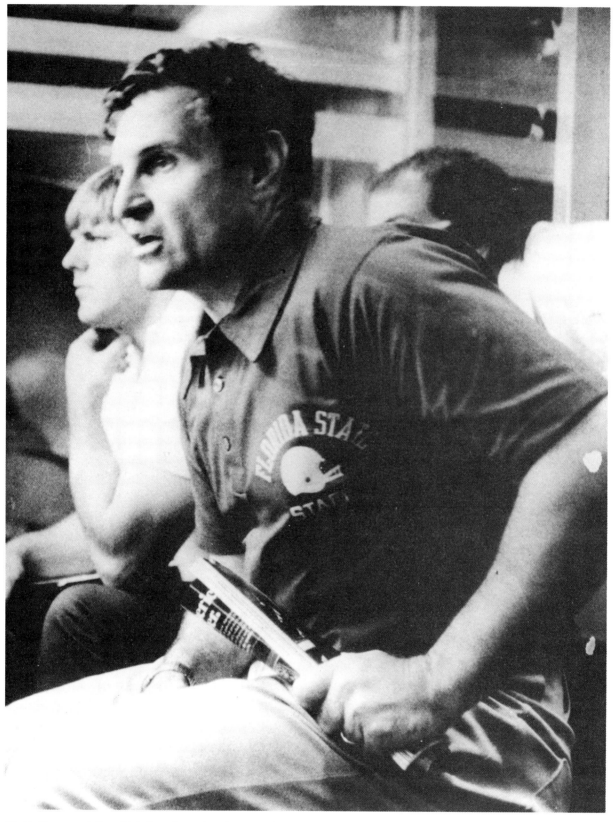

Florida State coach Darrell Mudra, who preferred to coach from up in the press box instead of down on the sidelines, watches as his Seminoles upset UM 21-14, to break a 20-game losing streak. (MIAMI HERALD)

sive tackle Bruce Harrison midway through the second quarter.

But by then, surprisingly, the Seminoles had actually taken the lead. Freshman running back Leon Bright ran 14 yards for a touchdown—deftly avoiding Miami cornerback Ernie Jones at UM's five-yard line—to give FSU a 7-0 lead with 3:57 to play in the first quarter.

Florida State increased its lead to 14-0 in the second quarter. The touchdown came on a 48-yard pass on third-and-10 from Steve Mathieson to Joe Goldsmith. It marked the 'Noles' longest scoring play to date for the season. Goldsmith avoided a jersey tackle by Miami's Paul Horschel at the 'Canes' 20.

After a scoreless third period, FSU entered the fourth quarter knowing it was only 15 minutes away from shedding the shackles of a 20-game losing streak. Elliott made a switch at quarterback, replacing junior Kary Baker with sophomore Frank Glover. The substitution looked like a masterstroke when Glover threw a 77-yard touchdown pass to senior Witt Beckman, brother of FSU tight end Ed Beckman, to get the Hurricanes on the scoreboard.

But Florida State responded with a scoring drive capped by a one-yard touchdown run by Jeff Leggett of Miami Norland High School. He had not been included on the original travel roster. But when FSU injuries mounted during the week, Leggett was summoned from Tallahassee and made the flight to Miami on a private plane. With Leggett's touchdown, the FSU lead was again at 14 points, 21-7.

The Hurricanes then scored on an 80-yard touchdown pass from senior wide receiver Steve Marcantonio to sophomore Phil August with 5:55 left in the game. The play almost didn't come off because Marcantonio nearly fumbled the lateral from Glover. August made the catch at FSU's 25 and kept his balance despite being pushed by Andy Stockton.

Within a touchdown of tying the score, Miami again pushed into Florida State territory. The 'Canes reached FSU's 38 in the closing minutes but were stopped on an inter-ception by Joe Camps at the 20. Camps had played deeper on orders from assistant coach Deek Pollard following Marcantonio's surprise touchdown pass. The Hurricanes got the ball back in the final minute at the Seminoles' 48. Glover was sacked by defensive tackle Greg Johnson for a 15-yard loss on first down, and Miami completed two passes to return to the original line of scrimmage when the game ended.

Under normal circumstances, a coach breaking such a long losing streak for his school would merit a triumphant ride from sideline to midfield atop the shoulders of his players. But Darrell Mudra was, of course, up in the press box, high above the Orange Bowl field. FSU players settled for the next best thing and grabbed offensive coordinator Dan Henning.

When the jubilant Seminoles reached the locker room, the game ball for Florida State's first win in almost two seasons was presented to senior offensive guard Bob Jones from Pompano Beach. Jones had cried openly earlier in the season following the loss to Alabama. Tears again streamed down his face when he was given the game ball in Miami.

*   *   *

The stunning loss to Florida State dropped Miami's record to 5-3. And with the opponents they had ahead—Alabama, Syracuse and Florida—the 'Canes must have known it would have been difficult to finish 7-4 and well within bowl contention. A 6-5 finish usually means a bowl bid only for a school that can deliver huge numbers of fans, which Miami certainly was not in a position to do.

Indeed, the 'Canes were able to win only one of their three remaining games. They lost to Alabama, 28-7, and beat Syracuse, 14-7, to take a 6-4 record into the regular-season finale at Florida. The Gators had clinched their first Sugar Bowl berth in nine years by beating Auburn in early November to go 7-1. But they were

Darrell Mudra said he was "stunned" when he was fired by Florida State, despite recording only four wins in two seasons. (FLORIDA STATE UNIVERSITY)

stunned by Georgia, 17-16, then lost to Kentucky and coach Fran Curci, 41-24, to carry a 7-3 record into the Miami game. UF couldn't afford the embarrassment of taking a three-game losing streak to New Orleans and was more than Miami could handle, winning easily, 31-7.

There were problems off the field for Miami. Running back Johnny Williams, who had been benched, aired his grievances to the press, charging that Elliott and his staff lacked discipline with the players and lacked imagination in their game plans. Shortly thereafter, quarterback Kary Baker was charged with grand larceny in an alleged theft of $249 from a federally funded summer job program. He did not have to serve any time because his record was otherwise clean. But he was booed in the loss to Alabama, which prompted his teammates to extend to him a peculiar postgame vote of confidence.

The '74 finale against Florida turned out to be Pete Elliott's final game as UM coach. He had spent a year as combination football coach and athletic director, having been originally hired to perform only the latter's duties when he was brought on in 1972 as assistant athletic director to Ernie McCoy. Elliott agreed to serve as football coach at McCoy's request following Fran Curci's resignation. Having compiled an 11-11 record over two seasons and failing to bring home a bowl bid in '74, Elliott decided in February 1975 to give up coaching and concentrate his efforts on running the athletic department. Offensive coordinator Carl Selmer was promoted to fill Elliott's vacancy.

For Florida State, the euphoria of victory was short-lived. The Seminoles returned home to Tallahassee to face Virginia Tech in their Homecoming game—well, everybody's got to have a Homecoming game. The Hokies, though, proved quite rude to their hosts and ripped FSU, 56-21. The 'Noles closed the season at home with a 23-8 loss to Houston.

Darrell Mudra's first season as Florida State coach had produced a 1-10 record, a one-game improvement over the previous season. It took only two games to get a victory in

1975, following a 31-20 loss in the opener at Texas Tech with a 17-8 win at home against lightly regarded Utah State. The Seminoles fell back into a familiar losing pattern for the next five games, including a 34-8 defeat at Florida, before stunning Clemson, 43-7, to raise their record to 2-6.

The 'Noles dropped their two remaining home games to Memphis State and Miami before returning from Houston with a 33-22 victory in their '75 finale. The Mudra record for two seasons was a dismal 4-18.

Some players didn't believe Mudra took the job seriously enough, noting that there were times when he didn't remain through an entire practice and times when he didn't show up at all. Some players were left scratching their heads during Mudra's final weekend on the job in Houston. He took the team to see the movie "Patton"—and afterward proceeded to criticize the famous general. An odd form of inspiration.

Florida State president Stanley Marshall had told some people that he planned to announce during the radio halftime show being broadcast back to Tallahassee that Mudra was sure to return for the 1976 season. But Marshall never made that statement during the broadcast. A few weeks later, Mudra was fired.

"We were really shocked (by the firing)," Mudra recalls. "It was a great opportunity; we just didn't quite survive. Actually, most of the things that revolutionized the program took about three years to accomplish, and we never did actually get the facilities."

So the man who chose to coach from high above the field was gone. "Had we won a few more ballgames, they would have thought of me as a miracle worker," Mudra says. "It (coaching from the press box) was an issue but only because we had such a difficult time winning."

Mudra returned to the small-college ranks to coach Eastern Illinois to the NCAA Division II national championship. He later coached at Northern Iowa in Division I-AA before retiring only 15 miles south of Tallahassee in the town of Crawfordville, where he spends much of his time honing his fishing.

Florida State vs. Florida
FSU Ends Nine Years of Frustration

The 1977 season had blossomed into more than the most optimistic of Florida State fans could have hoped for. The Seminoles went into the last game of the regular season with an 8-2 record and a bowl bid. Neither had been seen on Tennessee Street in six years. In fact, the program had only registered nine total wins during the previous four seasons.

Five of those came in 1976 under first-year coach Bobby Bowden, who by this time was the toast of Tallahassee. He had injected a winning attitude, brought excitement with his wide-open style and won over many critics through his own warmth and personality.

Remaining hurdles were relatively few. The '77 season had brought a third consecutive loss to the Miami Hurricanes. That could be forgiven in light of the overall success.

But then there was the matter of beating Florida, which happened to be the Seminoles' season-ending opponent for the first time since 1973—and would be for years to come by design of the two schools. For nine consecutive years, Florida State coaches had had to offer their congratulations at midfield after being beaten by the Gators. From Bill Peter-

son to Larry Jones to Darrell Mudra to Bowden, FSU's futility in the series had reached new lows. Because of the long streak, the Gators had built a tremendous edge of 16-2-1 in the overall series. As Bowden put it: "We haven't turned it around until we beat Florida." And most FSU people would probably have agreed with him, 8-2 or no 8-2.

In Gainesville, earning a 10th consecutive win over FSU might heal some wounds following another one of those "What if?" years. The Gators were thought to have enough talent to contend for that elusive Southeastern Conference championship. The timing was perfect. Alabama had finally been knocked off in 1976 by Georgia, which had lost most of its nucleus to graduation. Kentucky had played surprisingly well in 1976 under former Miami coach Fran Curci. But when Kentucky had its choice to take a year's probation in '76 or '77, Curci chose '77. Surely he wasn't expecting as much out of this team. And with an SEC schedule that didn't include a game against Alabama, Florida stood a great chance of earning at least a co-championship with the Tide.

Instead, Florida floundered again. The Gators lost at LSU and at Auburn to virtually

Part of Florida's potent 1977 offense (from left): Terry LeCount, Earl Carr, Tony Green and Willie Wilder. (UF ARCHIVES)

end their chances of contending for the title. To make matters worse, Curci and the Wildcats came to Gainesville and hurt UF's bowl chances with a 14-7 win that gave Kentucky three wins in its last four games against the Gators. It also snapped Florida's 18-game unbeaten string at Florida Field. UF came back from Miami with a 31-14 victory over the Hurricanes, the game that ended with Miami coach Lou Saban refusing to shake UF coach Doug Dickey's hand because of Saban's displeasure over the officiating of the SEC crew, and carried a 6-3-1 record into the final game against Florida State. The Gators needed a win

to have any chance to play in a bowl. The game would mark the first time in the series that a complete SEC officiating crew was not used. Florida had agreed to use a split crew of SEC and independent officials.

Dickey opened the season using a Wishbone offense but integrated some I-formation plays as the year progressed. The team was quarterbacked by Terry LeCount, who came to Gainesville as a speedy wide receiver and was moved as part of the Wishbone plan. The top running back was senior Tony Green, who had led the team in rushing as a freshman before giving way to Jimmy Dubose.

111

Senior wide receiver Wes Chandler, considered one of the best in the country, had seen his reception total cut almost in half with the advent of the option offense.

Florida State boasted a balanced attack. Senior running back Larry Key was enjoying his best season, becoming the first Seminole to rush for more than 1,000 yards. At quarterback, Bowden was writing a typically unconventional story, platooning sophomores Wally Woodham and Jimmy Jordan. Going against standard coaching logic, Bowden played whoever had the hot hand. At 8-2, there wasn't much doubting Bowden's decision.

*   *   *

There was little collegiate interest in Tallahassee Leon quarterback Wally Woodham coming out of high school, even though he was named the state player of the year for 1974 and had guided the Lions to the Class 4A championship. So when his hometown school, Florida State, and coach Darrell Mudra expressed their willingness to take a chance on him, it was an easy choice for him to make.

Meanwhile, a year later back at Leon, the Lions were rampaging again with senior Jimmy Jordan at quarterback. Jordan, after considering Miami, Vanderbilt and Rice, also signed with FSU, assuming that he would fall in a year behind Woodham as he had in high school. What he didn't suspect was that new coach Bobby Bowden would elect to redshirt Woodham and play Jordan that fall, so that beginning in the fall of '77 they would both be sophomores.

Jordan won the starting job in '77 and got Florida State off to its first 2-0 start since 1972. The third game of the season was a 23-

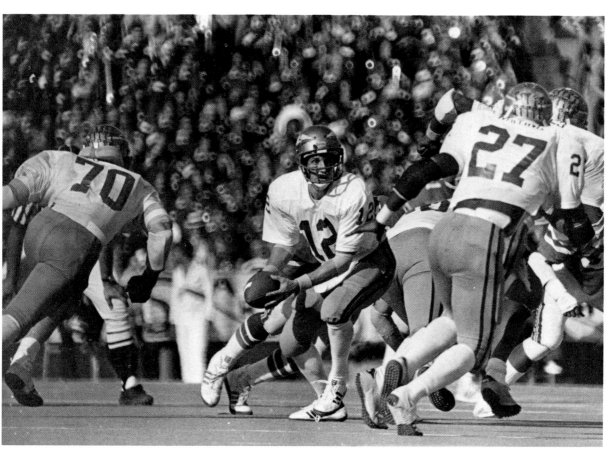

Florida State quarterback Wally Woodham (12) looks to pitch to running back Michael Whiting (27). (UF INFORMATION SERVICES)

17 loss at home to Miami, in which Woodham struggled when he came in to replace Jordan. After the game Woodham met with Bowden to make sure his coach wasn't going to give up on him after the one bad showing:

of them, it gave you one heck of a pitching duo. I used to call 'em 'Spahn and Sain and pray for rain.'"

With FSU building a successful program in subsequent years, the two quarterbacks

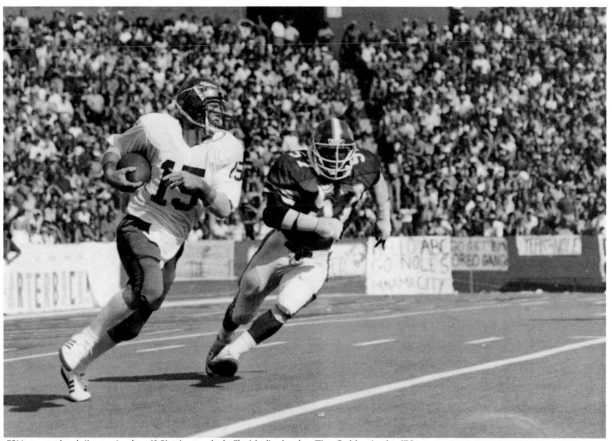

FSU quarterback Jimmy Jordan (15) tries to elude Florida linebacker Tim Golden in the '79 game. (UF INFORMATION SERVICES)

"I told him I could do better over time—I'm ready to step in."

And he did just that in the following game. With Oklahoma State leading FSU 17-0, Woodham came off the bench and led the Seminoles to a 25-17 victory. Thus began Bowden's tag-team approach to quarterbacking.

"We'd play one; as long as he's hot, we'd leave him in there," Bowden explains. "We'd put the other one in, and it seemed like he did well. Both of them were drop-back passers that couldn't run. Jimmy had more velocity on the ball. Wally had more instinct throwing the football. And between the two

began to receive national recognition. *Sports Illustrated* dubbed them "the two-headed quarterback—Wally Jim Jordham." In fact, in 1979 the duo would lead the Seminoles to their first-ever 11-0 regular season.

✳   ✳   ✳

On defense, Florida State appeared to have brought in someone who would become one of their all-time greats in middle guard Ron Simmons. When freshmen first reported in August, upperclassmen were taken aback by this 6-foot-1, 230-pound mass of muscle from Warner Robins, Georgia. "It was like there were all the freshmen, and there was Ron," recalls Kurt Unglaub.

Simmons actually recalls the same setting with the opposite perspective. "I was in awe of them," he says. "But once I started in with the drills, I started to feel more comfortable."

Simmons, one of seven children, had his mother die when he was nine years old and was abandoned by his father shortly thereafter. Most of the kids moved in with relatives in Detroit after their grandmother died three years later. But Ron stayed with an older brother in central Georgia because he thought that would improve his chances of earning a football scholarship. He started lifting weights in high school and grew to more than 200 pounds. Initially exposed to Florida State through Bill Franklin, a Warner Robins man who had known Bobby Bowden in his days coaching at little South Georgia College, Simmons visited the Tallahassee campus at first merely as a favor to Franklin. It turned out to be the school that he felt best at.

*　　*　　*

Wes Chandler had been bothered by a virus throughout the week. Still, he was shocked to learn the morning of the game that he would not be dressing out at all against the Seminoles.

The Seminoles took the field to kick off knowing they had a chance to become the first FSU team to register nine regular-season wins. On their first possession after stopping Florida, they certainly looked capable of achieving that goal. With Wally Woodham hitting four of five passes as the starting

Florida State's Ron Simmons and Florida's Cris Collinsworth pose for a publicity photo in conjunction with their being named to the 1980 Playboy preseason All-American team. (FLORIDA STATE UNIVERSITY)

"pitcher," the 'Noles moved 72 yards and scored on a 35-yard pass to Kurt Unglaub. Just like that, FSU had grabbed a 7-0 lead, and the Seminole fans tucked into the northeast corner of Florida Field were rejoicing.

The Gators, conversely, could accomplish little in their first four possessions. The result was that Florida State enjoyed excellent field position throughout the first quarter. Woodham took FSU back toward the UF end zone

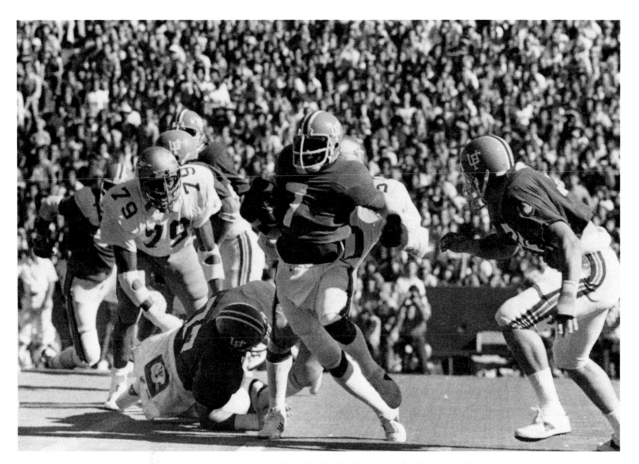

The tear-away jersey doesn't tear away soon enough on this play for Florida quarterback Terry LeCount (7).
(UF INFORMATION SERVICES)

on Florida State's second series, but the drive was halted by a diving interception by Chuck Hatch at the Gators' 15-yard line. The next time down, Florida State salvaged a 47-yard field goal by Dave Cappelen—his longest of the season—for a 10-0 lead.

Early in the second quarter, Florida's dormant offense finally began to awaken. Willie Wilder raced around left end for a 39-yard gain that set up a 32-yard field goal by Berj Yepremian. The Gators were on the board, pulling within 10-3.

But Bowden went to his "bullpen," much to Florida's chagrin. With Jimmy Jordan at quarterback, the 'Noles charged right back down the field for another touchdown—this one on a four-yard pass to senior receiver Roger Overby, whom Bowden had talked out of quitting the team the previous

spring. Cappelen's kick gave FSU a 17-3 lead. It was imperative for Florida to score a touchdown, not settle for a field goal, and to give Florida State a sign that it was prepared to stay in the game. Instead, two decent UF drives ran out of steam and resulted in a couple of Yepremian three-pointers, from 50 and 41 yards. The Gators left for the locker room at halftime with nine points on the scoreboard but without having proven they could get in the end zone.

In the third quarter, Jordan guided Florida State downfield for another touchdown, the drive capped by a 20-yard touchdown pass to Overby. But near the end of the period, it appeared FSU had given Florida a break that would allow the Gators to get back in the game. Unglaub, returning punts for the first time as a Seminole, fumbled at FSU's 30 and

Barry Walker recovered for the Gators. Tony Green raced to the nine, giving UF a first-and-goal. He fumbled back to the 12 on first down, then made it back to the seven. On third down, LeCount kept and was stopped at the five. Disdaining the field goal, LeCount tried to scramble for the score on fourth down but was stopped by linebacker Aaron Carter, among others, just inches short of the goal line.

Florida State then proceeded to march 99 yards in the opposite direction to send thousands of Florida fans to their cars. Mark Lyles scored on a one-yard run on a drive that spilled into the fourth quarter, giving Florida State a 31-9 lead with 12:30 to play.

Bill Capece, the Seminoles' other kicker, popped a short kickoff that a collection of Gators couldn't control at the UF 31. Mike Kincaid recovered for Florida State. Three plays later, Overby caught his third touch-down pass of the day, this one again for 20 yards. The PAT attempt failed, leaving the Seminoles with a commanding 37-9 lead with 11:25 still to play. That already marked the most points Florida State had ever scored against Florida. It nearly got worse, but FSU was left at the Florida one when time expired.

The way the Seminoles played, it looked like they might win nine in a row in this series. They racked up 578 yards total offense and held Florida to a paltry 200. Key rambled for 143 rushing yards. Jordan passed for 40 after Woodham warmed things up with 86 of his own. Bright spots for Florida were few. Green gained 71 yards, Wilder 61. But LeCount and backup quarterback John Brantley were a combined 6-for-19 for only 59 yards.

Ray Graves, the retired UF coach serving as athletic director, had high praise for the

Florida's Tony Green (33) runs down the line to pick up his blocking. (UF INFORMATION SERVICES)

Seminoles: "It's been a long time since I've seen a college football team come up with such a winning combination, on both offense and defense, like what I saw out there today."

Dickey lamented the third-quarter series in which Florida came away from first-and-goal at the nine with no points. "That was the ball game right there," he said.

For Bobby Bowden, another major hurdle was cleared. No longer would he have to attend booster functions and touchdown club luncheons and have to skirt the issue of Florida State's performance against Florida.

"This means we can look some kids in the eyes and say, 'Come to Florida State, son,'" he told reporters after the game. "We're not second-rate anymore."

✳   ✳   ✳

As for Simmons, he went on to become the most storied defensive player in Florida State history, earning All-American status for four years despite being bothered by a broken wrist as a junior and an injured ankle as a senior. As part of the school's publicity campaign for him, Simmons was photographed wrestling alligators.

An invitation to the postseason Walter Camp All-American banquet in Hartford, Connecticut, turned into more than just another night of plaques and long-winded speeches. Simmons learned before making the trip that there was a man in the Hartford area who was boasting to his friends that he was the father of that All-American linebacker from Florida State. Father and son, separated for so many years, were reunited on that trip.

"It's strange, how you can recall a man in some way after so long," Simmons says. "He had hurt me, but I wanted him to be there to share it the most."

Simmons was told by NFL scouts that he was too small to be considered a pro prospect, something he discounted since he was told the same thing about college coming out of high school. But Simmons' NFL career was a bust after being drafted by the Cleveland Browns. He played some in Canada and back in Tampa in the United States Football League before turning to a different line of business—pro wrestling. Instead of drawing paychecks from the NFL or the CFL, he's now paid by WCW—World Championship Wrestling. Based out of Atlanta, Simmons spends about 20 days a month out on the road trying to get his opponents into the "Spinbuster."

Those sessions with the alligators paid off, after all.

Miami vs. Florida
Farewell to Dickey and Saban

The white paint had been sprayed on the Florida Field Astroturf sometime during the night before Florida's November 4 game with Auburn, but the letters were still visible nearly a month later.

DUMP DOUG.

Nine years of frustration for Gator fans were succinctly summed up in the eight letters painted at the north end of the field. With all the great talent that had come through Gainesville, Doug Dickey wasn't able to win the Southeastern Conference as he did at Tennessee before returning to his alma mater in 1970. Three days before the '78 season finale against Miami, Dickey's critics got their way and Dickey was fired. The Miami game would be his last.

In Miami, the much-traveled Lou Saban was completing his second season as coach of the Hurricanes. At 5-5, the 'Canes had a chance to finish with their first winning season since 1974. A victory at Gainesville also would end a long streak of frustration against the Gators, whom they had not beaten since Dickey's first season.

"I hear Florida is going out and win one for their old coach," Saban told his players the week of the game. "Well, how about you guys winning one for *your* old coach?" Little did those players—or anyone connected with UM football, including the old coach himself—realize that this, too, would be Saban's last game with the Hurricanes.

Saban probably wished he was elsewhere at halftime. The Hurricanes straggled into the locker room trailing 21-3. "We kind of felt sorry for ourselves in the first half," he recalls. "I said I thought it was time for us to go on and pack our bags and go on home right there. And Jerry Anderson, one of our coaches (a Florida graduate and current UF assistant) said, 'No, we're not!' and started throwing players out of the locker room. I put my hand out and said, 'Jerry, don't do this. You'll hurt someone.' He took ahold of my arm and started throwing me out the door."

It was Florida, and its outgoing coach, that was hurt in the second half. Miami shut out the Gators and scored 18 consecutive points to score a dramatic 22-21 victory in front of a stunned crowd of 47,815. Ottis Anderson, Miami's star running back, couldn't contain his joy as he jogged to the visitors' dressing room. "Hey, man, 6-5!" he yelled. "We got some Gator tail today."

* * *

Doug Dickey based his success at Tennessee on a solid, physically dominating defense complemented by a ball-control offense. He moved to Gainesville in 1970, into a Florida program that lacked size on defense and based his offense around the Super Soph passing combination of quarterback John Reaves and wide receiver Carlos Alvarez.

"The Florida transition had not happened the way you would have wanted it to happen if you were the new coach," Dickey recalls. "I felt in some ways I had sort of been betrayed." Dickey came to Gainesville feeling almost apologetic, having to win his new players.

"I personally don't think there was a great deal of understanding of the passing game when he got there," Alvarez says of Dickey. "That hurt our offense quite a bit. He just had a different style. We both wanted to win, and I think out of necessity it made us work together."

Says Reaves: "My attitude was to keep my mouth shut and do what I was supposed to do. I do remember saying that I felt like I was a robot the first game my junior year because of the way they did the play calling. We worked an hour and a half in practice working on the running game and maybe 30 min-

The much-traveled Lou Saban became football coach at Miami in 1977 after serving 19 days as athletic director at the University of Cincinnati. (UNIVERSITY OF MIAMI)

utes working on the passing game. We would try to establish the running game and we couldn't, and revert back to the passing game and a lot of times we hadn't worked on it enough in practice."

Dickey continued to bring top-quality talent to Florida throughout the '70s but couldn't deliver the SEC title. The Gators, like many schools across the South, were signing more and more black athletes. But Florida was one of the first in the South to start a black quarterback, Don Gaffney (1973-74), followed by Terry LeCount. Assistant coach Jimmy Dunn believes Florida's increased signing of blacks and the use of the black quarterback contributed to turning off alumni and, therefore, decreased the athletic department's financial base. "They might disagree today," Dunn says of UF boosters in the '70s, "but at the time they were upset that Doug Dickey was signing the black athlete. Contributions started to decline. Season-ticket sales started going down. It wasn't because we weren't winning." Dunn also believes Florida was one of the first schools in the country to be troubled by agents signing players before their eligibility had expired. Some players, he says,

were disgruntled with what some of their teammates were receiving from agents. "They (the agents) denied it and our players denied it," Dunn says, "but something definitely was affecting them."

*　*　*

At Miami, there hadn't been time throughout the '70s to become very disenchanted with a coach; they all left too quickly for that to happen. First it was Fran Curci, the former UM quarterback, who believed Miami wasn't prepared to make a first-class commitment to building a winner and left in 1972 after two seasons. Pete Elliott, the UM assistant athletic director who coached at Nebraska, California and Illinois, coached the Hurricanes to records of 5-6 in 1973 and 6-5 in 1974 before quitting to devote all of his time

Florida coach Doug Dickey likes what he sees as the Gators build a 21-3 lead during the first half.
(UF INFORMATION SERVICES–JEFF ALFORD)

Lou Saban's predecessor at Miami was Carl Selmer, who compiled a two-year record of 5-16 and remains the only head football coach UM has fired. (UNIVERSITY OF MIAMI)

kept a job for long and the school that couldn't keep a coach. "They more or less issued an ultimatum of five years," Saban says, "and if they weren't able to get it started and get it going in five years, perhaps they would consider dropping the sport."

There was difficulty for Saban before he coached his first game at UM. On June 30, he underwent open heart surgery. In August, his wife Lorraine committed suicide in their Buffalo home while packing to make the move. His first season saw Miami finish 3-8. But Saban followed a dismal season with a recruiting class that started Miami on the road toward becoming a national power. A kid in Pennsylvania named Jim Kelly was told by Penn State that he might have to move to linebacker; Saban told Kelly that he was his quarterback. Others like Eddie Edwards followed. On the field in 1978, Miami showed enough improvement—its best game being a 17-15 road victory over nationally ranked Auburn—to carry a 5-5 record into the Florida game.

to being the school's athletic director. Next came Carl Selmer, who served Elliott as offensive coordinator. Selmer struggled through seasons of 2-8 and 3-8 before becoming the only football coach in Miami history to be fired. North Carolina's Bill Dooley agreed to replace Selmer, but changed his mind before making it to Coral Gables.

Enter Lou Saban, whose career in athletic administration included nine different positions on the college or professional level. Before coming to Coral Gables, he served as athletic director at the University of Cincinnati for 19 days during the summer of 1976 before resigning.

His acceptance of the Miami job created a provocative marriage: the coach who rarely

* * *

On the morning of his final game as Gator coach, Doug Dickey must have thought things couldn't get any worse. But they did. His starting quarterback, John Brantley, was bothered all week by a chest bruise that he suffered in the previous week's 38-21 loss at Florida State. And while Brantley was in particular pain on Thursday, Dickey assumed he would be able to play Saturday against the Hurricanes. Then Brantley told him before kickoff that he would be unable to start. That forced Dickey to go with sophomore Tim Groves, who had played little after starting in the Gators' season opener, a 35-25 loss to Southern Methodist. UF also would play without injured running backs Calvin Davis and Terry Williams and suspended running back David Johnson.

The Florida players sought some sort of psychological lift for the game and decided to wear their blue road pants to go with their blue home jerseys. Pants or no pants, Florida quickly had Miami on the run. Linebacker Scot Brantley returned an interception 12 yards to the Miami 13-yard line to set up an 11-yard touchdown pass from Groves to Cris Collinsworth in the first quarter. The Gators added another touchdown on their next possession, moving 57 yards and scoring on Groves' 37-yard touchdown pass to Tony Stephens.

Miami scored what would be its only points of the first half when Danny Miller kicked a 21-yard field goal. But before the half was over, Groves threw his third touchdown pass—a nine-yarder to a diving Collinsworth—to take a 21-3 lead to the locker room.

UM fans had little reason to expect much from their team in the second half. When the Hurricanes managed to beat Syracuse, 21-9, a week earlier, that marked the most points that Miami had scored in seven games. And here was UM trailing by 18 having shown little ability to stop a Florida team playing with its backup quarterback. But Miami scored on its first four possessions of the second half. Miami quarterback Kenny McMillan, threw a three-yard touchdown pass to Ottis Anderson on fourth down after Anderson had dropped a sure touchdown pass on the previous play. Next, Miller kicked a 37-yard field goal to cut Florida's lead to 21-13. Florida's John Smith fumbled the subsequent kickoff, which was recovered by Miami's John Swain at the Florida 29. Miller converted that into a 43-yard field goal, and Miami was within 21-16, still in the third quarter. Early in the fourth quarter, UM safety Rick Valerio cut in front of

Collinsworth on a sideline pattern for an interception at the Florida 23. Miami went ahead by one on an eight-yard touchdown run by Anderson. The two-point conversion pass failed.

While Miami's first four possessions of the second half resulted in scores, Florida's last four possessions of the second half resulted in turnovers. Dickey pulled Groves in favor of John Brantley. The Gators reached the Miami 18, but a clipping penalty pushed UF back and Miami's Fred Azrak made an interception at the goal line in front of Stephens. Florida later got the ball back at the Miami 42 only to have Tony Waters fumble on the first play. Interceptions by David Jefferson and Barry Gonzalez ended the last two drives.

Florida quarterbacks combined to go 8-for-29 with seven interceptions. Miami's passing wasn't much better, McMillan and Mike Rodrigue completing seven of 21 passes for 39 yards and three interceptions. Dickey's 4-7 finish marked Florida's worst since the '71 team that beat Miami in the Flop game to finish 4-7. Anderson carried a school-record 39 times for 149 yards for his eighth 100-yard game at Miami and a school-record 1,266 yards for the season.

In the Florida locker room, Dickey grimly summed up nine seasons as Florida coach by saying: "Somehow the horseshoe on the Tennessee walking horse didn't come with me." In Miami's dressing room, a beaming Saban said: "This is just the beginning of more good things to come."

*   *   *

While the Hurricanes could expect more good things on the field, the program still was lacking off the field. The '78 team attracted an average of only 20,978 to the Orange Bowl. The city's heart and soul still belonged to Don Shula's Dolphins. And Saban, as athletic director, was more immersed in the off-the-field details of the program. When he talked with officials at Army about whom to hire for its coaching vacancy, talk turned to Saban himself and he

Ottis Anderson's eight-yard touchdown run in the fourth quarter put Miami back in front of Florida, 22-21. (UNIVERSITY OF MIAMI)

accepted the job. Miami officially thought he was on a recruiting trip to Jacksonville when they discovered he was about to be introduced as the new coach at Army.

"You want a deserter, Army? You've got one," Miami *Herald* sports editor Edwin Pope wrote on January 5, 1979, the day after Saban took the West Point job. "Saban is a quitter." Saban insists he had no choice but to go. "Once Pete (Elliott) left, my responsibility reverted right back to the president (Henry King Stanford). And he and I apparently didn't see eye to eye on a couple of things, and things changed a great deal. I wasn't too pleased about the fact that I had to go, under the circumstances."

Pope encountered Saban a few days later and demanded a concrete explanation for the sudden departure. Saban offered a vague answer: "I thought I had done all I could . . . Things change. I can't explain. It's personal."

True to form, his stay at West Point lasted all of one year, a 2-8-1 finish followed by a resignation. He then hooked on with one of his assistant football coaching associates at Purdue in the early '50s, George Steinbrenner, and spent much of the early '80s working for the New York Yankees' owner at Tampa Bay Downs and with the Yankees themselves. He returned to football in 1983 with the Division II University of Central Florida Knights in Orlando, only to quit before the end of his second season, citing the school's lack of commitment.

Then came the surprising return to high school ball—two jobs in Florida and a third in South Carolina. Saban turned his sights back toward college by interviewing with the University of North Texas in 1991 before accepting a position at Peru State (an NAIA Division II school) in Nebraska. He guided Peru State into the playoffs—then suddenly resigned after the season.

✳   ✳   ✳

Doug Dickey had no immediate plans after his final game at Florida. He jokingly spoke of returning to school and running for student government president. Dickey went to work in private business in Lakeland. Then, in 1985, Tennessee athletic director

Bob Woodruff—the former UF coach who had spent seven dollars of the Vols' long-distance phone budget in 1963 to bring Dickey to Knoxville—brought Dickey back to college athletics to succeed him as athletic director.

"Once we went through a peak in about 1974, '75, and '76, and did not win the championship with our best teams, it went kind of sour with the press again," Dickey says. "And when that starts in Florida, it's trouble. I thought 1979 would be a hard year but that in 1980 the Florida program would be right back in the thick of it, and I think we were right.

"Charley Pell (hired in December 1978) brought an enthusiasm in fund-raising and total involvement of fans in the program, that he was accustomed to at Clemson, that Florida really needed. We didn't seem to be able, within our leadership, to do that."

Miami coach Lou Saban embraces assistant coach Joe Brodsky following what turned out to be his final game as UM coach. (MIAMI HERALD)

Florida State vs. Miami
Kelly and the 'Canes Arrive

The snow in western Pennsylvania was about two feet deep and still falling. Jim Kelly really didn't expect the head football coach from the University of Miami—Miami, of all places, in that weather—to make the 40-mile drive from the airport in Pittsburgh to his home in East Brady. Considering the driving conditions, it figured to take about three hours.

But UM coach Lou Saban was indeed a driven man. He knew young Jim Kelly had a tremendous arm. He knew young Jim Kelly had his heart set on playing quarterback at Penn State. He knew Penn State had told young Jim Kelly they were interested in him playing linebacker. He knew there were other schools interested in having young Jim Kelly play quarterback for them—namely, Notre Dame, Tennessee, Pitt and West Virginia.

That's why Saban and a Miami assistant made the drive, snow and all, from Pittsburgh to East Brady. And that convinced young Jim Kelly that Miami was the place to be.

Kelly's career at UM got off to a rough start. "When I went down there, they wanted to run the Veer offense," recalls Kelly, who was redshirted in 1978. "Jim Kelly is definitely not a Veer quarterback. I almost transferred out of the University of Miami to Tennessee. I decided to hold off."

He was a freshman under first-year coach Howard Schnellenberger in 1979 when the Hurricanes headed north to play Penn State. The Hurricanes had lost by three points at Florida A&M, an NCAA Division I-AA program, and dropped to 3-4 before making the trip to face No. 19 Penn State (5-2).

Schnellenberger decided he would bench starter Mike Rodrique in favor of freshman Kelly, who started the second half of the most recent loss to Syracuse. This news was not made public and not even revealed to the team—not even to Kelly himself—until only hours before kickoff.

Kelly recalls: "That morning, after the pregame meal, we head over to the stadium. And Coach Schnellenberger brought me (and fellow quarterbacks) Mark Richt and Rodrique together. He said the coaches talked it over, and they decided Jim Kelly's going to be our quarterback. I had a long time to prepare, about three hours."

"I knew that Jim was ready to go even before that," Schnellenberger says. "I was waiting for the offensive team to be ready. I

Jim Kelly chose not to attend Penn State in part because the Nittany Lions preferred for him to play defense. (UNIVERSITY OF MIAMI)

had a terrible experience at Baltimore when I had Bert Jones and Marty Domres and I knew that Jones was far and away the better quarterback. And I tried, as a young coach might do, to jump-start the winning process, and I started him (Jones) before the offense was ready to win. He had to bear the brunt of that ill-fated decision.

"I didn't want to do that with Kelly. So I waited and waited because I didn't want to ruin him. I suspect it was the right decision." With Kelly leading the way, Miami upset Penn State, 26-10. Kelly closed out the season with a 2-2 record as a starter, losing to Alabama and Notre Dame before closing with a victory over Florida. A team that managed to lose to Florida A&M and beat Penn State finished 5-6.

The doubts regarding UM football weren't limited to the on-the-field performance. After the 1980 Notre Dame loss, only 17,806 showed up at the Orange Bowl for the game against Mississippi State. During the entire season, no one appeared at the school's two ticket outlets in Palm Beach County.

In 1980, Miami opened by beating Louisville, 24-10, and exacting revenge upon Florida A&M, 49-0. The Hurricanes then traveled to Houston to face a team that was respected enough to be ranked 18th despite its 0-1 record. Miami responded with a surprising 14-7 victory. The 'Canes were off to their best start since 1962 at 3-0.

The Seminoles, rated 13th in the 1980 preseason poll, had met little resistance before coming to Miami. In what was expected to be a difficult opener, Florida State proved again that it could win in hostile conditions when it shut out LSU at Tiger Stadium, 16-0. Subsequent floggings of Louisville (52-0) and East

It was Jim Burt's block of a last-minute two-point try by Florida State that allowed the Hurricanes to beat the Seminoles, 10-9, in a game that both sides agreed meant a great deal to the turnaround of UM football. (UNIVERSITY OF MIAMI)

Carolina (63-7) left FSU with a combined scoring advantage of 131-7 in rising to ninth in the AP poll.

Florida State had accomplished this without the services of senior All-America nose guard Ron Simmons, sidelined with an injured ankle. Junior James Gilbert from Miami had proved to be an adequate understudy, and coach Bobby Bowden planned to start Gilbert again against the Hurricanes with the idea of possibly rotating him with a well-rested Simmons. Junior quarterback Rick Stockstill was also ailing, having bruised his throwing shoulder during the Monday practice before the game. But the injury situation that concerned Bowden the most was at center. Starter John Madden was questionable with a bad ankle. His backup, Bob Merson, had been lost indefinitely with a knee injury suffered on the play after Madden was hurt. The third-string center was junior offensive guard Redus Coggin.

With Miami undefeated and games with Nebraska and Pittsburgh looming in the near future, Bowden dubbed this stretch of games the "Mideast crisis."

"These next three will tell the story on Florida State," he said.

Miami fans had heard all about Simmons but liked to think their middle guard, Jim Burt, was better. UM went into the game leading the nation in rushing defense, allowing only 16 yards per game. Conversely, Florida State went into the game without having allowed a touchdown by the opponents' offenses all season. The lone touchdown registered against the Seminoles was scored by East Carolina on a kickoff return.

The Orange Bowl was rocking for a UM game for the first time since 66,000 were on hand to watch the 'Canes play Notre Dame in 1971. The gathering of 50,008 came out in 91-degree weather at 4:00 p.m. to see if Hurricane football really was back. Of course, some of the fans were hoping to see the Seminoles, favored by 4 1/2 points, try to stretch their winning streak in the series to three straight. They had also returned to the scene of the crime, the same stadium in which Florida State suffered its only loss of the entire 1979 season—to Oklahoma in the Orange Bowl Classic.

Madden started the game at center. But his ankle wasn't sufficiently healed, and he had to leave the game after only a few plays. With Merson out, Florida State had to resort to Coggin, who had not played center until being moved there that week.

Florida State's offense sputtered terribly in the first half, going six possessions before getting a first down. Miami, meanwhile, had no trouble pushing far into Florida State territory but was unable to capitalize once there. Miami's second drive reached the Florida State 35-yard line before running out of steam. Danny Miller, who had made only two of five field goals after hitting 14-of-17 the previous year as a sophomore, missed from 47 yards out.

The Hurricanes' next great opportunity came early in the second quarter after a fumble by FSU fullback Michael Whiting was recovered by UM cornerback John Swain at the Seminoles' 37. Six plays later, Miami fullback Greg Anderson made his first carry of the season—and fumbled on a busted play at the 15. Jarvis Coursey recovered for the 'Noles.

With 52 seconds left in the first half, Miami called timeout facing third-and-10 at the 50. Kelly dropped back and threw for the end zone, his intended receiver being Larry Brodsky. The ball was clearly overthrown as Brodsky and FSU defensive back Gary Henry bumped at the goal line. Henry was whistled for interfering with Brodsky, giving Miami first-and-goal at the FSU one with 41 seconds left in the half. The feeling on the Florida State sideline was that the penalty was a "makeup" call after no penalty was called on a previous long pass play during which Brodsky was jostled by FSU's Monk Bonasorte.

Kelly sneaked over for the touchdown, and Miami moved ahead, 7-0. That was the halftime score, as the Seminoles trudged off for the locker room with only one first down to show for the first 30 minutes of football.

Stockstill had attempted only six passes in the first half, completing three. Florida State

came out in the second half prepared to alter its game plan. The Seminoles moved quickly down the field, to the Miami 11, but settled for a 26-yard field goal by Bill Capece to cut UM's lead to 7-3 with 7:20 to play in the third quarter.

The Hurricanes responded immediately. Kelly passed them back down to the opposite end of the Orange Bowl—22 yards to Jim Joiner, two yards to fullback Mark Rush, 15 yards to Pat Walker and 11 more yards to Rush. Danny Miller capped the 75-yard drive by kicking a 22-yard field goal that Bobby Butler got his hands on, and the 'Canes' lead was again at seven points, 10-3.

Florida State finally got its offense going in the closing minutes of the fourth quarter. Stockstill guided the 'Noles 55 yards to a touchdown, the score coming on an 11-yard pass to tight end Sam Childers with 39 seconds left in the game. After completing only three passes in the entire first half, Stockstill completed nine on the scoring drive. The touchdown put the score at 10-9.

Bowden never hesitated in sending in his two-point unit. The plan was to pass over the middle, which had been the trouble area all day with Coggin so worried about UM's pass rush. On the Miami sideline, Bowden's decision came as no surprise. And the Hurricanes had dutifully practiced their two-point defense during the week. Defensive coordinator Rick Lantz had two defenses in mind and decided to use the formation that included a heavy pass rush down the middle. FSU wide receiver Phil Williams ran his route to the back of the end zone, but Stockstill's pass was batted down at the line of scrimmage by middle guard Jim Burt, leaving Florida State one very large point behind the Hurricanes. Miami only had to run out the clock to preserve one of its biggest victories in years. With it, Florida State's regular-season winning streak was snapped at 18 games.

"It's by far the biggest win I've ever been associated with at UM," Schnellenberger said. "We felt like if we could make them throw, we could win. But it almost didn't work that way."

Miami finished with 291 total yards to Florida State's 207, each team passing for 182

Jim Kelly (12) and Jim Burt (87) accept most valuable player trophies after Miami's 20-10 Peach Bowl victory over Virginia Tech following the 1980 season that gave UM its first bowl trip since 1967. (UNIVERSITY OF MIAMI)

yards. Averaging 225 yards rushing going into the game, the 'Noles were held to a measly 25. FSU was charged with seven fumbles, losing two of them. Five fumbles came on missed exchanges between Coggin and Stockstill. After the game, Coggin could barely bring himself to discuss his problems. "I don't know. I don't know," he said softly. "I guess I was just hitting his hand wrong."

Bowden could only shake his head and grimace when recalling how close Florida State had come to improving its record to 4-0: "He was open. We had 'em." On the pass interference play that set up Miami's only touchdown, Bowden had little to say: "I'm prejudiced."

Henry said: "All I did was turn around. It (the pass) was over everybody's head." Brodsky was candid in his assessment of the call: "It surprised me as well as everybody else."

One UM student said upon leaving the raucous scene at the Orange Bowl: "This is the first time I really feel like I'm in college."

Schnellenberger was asked how much the surprisingly large Orange Bowl crowd was worth to the Hurricanes. He pondered the questions and cleverly replied: "One point."

Looking back at the game, Bowden says: "That's the game I found out centers are more important than quarterbacks. Just couldn't get anything going offensively. To

※

me, that's the game that started Miami on their comeback."

* * *

Florida State did not lose another regular-season game, despite facing Bobby Bowden's "Mideast crisis." The Seminoles traveled to Nebraska and shocked the Cornhuskers, 18-14, then returned home to beat Pitt, 36-22. They made an encore appearance in the Orange Bowl Classic, but lost again to Oklahoma, 18-17.

Two losses by two total points in the Orange Bowl. Too much.

The Miami Hurricanes had felt in the locker room after beating Florida State that they were good enough to be ranked in the Top 10. The victory didn't vault them quite that high; they were ranked 13th the following week, three spots above the Seminoles. UM did not look like a Top-10 team in subsequent weeks. The Hurricanes tested their new-found status at Notre Dame and hobbled home after a 32-14 loss. Then Miami lost at home to Mississippi State, 34-31, and at Penn State in a homecoming of sorts for Jim Kelly, 27-12. At 4-3, Miami regrouped and won the remainder of its regular-season games to earn its first bowl berth (to Atlanta's Peach Bowl) since 1967. Says Schnellenberger: "I think that (beating Florida State) was what enabled us to get into a bowl game at 8-3."

Kelly finished with 1,519 yards passing. The 20-10 bowl victory over Virginia Tech enabled Miami to finish 18th in the nation.

With Kelly coming back as a junior in 1981, big things were expected of the Hurricanes—though they rated mention only as one of the "others receiving votes" in the preseason poll. But the 21-20 opening victory over Florida, Miller kicking a 55-yard field goal to win it, pushed Miami into the rankings. That's where the 'Canes stayed through mid-October. After falling out, Miami earned its way back into the poll in glorious fashion. With a 4-2 record, the unranked 'Canes stunned top-ranked Penn State on national television, 17-14.

Miami was also in the process of being investigated by the NCAA for alleged rule violations. Just before UM's trip to Tallahassee to face the Seminoles, the NCAA announced that the Hurricanes would be prohibited from playing in a bowl following the 1981 season. When interviewed in the UM training room the afternoon of the NCAA's announcement, Kelly angrily said: "I'm probably the only quarterback in the country who didn't get a car." Miami vented its anger toward the NCAA in the direction of Florida State and declared their date at Doak Campbell Stadium to be their bowl game for that season. The Hurricanes beat the favored Seminoles, 27-19. To close a season in which there would be no bowl game, the Hurricanes improved to 9-2 with a 37-15 drubbing of Notre Dame at the Orange Bowl. Without playing in a bowl, UM finished eighth in the final rankings for their best finish since placing sixth in 1956.

Kelly played only three games during an injury-shortened senior season and therefore didn't get any consideration in Heisman Trophy balloting. His career passing yardage of 5,228 broke George Mira's school record by more than 700 yards and was accomplished in virtually three seasons, the same as Mira's from the days before freshman eligibility.

Kelly became part of the famous 1983 class of quarterbacks selected in the first round of the NFL draft, along with Stanford's John Elway (picked first by the Colts before being traded to the Broncos), Illinois' Tony Eason (to the Patriots), Penn State's Todd Blackledge (to the Chiefs), UC-Davis's Ken O'Brien (to the Jets) and Pitt's Dan Marino (to the Dolphins). Kelly was picked by the Buffalo Bills but elected instead to sign with the Houston Gamblers of the United States Football League, where he proved his worth by becoming almost unstoppable in coach Jack Pardee's run-and-shoot offense.

Kelly eventually made it to the Bills and has guided them to a pair of Super Bowl appearances.

Miami vs. Florida
A Meaningful Meaningless Field Goal

This season was one that would be a watershed for college football in Florida. For all the seasons of past excellence at Florida, Miami and Florida State, 1980 would be the year in which fans recognized that all three could be powers concurrently, that the three Florida schools were capable of competing on a national level while rarely going beyond the state line to bring in players.

Florida State was on its way to a 10-1 regular season, coming on the heels of the 11-0 season of '79. Florida was rapidly exorcising the demon of its 0-10-1 finish of '79. In Charley Pell's second season as coach, the Gators would make the greatest turnaround in the nation, with a 7-4 record and a Tangerine Bowl bid in Orlando.

But that roar off in the distance in South Florida was a powerful engine being placed on the tracks in Coral Gables. And huffing and puffing at its head was Howard Schnellenberger, the ever-present pipe clenched in the side of his mouth. He would succeed where all others had failed since Andy Gustafson's glory days of the early '50s.

There would be no ignoring Schnellenberger and his 'Canes upon their trip to Gainesville in 1980, though. Gator fans probably shrugged off Miami's 7-3 record, considering that most of the victories had come against the likes of North Texas State and Vanderbilt and Division I-AA Florida A&M. The Gators came in at 7-2, but stinging from Georgia's 26-21 miracle victory in Jacksonville in which Lindsay Scott turned a desperation flip pass into a 93-yard touchdown in the closing seconds, a pass that would propel the Bulldogs to the national championship.

Who would have thought this would be Miami's day, especially after Florida opened the game with an incredibly easy 80-yard touchdown drive, capped by quarterback Wayne Peace's 15-yard pass to gangly receiver Tyrone Young? And who would have thought that Miami, after taking command with a 28-7 lead in the closing seconds, would tack on another three points with one second to play?

Certainly not ABC commentators Al Michaels and Frank Broyles, who were working the regional telecast from the TV booth above the west stands. They were befuddled when Schnellenberger sent in placekicker Danny Miller with one second left to attempt a 35-yard field goal. "I wouldn't do that even if my kicker was going for some kind of a record," Broyles drawled into the microphone.

Schnellenberger was going for a record, of sorts. The field goal that gave UM a 31-7 victory—though the Florida Field scoreboard continued to show only 28-7 until well after the teams had left the field—was Schnellenberger's way of getting on record his feelings about how the Hurricanes had become target practice all afternoon for the Gator student section, which is seated by the opponents' bench in the east stands.

Schnellenberger recalls: "One of our cheerleaders was hit in the stomach with something. One of my sons was hit with an orange, cut him in the eye. I was concerned somebody may have brought a bowling ball to the game. Knowing that the game was

iced, I turned to my offensive line coach, Chris Vagotis. As we shook hands, an orange was thrown and knocked him off his feet. And I don't know if I had a spontaneous reaction or what, but I wanted somehow to retaliate in that situation. My thought was that if we kicked a field goal at that time, it would draw attention to the fact that there was a dangerous situation."

Miller kicked the field goal, and Pell angrily waggled his right index finger at the Miami bench after the game.

✳   ✳   ✳

Howard Schnellenberger, a Miami Dolphins assistant coach, had his feet up in his Miami home when UM officials first called to

Wayne Peace (15) started at quarterback from midway through his freshman season in 1980 through his senior campaign in 1983. When he left, he was the second-leading offensive player in Southeastern Conference history. (UF SPORTS INFORMATION)

Howard Schnellenberger knew he had to do more than simply coach football at UM; he had to give the program presence in the community. On this occasion, it meant giving some passing pointers to a group of South Florida Boy Scouts. (UNIVERSITY OF MIAMI)

discuss the vacancy created by Lou Saban's sudden defection to West Point in January 1979. And Schnellenberger quickly, though politely, told them no. Just as quickly, he called back to say he indeed was interested. "I got to thinking about it, all the positives there were at Miami that could be put together if done right. The weather. The great number of high school athletes around there, if you could ever convince them to come there, that it could be a successful situation."

There also was a desire to prove himself again as a head coach. The former All-America end at Kentucky had been weaned as a coach under "Bear" Bryant at Alabama and through assistant positions in the NFL before he became the head coach of the Baltimore Colts in 1973. In the days in which the Dol-phins dominated the AFC East, Schnellenberger's '73 Colts went 4-10 and his '74 team was 0-2 when, on the sidelines of a game against the Philadelphia Eagles, team owner Robert Irsay thought he'd make a few coaching suggestions. Irsay was eager for Schnellenberger to play Bert Jones, a highly touted prospect out of LSU. Schnellenberger believed Jones would only be thrown to the wolves with inferior players around him and stuck with Marty Domres, whom Baltimore had acquired two years earlier in a trade that sent Colts legend Johnny Unitas to San Diego.

Irsay's sideline suggestion was more of an on-the-job order. But Schnellenberger wasn't about to let Irsay dictate X's and O's and said so, in so many words. The Colts lost the game, and Schnellenberger lost his job. He returned

Miami defenders John Daniels (36) and Fred Marion (31) break up a pass intended for Florida's Cris Collinsworth.
(UF INFORMATION SERVICES)

to the Dolphins, where he had been one of Don Shula's top lieutenants before taking the Baltimore job. Now he was leaving the security of the Dolphins to take on the challenge of the Hurricanes, who had plenty of coaches (six in the previous nine seasons) but not many fans (average attendance at the Orange Bowl was 20,978, up from 17,236 in 1976).

Saban had left some good players behind, but not enough. Schnellenberger's first season saw Miami struggle to a 3-4 start before the new coach decided it was safe to play freshman quarterback Jim Kelly. The strong-armed

enough good players in the state to support Miami as well as Florida and FSU. Schnellenberger decided Miami could compete to sign the best players in South Florida and called his recruiting concept the "state of Miami." The idea was that the territory from Tampa east through Orlando to the Space Coast belonged to the Hurricanes. No longer could the Gators and Seminoles expect to split the South Florida spoils between them.

Expectations for 1980 were tempered by the 5-6 finish of '79 until Miami scored the breathtaking 10-9 victory over Florida State

Miami's Jim Kelly gets his pass away despite heavy rush from UF linebacker Tim Golden. (UF INFORMATION SERVICES)

kid from Pennsylvania helped the Hurricanes split their final four games.

Off the field, though, Schnellenberger was winning plenty of battles. He expanded on Saban's idea that there were more than

to break the Seminoles' 18-game regular-season winning streak. But the 'Canes struggled with other top teams, losing at Notre Dame (32-14) and Penn State (27-12) as well as a 34-31 home loss to Mississippi State that

✳

135

lured all of 17,806 to the Orange Bowl. Same ol' Hurricanes.

* * *

Same ol' Hurricanes. That's what Gator fans must have been saying as Florida players punched fists into the air, coming to the sidelines with a 7-0 lead only minutes after kickoff. But Miami responded quickly with its own 80-yard touchdown drive, Kelly throwing 19 yards to Jim Joiner for the tying score. The Hurricanes soon were back on the offensive after Scott Nicolas intercepted a Peace pass at the Miami 10-yard line. The Hurricanes converted that turnover into a 32-yard field goal by Miller for a 10-7 lead. Miami's defense continued to stuff the Gators while Kelly moved the offense with ease. A one-yard plunge by Mark Rush and a 16-yard pass from Kelly to Pat Walker put the 'Canes ahead, 22-7, at halftime.

Peace says: "I thought we were in sync offensively (after scoring on the first series). Boy, from then on, they just killed us. I remember thinking at halftime, 'Boy, I'm just really getting killed out there.' They had Lester Williams and Kevin Fagan and Jim Burt, and they were just super."

The second half wasn't much different. The Gators had a chance to get back in the game early in the third quarter, recovering a fumble at the Miami 23. But on fourth-and-one at Miami's two, running back James Jones tried to go wide and was tackled at the seven. Later in the quarter, Gator receiver Cris Collinsworth—who had eight catches for 114 yards—couldn't hold onto an apparent touchdown pass in the end zone, and place-kicker Brian Clark's subsequent field goal attempt hit an upright.

Smokey Roan added Miami's final touchdown on a five-yard sweep around left end with 15 seconds left. It appeared to be of no consequence when Peace lost control of the ball while attempting to pass and fumbled at the Florida 18 with one second left. But few people outside of the Hurricanes' bench knew that Schnellenberger and Co. believed they had taken a physical beating from the fans.

The field-goal unit was ordered into the game. Miami assistant coach Kim Helton, a three-year Gator letterman and a UF assistant for six years before coming to Miami, tried to talk Schnellenberger out of his plan. No way. As Miami had felt the oranges and ice cubes, Florida would feel this swift kick. Now it was the Hurricanes with their fists and spirits raised high. Kelly—who completed 13 of 21 passes for 192 yards—walked off the field carrying a toy alligator hung in effigy.

Pell, in his postgame news conference, tersely said the Gators would respond to this in 365 days (actually, the '81 game had been moved to the first week of the season, on September 5). Many Gator players were enraged, pointing out that in a similar situation a few weeks earlier, Pell had ordered Peace to fall on the ball to finish a 21-10 victory over Auburn. Said noseguard Robin Fisher: "If I don't do anything else in football, I would like to run the score up on Miami. That field goal was bush-league." Peace, who was 19-for-41 for 329 yards passing, claims: "To me, it really wasn't that big of a deal. But the fans went crazy."

Which, of course, was Schnellenberger's original rationale for kicking the field goal. The scene kindled talk in the press of a Pell-Schnellenberger feud. Pell downplays such talk, saying he had a good working relationship with Schnellenberger. But of the relationship, even before the 31-7 game, Schnellenberger says: "We didn't have a good one to start with. I had coached him in college (at Alabama); he was one of the players on the national championship team. As we competed there at Miami, we had some situations in a lot of areas where we were meeting together with the press or recruiting together . . . well, he was doing some things that we didn't think were quite right. But that didn't have anything to do with the field goal."

Florida came back after an off-week to play Florida State tight, leading at halftime

An angry Charley Pell gestures toward the Miami bench shortly after the final whistle. (CARLA HOTVEDT)

but losing, 17-13. The Gators took a 7-4 record to Orlando and beat Maryland, 35-20.

The eight victories were the most by Miami since 1956. Schnellenberger had lobbied long and hard for a bowl bid, and while many schools would have snickered at going to the Peach Bowl, the 'Canes were thrilled to accept an invitation the week before beating UF. It was Miami's first bowl trip since Charlie Tate's '67 team played in the Bluebonnet Bowl. The 20-10 victory over Virginia Tech on January 2, 1981, allowed the 'Canes to finish ranked 18th in the AP poll.

But the best was yet to come for Schnellenberger and the Hurricanes. Miami kicked another late field goal against Florida in '81, but this one was from 55 yards by Miller and gave the Hurricanes a dramatic 21-20 victory.

Schnellenberger continued to promote Miami football tirelessly. He and Florida State coach Bobby Bowden often combined their efforts—one year preceding their meeting with a "weigh in," another year hyping their game with a one-round boxing "match." The two coaches had a common problem—fighting Florida. The Gators boasted the best facilities, the most alumni and all the advantages that came with being a member of a major conference.

A 7-4 finish without a bowl bid in 1982 preceded UM's national championship year of '83. But only a few months after the 'Canes and freshman quarterback Bernie Kosar stunned No. 1 Nebraska in the Orange Bowl Classic, 31-30, to win the national title, Schnellenberger made equally stunning news by announcing he was leaving UM to become coach and part owner of a proposed Miami franchise in the fledgling United States Football League. His plan for an on-campus football stadium having been voted down by the school in 1981, Schnellenberger didn't believe Miami was prepared to make a long-term, first-class commitment to the sport.

"Looking back, it was a dumb decision to make," Schnellenberger says. "We did it based on something that we felt was outstanding for the city of Miami, without hurting the University of Miami. We felt we had (the program) in great shape. When the situation came up, we had already recruited for '83.

"I thought they would elevate one of our assistant coaches and they wouldn't miss a beat. (Defensive coordinator Tom Olivadotti was the people's choice, but was passed over. He remained on Jimmy Johnson's staff before moving over to the Dolphins.) They missed a beat, but they obviously haven't missed much since. I think a professional football team in Miami in the spring would be another way that I could repay a city that had been very supportive of me."

Of course, there was never a USFL team in Miami. Schnellenberger's return to coaching came in his native Kentucky, at Louisville. Like Miami, it was struggling long and hard as an independent, but unlike Miami, it had neither the abundant talent nor football interest of South Florida. Schnellenberger signed a five-year deal for a reported $1 million beginning in 1985, and sloshed through seasons of 2-9, 3-8 and 3-7-1 before the '88 team went 8-3 (albeit ignored by bowl scouts). The highlight of his Louisville stint to date was the 1990 team that went to the Fiesta Bowl and smashed Alabama.

"You can't look back and say I wished I'd never done that," Schnellenberger says of his exit from UM. "I'll never do that, because what has come out of that—me coming to Louisville—is a great, great experience.

"The Lord leads in mysterious ways."

Miami vs. Florida State
Miami Takes Aim at a National Title

A little hype couldn't hurt, could it? There wasn't any harm in Miami coach Howard Schnellenberger taking a plane to Tallahassee to publicize UM's meeting with the Florida State Seminoles that week at Doak Campbell Stadium.

Schnellenberger and his friendly rival, Bobby Bowden, agreed to stage a mock boxing match for some publicity. Schnellenberger was wearing green boxing trunks as he and Bowden "squared off."

Harmless? Sure. Silly? No question. If there was one Miami-FSU game to date that didn't need any hype, it was this one. Miami was the talk of college football, winning nine consecutive games since losing its opener at Florida. A win over Florida State would send the Hurricanes to the Orange Bowl Classic against No.1 Nebraska.

There was even an outside chance that if the right set of circumstances fell into place, this Miami team that began the year with a 25-point loss could win the national championship.

But the boxing was still a lot of fun.

Of course, these teams were a lot of fun out on the field. And the series had become predictably unpredictable because it was dominated by the visiting team.

If the game's outcome hinged on any one individual, it was Miami's sensational freshman quarterback Bernie Kosar. Judging by the Hurricanes' record and national ranking, it was difficult to believe there was any question back in August about just who should quarterback the Miami Hurricanes in 1983.

But there was.

* * *

There was one bit of silver lining to the injury that cut short Jim Kelly's senior season at Miami in 1982. It was that Kyle Vanderwende got the opportunity to start a couple of games as a freshman and show Howard Schnellenberger and the rest of the UM coaching staff just what he could do under game conditions. What he did was deliver a 2-1 record, suffering only a one-point loss to Maryland.

Vanderwende's competition consisted of fellow sophomore Vinny Testaverde and redshirt freshman Bernie Kosar. Schnellenberger was unable to name Vanderwende as his '83

starter at the con-
clusion of spring
drills, which made
for a rather uncom-
fortable and anx-
ious summer for all
three of them. It
wasn't until the
week of the opener
at Gainesville that
he called the three
of them into his
office and told
them of the deci-
sion that had been
reached in consul-
tation with offen-
sive coordinator
Gary Stevens and
quarterback coach
Marc Trestman.
Kosar, who had last
played for Board-
man (Ohio) High
School, would start
in front of 72,000
fans at Florida Field.
Vanderwende
would be No. 2,
and Testaverde would be redshirted and
return as a sophomore in 1984.

UM quarterback coach Marc Trestman (white shirt and shorts)
poses with the three starting candidates going into fall drills in
1983: Bernie Kosar (20), Kyle Vanderwende (13) and Vinny
Testaverde (14). (UNIVERSITY OF MIAMI)

"It was down to an eyelash," Schnellenberger recalls. "My first gut feeling on something like that was to go with the guy who
was there before, and that was Kyle Vanderwende. I leaned toward Kosar because of his
mental toughness."

Kosar, who had switched from uniform
No. 1 to No. 20 because he didn't want to
project a cocky image, did not act like the
winning contestant on "Jeopardy." Feeling
more awkward for how the others felt, he
didn't celebrate. Vanderwende was particularly bitter about the outcome, telling reporters
he really didn't hear anything that Schnellenberger said after the word "Bernie" exited his
mouth. He considered transferring but
thought better of it.

In the opener, Kosar struggled against a
ferocious Florida pass rush that forced him
into three interceptions. He was also betrayed
by a running game that managed only 75
yards. Most folks left Florida Field not knowing whether Florida was that good or Miami
that bad.

"This is not my proudest moment,"
Schnellenberger told reporters after the game.
"But this is the beginning, our first test. We
had to get this one out of our system."

But what any UM watcher should have
gathered from the opener was that Kosar was
the quarterback through thick and thin. Why
else would Schnellenberger leave him in for

the duration instead of getting some time for Vanderwende? Said Schnellenberger the following day on his television show: "I think he's the guy we're going with, and he needed the work." Case closed.

Next stop was Houston, where there was talk that the Houston Cougars might challenge Texas for the Southwest Conference championship. None of that mattered to the 'Canes; they just needed a victory, plain and simple, to erase the memory of the demolition in Gainesville. And a win they got, 29-7. The UM running game was still missing, but the combination of passing and defense was enough to dominate the Cougars. Kosar only threw about half as many passes as he did against the Gators (26 compared to 45) yet threw for almost the same yardage (197 compared to 223). Plus, he threw for two touchdowns and had no interceptions.

A 35-0 blanking of Purdue at the Orange Bowl set up next week's game with another team from Indiana, the 13th-ranked Fighting Irish of Notre Dame. This was not vintage Irish, though, despite the ranking. Notre Dame was 1-1 under Gerry Faust and was unable to harness its great individual talent. This game was a classic example. The Irish gained 335 yards yet didn't score, losing to the 'Canes, 20-0, as Kosar passed for 215 yards. The win improved Miami's record to 3-1 and moved it into the AP rankings for the first time that season, at No. 15.

Miami had built up steam and confidence. The 'Canes toyed with the likes of Duke (56-17), Louisville (42-14) and Mississippi State (31-7). In the meantime, Albert Bentley showed signs of giving Miami the running threat that would make its offense complete. He ran for 83 yards against Duke and 152 against Louisville.

The next three weeks saw the Hurricanes struggle through relative squeakers. They were outgained by Cincinnati 290 yards to 144, yet still won 37-7. UM held West Virginia to two yards rushing in a 20-3 victory. Then East Carolina, Miami's Homecoming opponent, almost pulled off a stunning upset. The 'Canes

had to break up a last-minute pass near the goal line to come away with a 12-7 victory.

That left Miami at 9-1 and ranked sixth in the nation. Next up for UM was Florida State, which was in the uncharacteristic position of being unranked with a record of 6-3. The 'Noles were picked seventh in AP's preseason poll and even received one first-place vote. Five games into the season, FSU was 2-3 and not even thinking about national rankings, losing consecutive games to Tulane, Auburn and Pittsburgh on the road. In winning their last four games, Florida State's offense returned to form, averaging 42 points and ranked fourth in the nation. Miami's defense was ranked second in the nation.

And then there was Kyle Vanderwende. The 'Canes' No. 2 complained during practice that week that he had suffered a fractured rib. If he couldn't play and Kosar got hurt, who would play quarterback? Not only did Schnellenberger want to keep Testaverde out to complete the redshirt year, but Testaverde was also hurting, with a sore passing arm. Schnellenberger decided that if Kosar had to come out of the game for a couple of plays that receiver John Smatana, who had passed some on trick plays, would serve as a temporary quarterback. A more prolonged absence might require more drastic measures.

A heavyweight matchup? Put on the gloves.

✻ ✻ ✻

Before the game, in the visitors' dressing room beneath the east stands at Doak Campbell Stadium, Howard Schnellenberger wrote, "It takes everyone to be No. 1" on the chalkboard. He and his coaches left the players alone in the dressing room to ponder that thought for five minutes before taking the field.

In Florida State's locker room beneath the north end zone bleachers, Bobby Bowden challenged his team, challenged a defense that had trouble keeping up with the offense: "I don't like your image. You don't like it

The week before the 1983 opener against Florida, Miami coach Howard Schnellenberger chose redshirt freshman Bernie Kosar (20) as his starting quarterback. (UNIVERSITY OF MIAMI)

FSU coach Bobby Bowden and Miami coach Howard Schellenberger playfully square off during a publicity session in Tallahassee the Monday before their teams' showdown. (TALLAHASSEE DEMOCRAT–MARK WALLHEISER)

either, do you? It's an image of patsies. . . People say anybody can score all they want on Florida State. And that's ridiculous."

Kosar wasted little time guiding Miami downfield after the opening kickoff for the initial score of the game. Kosar threw a 17-yard pass to Glenn Dennison and a 19-yarder to Eddie Brown. Then came the game's first critical play, a pass interference penalty called against FSU defensive back Eric Riley on UM receiver Stanley Shakespeare that gave Miami first-and-goal at the Seminoles' one-yard line. Bentley took it in from there to give the 'Canes a 7-0 lead with 13:03 to play in the first quarter.

Miami forced Florida State to punt and appeared headed for another touchdown when UM took over at its 30. Seven plays later, the Hurricanes were on the FSU 29 facing third-and-three. Kosar was hurried by a three-man rush and his pass to Smatana was intercepted by FSU safety Brian McCrary at the 'Noles' one.

Florida State still couldn't muster much of an offense and punted again. But Miami's Ron Harris was blocked into Seminoles punter Louis Berry to give FSU a first down. All that did was gain Florida State a little breathing room before punting again. But Brown made a fair catch at the 'Canes' three.

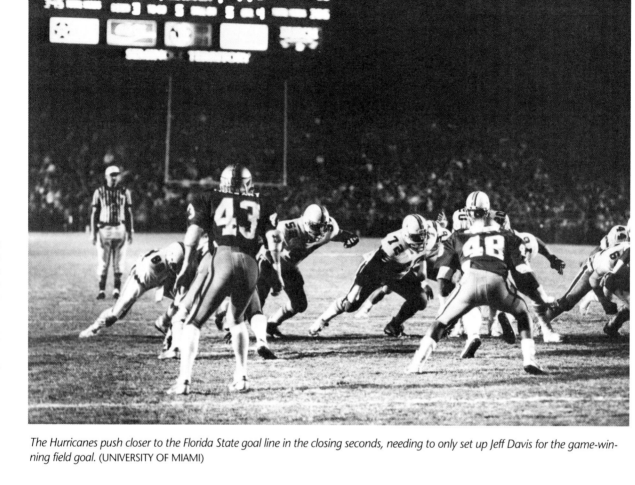

The Hurricanes push closer to the Florida State goal line in the closing seconds, needing to only set up Jeff Davis for the game-winning field goal. (UNIVERSITY OF MIAMI)

Kosar had Shakespeare wide open at the Miami 45 but the receiver dropped the ball. Rick Tuten stood inches from the back line of the end zone as he prepared to punt. Florida State let loose a 10-man rush, and David Ponder blocked the kick out the end of the end zone for a safety, cutting Miami's lead to 7-2 with 57 seconds to play in the first quarter.

A succession of punts led to a 46-yard field goal attempt by Miami senior Jeff "Flea" Davis. His kick was short and wide left. Florida State converted the miss into a go-ahead touchdown. The 'Noles moved 70 yards in 12 plays, the key play being a 21-yard pass from Bob Davis to Hassan Jones to Miami's 33. Greg Allen's three-yard touchdown run, and

Phillip Hall's extra point put the Seminoles ahead, 9-7, with 7:50 left in the first half.

The Hurricanes put together a drive to Florida State's 12 early in the third quarter, but Kosar was sacked for a 12-yard loss and didn't look stable as he walked to the sideline. John Smatana, anyone? Kosar assured those on the UM sideline he would be ready to go in for the next series. In the meantime, Jeff Davis went in to try a 41-yard field goal but missed again.

FSU took over and built its lead to 16-7 with a one-yard touchdown run by Bob Davis and Hall's kick with 3:23 left in the third quarter. But the Hurricanes answered immediately with a seven-play, 64-yard drive capped by a 37-yard touchdown pass from Kosar to Brown. With only 31 seconds left in the third quarter, Miami had cut the FSU lead to 16-14.

Next, it was FSU's turn to miss a field goal attempt. Hall missed a 47-yard effort that would have given the 'Noles a five-point lead with less than three minutes to play and forced Miami to score a touchdown to win.

With 2:12 to play, the Hurricanes assumed possession at the FSU 49. Kosar completed two 10-yard passes to Shakespeare, putting the ball on the Florida State 29 with 1:41 to go. The next play was a sprint draw to running back Keith Griffin, who darted his way to the FSU nine and was pushed out of bounds to stop the clock. It then became a matter of getting a good spot for Jeff Davis to attempt his field goal and also not allowing Florida State any time afterward to move the ball downfield. Three plays got Miami seven yards to the FSU two when time was called with three seconds left. The spot of the kick would be the nine, giving Davis a 19-yard attempt. Florida State used its final timeout in an attempt to rattle Davis into a third consecutive miss.

What Davis thought about was the Maryland game of 1982. In that game, Davis missed a 41-yard try with 12 seconds to play. Miami lost, 18-17, and was immediately dismissed by the bowl scouts who had maintained even the slightest interest in UM. After that miss, Schnellenberger had only encouraging words for his distraught soldier: "Don't worry about it. I know you'll have another chance some day, and I know you'll make it."

Before he jogged back out onto the field, Davis turned to Schnellenberger and said: "Coach, this one's for you."

Davis lined up the kick taking the attitude that this was just a glorified extra-point attempt. The snap was good, the spotting true, and the kick sailed between the uprights. The east sidelines of Doak Campbell Stadium looked like New Year's Eve. Except for Albert Bentley. He walked around in a circle, as if in his own world, and cried. "Oh, Jesus," he said softly.

The official invitation wouldn't come for another week, but the 'Canes and their freshman quarterback would play No. 1 Nebraska with a chance of winning the national championship.

Florida State had lost its fourth game of the season—six points to Tulane, three to Auburn, one to Pitt and one to Miami. That was good enough for the Peach Bowl, which invited the 'Noles to Atlanta to play North Carolina. No one counted on a total collapse in the season finale against Florida, a 53-14 defeat that had Bowden mumbling afterward that maybe someone else should have a shot of coaching FSU past the Gators.

Miami had won despite a Florida State rushing attack of 282 yards against the nation's second-ranked defense. The passing edge went to Kosar—21-for-35 for 243 yards, one touchdown and one interception. Seven times had Kosar passed for 200 or more yards. Only once had he thrown more interceptions than touchdown passes—that, in the opening loss to the Gators. He set school records for completions and touchdown passes in a season. His 2,329 passing yards were second only to Jim Kelly's 2,403 yards in 1981.

✳ ✳ ✳

It would take a domino of bowl wins and losses for the Miami Hurricanes to be thinking national championship by the time they took the field on the night of January 2, 1984. First, second-ranked Texas would have to be upset by No. 7 Georgia that afternoon in the Cotton Bowl. Then, No. 4 Illinois would have to lose to unranked UCLA in the Rose Bowl. Even after all that, there was No. 3 Auburn—which would play No. 8 Michigan in the Sugar Bowl—to be considered.

The dominos began to fall in an incredible fashion. Texas controlled Georgia for most of the afternoon, only to give up a late touchdown after fumbling a punt return and lose to the Bulldogs, 10-9. Scratch the Longhorns from the chase for No. 1. Illinois? It not only lost to UCLA, it was crushed—45-9.

With FSU leading 16-14 and time for only one play remaining, Miami kicker Jeff Davis prepares to get his right foot into the 19-yard field goal that won the game for the Hurricanes. (TALLAHASSEE DEMOCRAT–MARK WALLHEISER)

As the Orange Bowl began to fill, there were, realistically, three teams still eligible to win the national title—Nebraska, Auburn and Miami. The Huskers were 12-0 and were being called one of the great college football teams ever assembled; few folks outside Miami had even considered the prospect of their losing. As for Auburn, the Tigers had one loss—at home in September to Texas. If Auburn and Miami were to win that night, Auburn's claim to No. 1 would be that it finished 11-1 just like Miami and played an overall tougher schedule. Miami's claim would be that it had just beaten the No. 1 team, despite the fact that the 'Canes would be making a leap from No. 5 to the top.

Miami stunned the crowd and a national television audience by building a 17-0 lead.

The 'Canes took a 31-17 lead into the fourth quarter, but Nebraska wasn't about to give up. With Jeff Smith replacing Heisman Trophy winner Mike Rozier in the backfield, Nebraska started back. Smith scored on a one-yard run with 6:55 to play. The subsequent PAT cut Miami's lead to 31-24. The 'Canes moved far enough downfield afterward for Davis to attempt a 42-yard field goal with 1:53 to play. The kick fizzled off to the left, leaving Nebraska the opportunity to win with a touchdown and a two-point conversion.

The Huskers took over at their 26. Quarterback Turner Gill guided Nebraska to Miami's 24, where Nebraska faced fourth-and-eight. That's where Gill pitched off to Smith at the last minute. Smith raced in for a touchdown with only 48 seconds to play.

Miami 31, Nebraska 30 with a two-point conversion to play.

In what became arguably the most significant college football play of the '80s (apologies to the Stanford band), Gill rolled out to his right looking for Smith amid a crowd of Nebraska receivers in the area. Miami defensive coordinator Tom Olivadotti had noted such a tendency on film only the previous

But Miami was able to gain control, run out the clock and wait for the results of the balloting. Auburn had also won its game, relying on three field goals to outlast Michigan 9-7.

As it turned out, there were few writers who liked Auburn's argument over Miami's. Auburn received seven first-place votes but finished third in the balloting. Nebraska was second, receiving 4 1/2 firsts. Miami captured

A moment of celebration for Bernie Kosar. (UNIVERSITY OF MIAMI)

day and boned up on the appropriate defense. Three Miami defenders were waiting in the area. Gill's pass was batted to the ground by defensive back Kenny Calhoun. Miami 31, Nebraska 30.

In the UM coaches' box, there was fear that UM's subsequent 15-yard penalty for the mass celebration could put Nebraska in field goal range if the Huskers recovered an onside kick.

the other 47 1/2 first-place votes to easily win the first national championship in the history of the school—and the first for a school from Florida, for that matter.

Kosar, who set an Orange Bowl record by passing for 300 yards, had quarterbacked Miami to the national championship as a freshman.

When Jimmy Johnson came in to replace Schnellenberger the following year, the 'Canes finished 8-5, closing with a Fiesta Bowl loss to UCLA. That turned out to be Kosar's last game as a 'Cane. He was eligible for a special supplemental round of the NFL draft because he would be graduating before the next college season. With that, Kosar was not only able to leave college after only two seasons but all but arranged to play with the favorite pro team of his boyhood, the Cleveland Browns.

In the NFL, the closest Kosar has come to duplicating the glory he experienced at UM was getting the Browns into two AFC championship games, a pair of heartbreaking losses to the Denver Broncos.

But in Miami, there will always be memories of No. 20 and the year that he barely won a starting job in August, barely won a bowl game in January and won a national championship.

✳

Florida vs. Florida State
"We've Got Your Number"

The white jerseys that the Florida Gators had worn to Tallahassee had long since turned to brown, transformed by the mud and the muck that was Doak Campbell Stadium's turf on this horrendously rainy night.

Deion Sanders, Florida State's budding All-America cornerback, didn't have any trouble finding Florida quarterback Kerwin Bell, though his jersey number was covered with mud. Sanders was a man on a mission. The Seminoles were leading 13-10 in the fourth quarter and Sanders had a message he wanted Bell to hear.

"We've got your number this year," Sanders told Bell. "You ain't gonna do it."

Bell, who often sounded like Opie Taylor, could only think to say, "OK, just wait until the end of the game." But Bell and his teammates were about to give Sanders a much more forceful response.

*   *   *

Valdosta State football coach Jim Goodman liked what he saw of Kerwin Bell, the kid from the tiny north Florida town of Mayo (population 500). Goodman told Bell he thought he would be able to offer the young quarterback a scholarship to play for the Blazers in 1983. But by the time signing day came, Goodman had found players he liked better, and the offer never came through.

Now faced with the choice of walking on at either Florida State or Florida, Bell chose Florida because he considered himself something of a Gator fan and because he knew that starting quarterback Wayne Peace would graduate following the '83 season.

After spring practice 1984, Bell was fifth on the depth chart. That fall, six quarterbacks took the green flag in the race to succeed Peace. Dale Dorminey, a fifth-year senior, won the starting job only five days before the season opener. Walk-on Bell was the surprising choice for the second team. Second team, that is, for about 24 hours. At Tuesday's practice Dorminey was standing on the sidelines when reserve fullback Joe Henderson rolled out of bounds during a drill . . . out of bounds and right into Dorminey, who sustained a knee injury that ended his career.

Suddenly, Bell found himself the starter, and who was UF's opponent on opening day? None other than defending national champion Miami. Bell shrugged off the challenge, saying he just wanted to play the best game possible. That he did, leading Florida to within seconds of an upset of the Hurricanes. Bell's five-yard touchdown pass to Frankie Neal gave the Gators a 20-19 lead with 41 seconds to play. Unfortunately for the Gators, UM quarterback Bernie Kosar answered with some heroics of his own. UM scores twice in the Closing seconds for a dramatic 32-20 win.

nation before stumbling against Georgia and finished at No. 5. Bell's quarterback rating was second only to that of Iowa's Chuck Long, and he again led the SEC in passing. The 2,687 yards would be his career best and second in UF history to the 2,896 yards that Reaves threw for as a Super Soph in 1969.

The 6-5 finishes during his junior and senior years weren't enough to prevent Bell from becoming the SEC's career passing lead-

Walk-on Kerwin Bell finished spring practice in 1984 as the Gators' No. 5 quarterback, but circumstances allowed him to start the opening game against Miami's defending national champions. (UF SPORTS INFORMATION)

In spite of the loss—and in spite of Florida's ongoing problems with the NCAA, Bell flourished with the Gators. As a freshman he led the team to a 9-1-1 record and a No. 3 ranking, and he was named Southeastern Conference Player of the Year. During his sophomore year, Florida rose to No. 1 in the

er, his four-year total of 7,585 yards surpassing Reaves' three-year total of 7,549.

But it isn't the numbers that made Kerwin Bell memorable. It was the humility of a walk-on, the son of a small-town tobacco farmer, the guy who marries the head majorette, leading the program that had been typecast as a bunch of cheaters. Says Bell: "The way I got the starting job was unbelievable in itself. I think people thought, 'When he did earn it, he stayed the same person.' That was always my biggest goal, and still is, to be the person I've always been."

* * *

Bell's presence notwithstanding, this did look like the year in which FSU would finally end its frustrating losing streak to the Gators. Since the 1981 meeting that settled which team would go to the Peach Bowl and which would stay home, Florida had beaten Florida State. For all of Bobby Bowden's success in giving Florida State a national football presence, he had a 4-6 record against the Gators.

But that was supposed to change in 1986, based on how each team fared in reaching the season-ending showdown. Florida had staggered through the season to a 5-5 record. Following their opening win over Georgia Southern, an NCAA Division I-AA school, UF dropped four in a row to Miami, Alabama, Mississippi State and LSU. The loss to the Hurricanes broke Florida's 19-game unbeaten streak at Florida Field.

The Gators were all but left for dead at 1-4 with the likes of Auburn, Georgia and FSU still remaining on the schedule and starting quarterback Kerwin Bell lost indefinitely with a knee injury. After beating Kent State and Rutgers, the Gators pulled off a stunning upset by rallying from a 17-0 deficit in the second half, with Bell coming off the bench, to beat Auburn 18-17. Florida then headed to Jacksonville and knocked off Georgia, 31-19, to suddenly rekindle bowl thoughts. With that motivation, UF promptly went out and lost to Kentucky, 10-3. No bowl could take a chance on the Gators at that point. It didn't help that Florida had played five nationally ranked teams, going 2-3.

Florida State had come through a relative struggle itself, going 6-3-1. The Seminoles had finally buckled beneath the weight of a heavyweight road schedule. They lost at Nebraska, Michigan and Miami and were tied at home by North Carolina. With one game to play, FSU had accepted a bid to play Birmingham's All-American Bowl against Indiana. The Seminoles were favored to beat the Gators by seven points.

* * *

Charley Pell arrived at the University of Florida in December 1978 armed with the mission to deliver the elusive SEC championship. What followed was a wild ride that no Gator fan will forget, for both the good and the bad.

A three-year starter at Alabama, Pell had made a coaching name on the small-college level at Jacksonville (Alabama) State. It was his years at Clemson, though, that first brought him national attention. Pell took the Gators job, saying that he thought there was a better chance to win a national championship with Florida than with Clemson. Ironically, Clemson won the 1981 national title under Pell's chief aide and successor, Danny Ford.

In Gainesville, Pell discovered a program that was sorely lacking in facilities and funds. Not to mention players. For all the NFL players that had come through UF during Doug Dickey's tenure, the 1979 roster didn't figure to scare too many opponents in the SEC. The most talented player on the team was junior Cris Collinsworth, who had come to Florida as a highly sought quarterback and was converted to wide receiver.

An episode in the spring of '79 typified what would become an era of conflict and internal strife. Athletic director Bill Carr was giving an NCAA representative an unofficial tour of the athletic facility when the two came to a football practice session. The problem was that Florida was not yet supposed to be in spring football. For this relatively minor violation, the Gators were docked some spring practice dates. The appearance in Gainesville was that one hand didn't know what the other was doing.

Pell's first team suffered through an 0-10-1 campaign, but Pell's rebuilding program began paying dividends the next year, when UF made the single greatest one-year turnaround in NCAA history by going 7-4 and beating Maryland in the Tangerine Bowl. The Gators traveled to the Peach Bowl in 1981, after breaking a four-year losing streak to Florida State, and to the Bluebonnet Bowl in 1982.

Off the field, Florida was also making impressive gains. One of the weakest aspects of the athletic department when Pell arrived was the financial infrastructure. He had seen what a well-oiled fund-raising machine could do at Clemson, and at UF Pell's presence brought about the growth of Gator Boosters. The group suddenly came to life after so many virtually dormant years. With Gator Boosters thriving and Pell producing victories, UF was able to set into motion renovations and expansions to Florida Field that saw seat-

ing capacity increase from 62,800 to 72,000 in 1982 and to 83,000 in 1991.

But before Florida left on its Bluebonnet Bowl trip to Houston, university president Robert Q. Marston acknowledged that he had received word from the NCAA that the school was under a preliminary investigation of its football program. Only three weeks earlier, Clemson had been placed on probation with some of the rule violations dating to Pell's term there as assistant coach and head coach.

The entire 1983 season was played beneath the shadow of the NCAA investigation–and a flurry of reports in state newspapers of wrongdoing in the UF program. Most stinging was a package of stories published in April 1983 by the St. Petersburg *Times,* charging that players had sold game tickets and received summer jobs improperly through the football program in violation of NCAA rules.

Charley Pell, with wife Ward at his side, speaks with reporters after Florida president Marshall Criser has announced that Pell will leave the Gators after the '84 season.

Pell maintained the innocence of himself and his staff.

The NCAA cloud continued to hover over Florida Field in 1984, through spring drills and after the Gators reported for fall practice in early August. Actually, plenty was going on behind the scenes. UF officials determined that the football program had committed serious violations and they expected the NCAA to bring down the hammer. Pell met with university lawyer Jim Quincey to discuss what exactly happened and why. Pell said he was unaware of most of the transgressions, maintained that others couldn't have been helped. A new university president, former south Florida lawyer Marshall Criser, was about to take office at UF. He talked tough and promised to get to the bottom of the problem and run an athletic program with integrity.

Criser convinced Pell to quit on Sunday night, August 26. Pell told his players the following day that he would resign for the good of the program effective at the end of the season. Criser and Pell made the official announcement that Monday morning, neither providing further details of the NCAA investigation.

The Gators opened the season on September 1 at Tampa against Miami. UF gave up two touchdowns in the final minute to lose 32-20, and was further frustrated by a 21-21 tie at home to LSU the following week.

On Tuesday, September 11, UF revealed that the NCAA had charged it with 107 rule violations. The school's hearing before the infractions committee was scheduled for September 21-22, an off week on the UF football schedule, in Kansas City. The Gators vented their frustration on the field the following Saturday in the last game before the hearing, improving their record to 1-1-1 with a 63-21 flogging of Tulane.

It turned out to be Pell's final game as Gator coach; Criser summoned Pell to his home the next evening and told him that he would not continue as football coach. At the news conference on Monday, September 17, Criser introduced offensive coordinator Galen Hall as the interim coach.

The NCAA found Florida guilty of various rule violations. Of the approximately 1700 pages in the initial NCAA report, 64 referred to a rather obscure individual named Mike Brown. It turned out that Brown, a football aide who didn't even get his photo printed in the annual football brochure, admitted to the NCAA that he spied on some opponents' practices. He obtained a student I.D. on his "mission" to the University of Mississippi. At Auburn, he even chatted openly with former Auburn coach Doug Barfield, who thought he was a student. Florida AD Bill Carr questioned Brown about his absences, the NCAA files stated, and Brown simply said he had to go visit his sick grandmother in North Carolina.

Pell has been out of college football since leaving UF, getting into real estate in the Pensacola area. There have been times when he has discussed the NCAA affair in general terms in interviews and public speaking engagements, but he has never expounded on the NCAA dealings at Florida or Clemson, the latter of which he says he has been wrongly connected with.

"Someday, somehow, the whole truth of the situation's going to come out," he says. "I think Marshall Criser resigning as president after only two years there–whatever, three years–that makes the hurt go even deeper because of the way things were and why they happened.

"When it does, I just think it'll be far more understandable. As each year goes by, It becomes absolutely more absurd the way it happened."

* * *

Florida football had been in the hands of Galen Hall since the dismissal of Charley Pell. Hall's hiring as interim coach was a classic case of being in the right place at the right time. Hall had come to Gainesville the previous February to replace Mike Shanahan as offensive coordinator after serving in that capacity for years at Oklahoma. He had been looking for a change of scenery following a second marriage.

Galen Hall had plenty to smile about during his first few years as Gators coach. He completed the '84 season for Charley Pell by winning all nine games to finish No. 3 in the country, then went 9-1-1 in '85 to finish No. 5. (UF SPORTS INFORMATION)

Hall was Criser's logical choice for interim coach because he was in no way connected with any of the transgressions that had brought about the NCAA probation. Hall was a dramatic contrast to Pell in personality. Pell was the picture of intensity, approaching the game with an almost religious fervor. Hall contained no such fire. He looked more like a chemistry professor: bald, pudgy, with eyeglasses and a little mustache, constantly chewing his fingernails. While Pell was a fiery speaker, Hall spoke with an occasional stutter, but he did have a keen sense of humor that allowed his players to relax.

He took over a UF team in 1984 with a 1-1-1 record. His first game was a 27-12 victory against Mississippi State beneath a blazing sun at Florida Field. Having come down out of the coaches' booth for the first time in years, Hall noted in his postgame news conference that he would need to wear a hat to prevent a serious sunburn atop his head.

The Gators began to march through the balance of their schedule. That included surprising Tennessee at Knoxville. UF was still in the hunt to win the SEC. What remained in doubt was whether the Gators would be allowed to play in a postseason bowl. Florida had appealed the NCAA's guilty verdict, and it was possible that the time it took to answer such an appeal might allow the Gators to play in a bowl after the '84 season.

UF closed its Florida Field schedule against Auburn, with Charley Pell on hand sitting in one of the luxury boxes high atop the west stands. Moments after Florida's convincing 24-3 win, most of the players looked up toward the skyboxes and saluted their former coach. In Jacksonville, the Gators pummeled Georgia, 24-3, to keep alive their hopes of winning the conference title.

That left only one game, at Kentucky, on their SEC schedule. Both Florida and LSU went into the weekend with records of 4-0-1 in the league. If Florida could beat Kentucky while LSU lost to Mississippi State, the Gators would be alone atop the conference at 5-0-1. Despite this success, school officials had said

nothing about whether Hall would be retained beyond the end of the season. The team's success had actually painted school officials into a corner. As long as Hall could still deliver UF's first SEC title ever, there was no way they could decide to hire anyone else. Only a few days before Florida's game against Kentucky, Gator athletic director Bill Carr acknowledged to a booster group in Orlando that Hall was about to be named as Florida's permanent coach.

In Lexington, Kentucky, the Wildcats put up a strong fight against the Gators. Florida held off Kentucky behind the kicking of Bobby Raymond and a last-minute defensive stand keyed by defensive back Adrian White to win, 25-17, and clinch at least a share of the conference title for the first time since Florida became a charter member in 1933. In the joyous locker room after the game, Criser announced to the players that Hall was their coach—period. Later that day, Mississippi State stunned LSU, 16-14. That meant Florida owned first place in the league outright.

With Gator fans thinking SEC trophy and Sugar Bowl trip, the conference hastily convened a meeting at its Birmingham headquarters to discuss Florida's eligibility to be recognized in either area. The conference voted not to recognize UF as the official champion and that it could not represent the league as champion in the Sugar Bowl or play in any bowl that year. All connected with the Gators were enraged. Revenge was the frame of mind going into Tallahassee. UF beat Florida State, 27-17, to finish the year with a school-best No. 3 ranking in the AP poll. Hall's record as coach was 8-0.

Florida, ineligible for bowl play or official SEC consideration in 1985, opened with a 35-23 victory at Miami before stumbling into a 28-28 tie against Rutgers. Afterward, UF reeled off wins over Mississippi State, LSU, Tennessee, Southwestern Louisiana, Virginia Tech and Auburn—to reach the No. 1 ranking for the first time in school history. Even without playing in a bowl, Florida had a chance to win the national championship if it could win the remaining three regular-season games against teams it had beaten the previous year.

Instead, the Gators promptly went out and were tripped up in Jacksonville by Georgia, 24-3. Forget the national title. Still, the Gators won out against Kentucky and FSU to finish 9-1-1 for the second consecutive year and fifth in the final poll. For two seasons, Galen Hall's record was an incredible 17-1-1.

But while Hall played no role in the rule breaking that brought about the NCAA sanctions, he would feel the brunt of scholarship restrictions. UF was cut back in both the total number of scholarship players allowed on the team and the number of scholarships that could be awarded. In 1986, every team that Florida played boasted more players. Hall, for instance, couldn't afford to offer scholarships to punters and kickers.

*　*　*

The sopped, muddy turf at Doak Campbell Stadium indicated that defense and the running game would dominate this latest chapter of Florida-FSU. Florida State had the first chance to score on a 47-yard field goal attempt by Derek Schmidt five minutes into the game, but the kick missed to the right. Florida in turn moved downfield with freshman running back Octavius Gould scoring on an eight-yard run with 4:06 to play in the period to give UF a 7-0 lead.

On the ensuing kickoff, Keith Ross brought the Seminole fans to their feet with a spectacular 71-yard return. Ross was a familiar name to Gator fans. He originally signed a football letter of intent with Florida but instead decided to sign a professional baseball contract with the Philadelphia Phillies. South-

UF's Ricky Nattiel broke the hearts of many drenched Seminole fans with an 18-yard touchdown catch in the closing minutes that gave Florida its sixth consecutive victory over FSU. (UF SPORTS INFORMATION)

eastern Conference rules prohibited any SEC athlete from competing in sports professionally, even if he didn't compete in that sport collegiately. Most schools and independents had by then changed their rules to allow athletes to cross over. For instance, John Elway could continue to play football for Stanford even after playing minor league baseball for the New York Yankees. The SEC also prohibited such athletes from returning after they had played professionally. So when Ross was ready to give up his pro baseball career after a couple of seasons in the Phillies' organization, he couldn't come back and play at Florida. He did what he thought was the next best thing and signed with FSU.

Even with Ross's return, Florida State could do no better than attempt a field goal. Schmidt came back on and kicked a 36-yarder with 2:09 left in the second quarter to pull the 'Noles within 7-3.

Florida came right back with a 66-yard march that stalled at the Florida State 3. Walk-on kicker Jeff Dawson was summoned and kicked a 19-yard field goal. That boosted the UF lead to 10-3 with 10:18 to play in the half.

The Seminoles answered with an impressive drive that featured the passing of sophomore Danny McManus and the running of freshman tailback Sammie Smith. Smith carried eight times for 44 yards on the 73-yard drive, including the one-yard touchdown run. FSU tied the score at 10-10 with 3:37 left in the half.

The most spectacular play of the game came early in the third quarter but was negated by a penalty. FSU's Smith turned a simple cutback on third-and-four at the Seminoles' 48 into a slashing 52-yard touchdown run in which he broke two tackles near the line of scrimmage and even got a crucial block from McManus. The play, though, was called back for offensive holding on receiver Herb Gainer. The drive ended with a fake punt that failed to gain a first down.

Later in the period, with the rain coming down harder than ever, Smith's rushing led Florida State to the UF four, where the Gators' defense held. Schmidt came on and kicked a 21-yard field goal. That put the 'Noles ahead, 13-10 with 3:06 to play in the third quarter. Florida pushed downfield in the closing minutes of the quarter thanks in part to an FSU penalty that kept the drive alive. Facing fourth-and-one at the FSU 36, Hall chose to go for the first down with 16 seconds left in the period. Bell took the snap and hopped forward, trying to squirm for as much yardage as he could, but was stopped for no official gain.

It was while Bell was waiting for the officials' measurement that Sanders strolled up, patted him on the rump and delivered his proclamation that the game was over.

On FSU's next possession, Smith continued to run through and around the Florida defense. He passed the 100-yard mark in the third quarter. But midway through the fourth quarter, Smith was caught for an eight-yard loss—he came up limping but stayed in the game—and Florida State faced fourth-and-15 at the UF 29. Bowden sent in Schmidt to attempt a 46-yard field goal, but the ball came off his foot low and was blocked by the Gators' Louis Oliver. Florida took over at the UF 40 with under eight minutes to play.

Wayne Williams got the possession off to a booming start with an 11-yard carry to the FSU 49. Florida stayed primarily on the ground, and on third-and-six at the Florida State 18, Bell dropped back, looked first for Eric Hodges, then spotted Ricky Nattiel who had beaten two FSU defenders in front of the goalposts. Bell fired the ball to him for a touchdown with 3:50 to play. Before the TD catch, Nattiel had caught three passes for a measly five yards. Dawson's initial PAT kick slipped off to the side. But FSU was penalized, and Dawson made good on his second chance to give Florida a 17-13 lead.

Now, not only would FSU have to score a touchdown to win, but it would have to do so without its top runner. Smith was sidelined with an injured ankle. The 'Noles got the ball back twice in the muck and slop and rain but were unable to get anything going.

FSU was penalized 116 yards during the game, a school record. This all left Bobby Bowden shaking his head over a sixth consecutive loss to the Gators: "They all hurt the same."

Hall, who shunned reasonable rain gear throughout the game and instead faced the elements with a long-sleeved T-shirt beneath his orange coaching shirt, had managed another winning year with the Gators despite falling into the early 1-4 hole. His mark in Gainesville was 23-6-1.

The muddy victory at Tallahassee turned out to be one of the last bright moments of Hall's stay at UF. With the scholarship restrictions continuing to hamper the squad's effectiveness and depth, Florida finished 6-5 again in 1987. With the exception of an impressive win over Alabama in Birmingham, the Gators lost to the teams that counted the most to their fans—Miami, LSU, Auburn, Georgia and Florida State. The star of the team was freshman tailback Emmitt Smith. Having served their time in the NCAA doghouse, the Gators were free to play in a bowl and traveled to the Aloha Bowl in Hawaii, where they lost to UCLA, 20-16. The following season brought about another 6-5 finish in the first year after the Florida-Miami series was discontinued. Again, UF lost to Auburn, Georgia and FSU. Florida finished on a happy note by beating Illinois in the All-American Bowl, 14-10.

In 1989, Hall found himself in a mess that was remotely similar to that of his predecessor. He was found guilty of violating NCAA rules, in this case paying his assistants an additional stipend. Five games into the season, Hall announced his resignation for the good of the program. Defensive coordinator Gary Darnell was elevated to interim coach in what was becoming something of a Gator tradition.

Hall stayed in the business by latching on as a graduate assistant at his alma mater, Penn State, under Joe Paterno before becoming the head coach of the Orlando Thunder of the World League of American Football in 1991.

Miami vs. Florida State
Bowden Goes for Two

Bobby Bowden's reputation was that of the gambler. Double reverses. Quarterback sneaks on fake field goals. Halfback passes. Fake punts.

With 1:40 remaining on October 3, 1987, this noted gambler had to decide to go for a tie against the Miami Hurricanes or take dead aim on victory. With the stands at sun-splashed Doak Campbell Stadium filled with crazed Seminole fans, fourth-ranked Florida State had just scored a touchdown to pull within 26-25 of the third-ranked 'Canes.

One fact of college football life is that a tie in early October will probably be forgotten by the pollsters who choose a national champi-on after New Year's Day—as long as you go unbeaten for the balance of the season.

But there were other factors to consider. FSU senior kicker Derek Schmidt, while on course to become the NCAA's career scoring leader later that season, had struggled with a stubborn north Florida wind that day.

And there was Bobby Bowden. Kick for a tie?

He sent in his kicking unit—then replaced it with his two-point conversion unit. From Doak Campbell's east sideline, UM coach

Jimmy Johnson, squinting into the sun, sent in his defense.

*　　*　　*

A shadow had been cast over the Miami athletic department in May 1984 when Howard Schnellenberger, fresh off delivering a national championship, shockingly announced his resignation to join a profes-sional franchise that existed only in theory. Claiming dissatisfaction with the university's commitment to football, he accepted a job to put together a United States Football League team in Miami.

In college football terms, having a coaching vacancy in June was akin to realizing on Christ-mas Eve that you had no presents to give the children. Most coaching changes are made in the weeks following the season, with coaching staffs subsequently hired in time to put in the new regime's philosophy during spring practice.

Miami was not afforded that luxury for 1984, the year in which the nation would watch how it planned to defend this surpris-ing national championship. UM athletic director Sam Jankovich, who had been con-

It didn't take Jimmy Johnson long to figure out that coaching the Hurricanes would be a blast. (UNIVERSITY OF MIAMI)

centrating his efforts on giving the department a sound financial foundation, suddenly had to turn his attention to hiring a football coach—and a good one—fast.

His choice was the head coach at Oklahoma State, who had built his reputation on defense. Jimmy Johnson was young, charismatic and he won football games. His five-year record with the Cowboys was 33-25-2, with 10 of the losses coming to the Big Eight Conference's warlords, Nebraska and Oklahoma. Johnson's resume was even impressive in defeat; in facing Nebraska and OU in consecutive games in 1983, Johnson had come within a point of beating the Cornhuskers and four points of beating the Sooners.

And Johnson did have some beach in his blood. He was reared in Port Arthur, Texas, 15 miles from the Gulf of Mexico. While some coaches might have shied away from expressing interest in the UM vacancy for fear of being compared with a coach who just won a national title, Johnson eagerly sought such a challenge. The basic design he had established for his coaching career included the logical promotion from head coach in college to head coach at a "major" power. Based on the 1983 season, Miami—with quarterback Bernie Kosar returning for his sophomore season—was such a power.

He first met with Jankovich at the annual summer football coaches' meetings the first week of June in Dallas. In seeking feedback from close associates, Johnson was told he would be crazy to move this late in the year and to succeed a coach who finished No. 1.

On June 5, Johnson was introduced as Miami's new coach. Introduced was the right word; many of Florida's media and some of the UM football players themselves had never heard of this guy from Oklahoma. He signed a reported five-year deal worth $1 million, not bad for a kid from blue-collar Texas who once washed cars for free on the used-car lot next door to his house. "Maybe I can add something," Johnson said during his first speech as UM coach. "Maybe I can make something a little better."

But there were strings attached to the deal. While a coach usually will come in and retool the staff to his liking, Johnson agreed to retain Schnellenberger's assistants since the chances of them finding jobs three months before the season were scant. Some assistants had no problem with this deal, but others weren't about to hide their displeasure. That included defensive coordinator Bill Trout, who displayed his feelings during Johnson's first staff meeting by annoyingly jingling his keys. The friction didn't subside.

The '84 season got off to a successful start when Miami headed to the Kickoff Classic in New Jersey and rallied to beat top-ranked Auburn, 20-18, then pulled off another rally in the closing minutes in Tampa to beat Florida, 32-20. And even after losses to Michigan and Florida State (the latter a 38-3 thumping at the Orange Bowl), Miami stood at 8-2 with two games to play, ranked sixth in the nation, and was invited to play in the Fiesta Bowl on New Year's Day against UCLA. True, they were not going to play for the national title. But remember that the trip to the '84 Orange Bowl was UM's first New Year's Day invitation in 33 years. And now a second was coming the next season.

But such an optimistic view of the first post-Schnellenberger season began to crumble the next week when Maryland visited the Orange Bowl. The 'Canes had the Terrapins put away at the half, 31-0, and with No. 1 Washington and No. 2 Texas both losing that same day, UM stood a chance to move up to fourth in the poll. The second half, though, proved to be one of the darkest hours in Miami football. Maryland had its way with the UM defense and rallied for an incredible 42-40 victory.

After an off week, there was more embarrassment. Boston College, with Heisman Trophy favorite Doug Flutie at quarterback, came to the Orange Bowl and stole a 47-45 win with the famous 48-yard desperation heave into the end zone on the final play that Gerard Phalen somehow caught for the winning score. The 39-37 Fiesta Bowl loss left Miami at 8-5—18th in the final rankings.

Johnson then suffered the additional setback of having Kosar, academically eligible to enter the NFL draft, declare he was leaving

UM after two seasons to go pro. But Johnson was free to put together a new staff, which he promptly did, and was not exactly devoid of quarterbacks with Vinny Testaverde available for two seasons. After opening the '85 season with a loss to Florida, Miami won the remainder of its regular-season games, including a 58-7 thrashing of Gerry Faust's struggling Notre Dame program that brought cries of Johnson blatantly running up the score. Miami found itself in position to win another national championship. If No. 1 Penn State lost to No. 4 Oklahoma in the Orange Bowl and No. 2 Miami beat No. 8 Tennessee as expected in the Sugar Bowl, Miami could finish on top.

But while Oklahoma was beating Penn State, Miami was stunned by Tennessee, 35-7. Make Johnson 0-for-1 when playing for the national title.

Make him 0-for-2 following the 1986 season. The Hurricanes won all 11 regular-season games and were matched with No. 2 Penn State, likewise 11-0, in a Fiesta Bowl game that was moved to January 2, 1987 to command the national spotlight.

The '86 season, by the way, had been the year of Vinny Testaverde, who two years earlier had gotten just about fed up with being Bernie Kosar's understudy. But when Kosar confided to him that he would graduate before the following season and enter the supplemental phase of the NFL draft, Testaverde saw—and grabbed—his chance to become UM's starting quarterback for the '85 and '86 seasons.

In fact, '85 wasn't exactly a bust for Testaverde. He threw for 3,238 yards, second-best in school history behind Kosar's 1984 total, and finished fifth in the Heisman Trophy balloting. But in '86, despite 700 fewer yards pass-

Vinny Testaverde accepts the 1986 Heisman Trophy, the pose of which doesn't at all resemble Testeverde's running style when he rumbled around right end for a touchdown in his first start against Florida as a junior. (DOWNTOWN ATHLETIC CLUB)

ing, Testaverde was the runaway Heisman winner, the first in UM history. He captured 678 first-place votes, while the runner-up totaled 32. Accepting the award, Testaverde looked out into the audience at New York's Downtown Athletic Club and told his father, Al: "Dad, we dreamed it together. We did it together."

Before kickoff back at the Fiesta Bowl, Miami held the spotlight in ways it would not have wanted. The team's renegade reputation was cemented when a group of players wore battle fatigues to a bowl luncheon and later walked off, claiming they weren't obligated to fraternize with the team that stood in their way of finishing No. 1.

In one of the best 1 versus 2 bowl matchups ever, Miami fell behind in the fourth quarter, 14-10, then set out on what looked like a game-winning drive in the closing minutes. Testaverde took the 'Canes to the Penn State six-yard line, but with 18 seconds to play was intercepted at the goal line by Penn State linebacker Pete Giftopoulos.

*   *   *

Miami was ranked 10th in the 1987 preseason poll, not even the best in the state (FSU was No. 9). There were questions about whether new quarterback Steve Walsh could adequately succeed Testaverde. But the Hurricanes were particularly impressive in their first two games, handcuffing Florida senior quarterback Kerwin Bell for a 31-4 victory at the Orange Bowl and traveling to Arkansas to humble Johnson's alma mater, 51-7. There were further claims of Johnson needlessly embarrassing an opponent, this time the school that had twice passed him over when it had a coaching vacancy. All that mattered to Johnson was that his 2-0 Hurricanes had a date the following week at Florida State.

The Seminoles came into the Miami game having already played four times. That was more than enough time to display one of the country's most potent offenses: 40-16 over Texas Tech, 44-3 over East Carolina, 41-24 over Memphis State and 31-3 over Michigan State. Sophomore tailback Sammie Smith

missed the opener with a knee sprain, then raced for 244 yards against East Carolina. Against Michigan State, the 'Noles ran five reverses. That included one by wide receiver Ronald Lewis that went for a 56-yard touchdown, enabling Lewis to become FSU's top rusher that day with 66 yards. At quarterback, senior Danny McManus had a gifted set of young wideouts—sophomores Lewis and Terry Anthony and freshman Lawrence Dawsey—to go along with senior Herb Gainer.

McManus had completed 53 of 106 passes to date with six touchdowns and three interceptions. Not pleased with those figures, he spent part of the week before the Miami game practicing his passing motion in his apartment, checking technique from the feet up. "Right now, things aren't going that well for me," he said. "I'm the weakest part of the passing game." The previous year, McManus was knocked out of the UM game at the Orange Bowl with a thumb injury in the second quarter with the Seminoles leading, 17-14. Miami went on to a wild 41-23 victory.

Bobby Bowden didn't mince words when asked about the '87 game's importance to the national rankings. "I don't think there has been any game more important than this," he said. "Whoever gets this one is going to be really visible in the polls."

Before kickoff, CBS announcer Brent Musburger—the same Musburger who chastised Johnson for running up 58 points on Notre Dame two years earlier—asked the Miami coach about playing for a tie or a win if the game came down to a PAT or two-point conversion. Johnson told him Miami was not very good at two-point plays.

Bowden likewise told Musburger he would kick in just such a situation. Just that week, Tennessee coach Johnny Majors had been criticized for kicking to tie Auburn in a battle of nationally ranked teams. Bowden telephoned Majors that week and assured him that he had made the right decision.

*   *   *

Danny McManus' 18-yard touchdown pass to Ronald Lewis pulled Florida State to within a point of Miami with 42 seconds to play, but his two-point pass intended for tight end Pat Carter fell short.
(FLORIDA STATE UNIVERSITY)

A record Doak Campbell Stadium crowd of 62,561 came prepared to see how Bobby Bowden intended to confuse Miami, a three-point favorite. But Bowden's first gamble of the day backfired. Florida State had ridden its rushing game from its 17-yard line to the Miami 45 on the game's first possession. Facing third-and-three, Bowden turned to one of his trusty reverses—Ronald Lewis, naturally. But the play gained only one yard, and the Seminoles were forced to punt.

After forcing a UM punt, Florida State reached the Miami 22, where Derek Schmidt was brought in to attempt a 33-yard field goal. But long snapper Marty Riggs let fly before McManus and Schmidt were ready, resulting in a 51-yard loss back to the FSU 26, where the Hurricanes took over. The result was a 29-yard field goal by Greg Cox that gave the 'Canes a 3-0 lead late in the first quarter.

Florida State responded, thanks to the combination of power and speed that was Sammie Smith. He rambled 64 yards from the 'Noles' 19 to the 'Canes' 17. Smith was chased down from behind by UM defensive back Bubba McDowell, playing in place of the injured Don Ellis. Four plays later, fullback Dayne Williams bulled into the end zone for the touchdown. Schmidt added the extra point, and the Seminoles owned a 7-3 lead four seconds into the second period.

FSU's defense frustrated Walsh and the 'Canes for the remainder of the half. Only once during three possessions did Miami cross midfield. The Seminoles, meanwhile, added another field goal, Schmidt hitting from 36 yards late in the second period. At halftime, Florida State led, 10-3, and had held Miami to eight rushing yards. While Walsh had thrown for 73 yards to McManus' 45, McManus had completed five of seven passes. There was every reason for Florida State fans to be optimistic about the second half.

But what followed, no one could have anticipated.

FSU elected to take the ball in the third quarter going into the wind and drove to Miami's 12, where Schmidt set up for what seemed to be a routine field goal. But kicking into the wind, Schmidt's attempt drifted to the right of the goalposts.

Despite this break, Miami stalled on its first possession of the half. Jeff Feagles punted from the UM 22, but the kick was blocked by Martin Mayhew—the fourth time in five games against Florida State that the 'Canes had had a kick blocked. Alphonso Williams returned the ball for a touchdown. Schmidt then missed the PAT attempt to the left, the first time the FSU senior had missed since his junior year of high school. It was considered hardly consequential at the time, leaving the Seminoles with a 16-3 lead midway through the third quarter.

Walsh couldn't get anything going on the 'Canes' next drive, and a 34-yard punt return by Deion Sanders set up Florida State at the UM 44. The Seminoles drove inside Miami's 10, aided by a roughing-the-passer penalty, but settled for a 25-yard field goal by Schmidt. With 2:45 to play in the third quarter, Florida State had built a 19-3 lead. Miami's rushing game had amassed 17 yards. Walsh had failed to complete a pass on his first four attempts of the second half, leaving him 6-for-16 in the game. Florida State's Deion Sanders told Miami's Michael Irvin to stop blocking so hard, that the game was over. There was reason to rejoice if you were wearing garnet and gold.

But Miami came to life on its next possession. Walsh threw 11 yards to Brian Blades to the 'Canes' 35. Melvin Bratton carried six yards to the 41, and an offsides penalty against FSU on third down gave the Hurricanes a first down at the 46. Walsh threw five yards to Charles Henry to the Florida State 49. On third down, he went deep over the middle to Bratton, who made the catch for a 49-yard touchdown. With a two-point pass to Blades, Miami was suddenly revived, having cut the deficit to 19-11 with less than a minute to play in the third quarter.

Florida State pushed back into Miami territory as the fourth quarter began. But on first down at the Hurricanes' 36, McManus failed to get a screen pass high enough and it was

Sammie Smith gets outside of Miami linebacker George Mira, Jr. (45), to gain some yardage for Florida State. (UNIVERSITY OF MIAMI–ROBERT DUYOS)

intercepted by linebacker Daniel Stubbs, who returned the ball to the FSU 41. Walsh came up big again, this time finding wide receiver Michael Irvin over the middle despite a hard charging rush for a 26-yard touchdown pass. Irvin had beaten redshirt freshman John Wyche, a third-stringer who was inserted in FSU's five-man secondary after Eric Williams hurt a foot.

The touchdown pulled Miami within 19-17 with 11:39 to play in the game. Johnson elected to go for the two-point conversion to tie the score. Walsh hit running back Warren Williams, and Miami, which had looked like

a beaten team midway through the third quarter, had tied the score, 19-19.

Florida State answered with a drive that was highlighted by a 23-yard pass from McManus to Dawsey to the Miami 23. Three plays later, Bowden was faced with a fourth-and-1 at the 'Canes' 14. He sent in Schmidt for a 31-yard field goal attempt. But Schmidt missed his third kick of the day—two short field goals and a PAT—leaving the score tied with 6:17 to play.

Miami was finally slowed offensively, forced to punt from its 26. FSU took over at its 41, and McManus opened the drive with a 21-yard pass to freshman running back Edgar Bennett. Three plays later, the 'Noles had a first down at the Miami 26. Barring another Schmidt misfire, Florida State appeared to be in good shape to add either a touchdown or a field goal and move ahead with less than four minutes to play.

Smith carried on first down for nine yards to the UM 17. But on second down, McManus fumbled the snap. Bennie Blades recovered at the Miami 11 with 3:29 to go.

Warren Williams ran for 12 yards and a first down to the 'Canes' 23. He carried another four yards, followed by an incomplete pass intended for Bratton. On third-and-six at the Miami 27, Irvin outraced the FSU secondary

again. This time, it was for 73 yards, Irvin getting behind Mayhew and Dedrick Dodge. The touchdown put the Hurricanes in the lead for the first time since the game's early minutes. With Cox's conversion, Miami had taken a 26-19 lead with only 2:22 to play.

The Seminoles began their next drive on their 27. On third-and-ten, after two incompletions, Bowden decided to stay on the ground, but Smith was held to two yards. The Seminoles had no choice but to go for the first down on fourth-and-8 at the FSU 29. McManus dropped back and found Gainer open for a 10-yard gain to the 'Noles' 39 for a first down. He then threw 12 yards to Dexter Carter to the

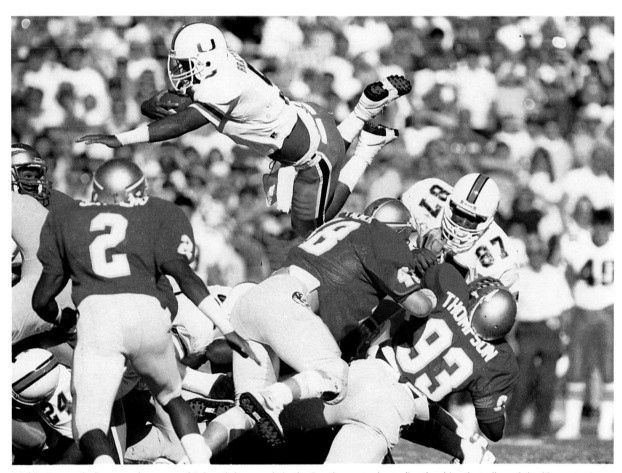

Melvin Bratton's dive over the top on third-and-three early in the fourth quarter kept alive the drive that allowed the 'Canes to tie the score at 19-19 with a touchdown and two-point conversion. (TALLAHASSEE DEMOCRAT–MARK WALLHEISER)

✳

Miami wide receiver Michael Irvin outraces Florida State's Dedrick Dodge (28) to put the Hurricanes back into the lead with 2:22 to play. (UNIVERSITY OF MIAMI–STEVEN MURPHY)

Miami 49. On second down, he found Carter for a 31-yard gain to the Miami 18. With another first down, McManus went for the end zone. The result was an 18-yard scoring pass to Lewis with only 42 seconds to play.

Florida State was trailing by one point. Bowden called the last of FSU's three second-half timeouts. For a fleeting second, he thought back to 1980, when a failed two-point conversion against Miami in the closing minutes resulted in FSU's only loss of the season. Bowden decided to go for the tie with Schmidt and sent out the kicking team. As McManus trotted over to the sideline, some of the members of the kicking team said to him, "Tell him (Bowden) to go for two."

By the time McManus reached the sideline, Bowden already had changed his mind. Even though Schmidt would be kicking with the wind—his three misses had been into the wind—Bowden brought back the kicking team and sent out the two-point unit. The call was for McManus to roll out to the right and look for 6-5 Pat Carter in the far right corner of the end zone. Johnson watched Florida

State line up and called his own timeout. Noticing that Smith wasn't lined up in the backfield with a two tight-end set, the UM staff figured Florida State planned a rollout pass to the strong side of the formation.

The play unfolded as planned. Wide receiver Ronald Lewis lined up with Carter on the right side and attracted man-to-man coverage from McDowell. But when Lewis ran to the middle of the end zone and McDowell saw McManus look to the right side in the direction of Carter, McDowell dropped off Lewis. Carter was being covered by strong safety Selwyn Brown. McManus lofted the pass toward Carter, who by this time was virtually double-covered by Brown and McDowell. The pass fell short; Carter didn't even have a chance to react and come back toward the ball. McDowell jumped in front of Brown and batted the ball to the ground, leaving Miami ahead by one point. Similar circumstances at the conclusion of the 1984 Orange Bowl Classic—Kenny Calhoun knocking down a two-point pass by Nebraska—left Miami as the national champion for 1983.

FSU attempted an onside kick, but the ball was recovered by Miami. With Florida State out of timeouts, Walsh only needed to take a knee twice to kill the clock and end the game.

Miami had won despite running only 53 offensive plays to Florida State's 84. Miami had won despite holding the ball for only 19:28 compared to 40:32 for Florida State. Miami had won despite being outrushed 225 yards to 52. Miami had won despite yielding 426 yards, three short of the combined total gained by Florida and Arkansas in UM's first two games. Miami had won despite not sacking Danny McManus once. Miami had won despite going four for 13 on third downs—three of the conversions resulting in touchdowns.

Miami had won; that's what mattered most.

"I don't think about championships yet," said an exhausted and elated Johnson, "But I know this win puts us on a different plateau."

Bowden was immediately asked about going for the win instead of the tie—and immediately second-guessed himself.

"If I had it to do over, I'd kick it for the tie," he said. "I thought we had the game won. We lost it—and I can't tell you how."

Johnson, despite what he told Musburger before the game, looks back and agrees with Bowden's call. "I would be surprised if any coach kicks the extra point," he says. "If you're to keep the respect of your players, you've got to go for two."

McManus was among the Florida State players who supported the decision to go for two. "We don't practice ties," he said. "I didn't spend all that time sweating during two-a-days to play for a tie."

Schmidt maintained that he would have made the final PAT had the coaches decided to go for it—and that the coaches had every confidence in him. He also insisted that the PAT that was ruled wide to the left was good.

"It was ridiculous," he told reporters after the game in a calm voice. "You kick 108 in a row, and you ought to know what they look like."

Bowden met with reporters as usual the following morning and admitted that this loss had affected him like few others had. "I don't believe I've lost one like that since I've been at Florida State, have I? . . . It was one of those 'Why me?' games. You can't explain why."

Johnson recalls: "We really went into the game overconfident. Just through sheer determination and belief that we were the better team were we able to come back."

* * *

The victory extended Miami's regular-season winning streak to 24 games, best in the nation, and their road winning streak to 17 games. The Hurricanes remained third in the AP poll behind Oklahoma and Nebraska and remained there until the Big Eight rivals' meeting in late November. When OU beat Nebraska, that set up the Orange Bowl Classic meeting between the Big Eight champion Sooners and the second-ranked 'Canes, each 11-0. Johnson would be matched against Barry Switzer, who had coached him at Arkansas two decades earlier.

Florida State did not lose another game that season—didn't really come close until bowl time. With a 7-1 record, the fourth-ranked Seminoles traveled to Auburn to face the sixth-ranked Tigers. It was no contest, a 34-6 FSU victory in which Schmidt became the NCAA's career scoring leader. After clinching a berth in the Fiesta Bowl, the 'Noles closed the season by rallying from a 14-3 deficit to beat Florida, 28-14, to end a six-game losing streak against the Gators. That raised Florida State to No. 3 in the country.

With No. 1 Oklahoma playing No. 2 Miami in the Orange Bowl Classic, the Seminoles went into the Fiesta date on the afternoon of January 1, 1988 with No. 5 Nebraska, knowing there was no chance to steal a national title. FSU fought back from a 14-0 deficit to beat the Cornhuskers, 31-28.

That night in Miami, the Hurricanes put the clamps on OU's option offense and beat the Sooners, 20-14. Linebacker George Mira, Jr., was suspended for the game, and his replacement, Bernard Clark, was named the game's most valuable player. Jimmy Johnson, his coiffure still in place despite a liberal dose of Gatorade, thrust a fist triumphantly skyward as his players carried him to midfield after the game.

The final poll of the 1987 season listed Miami a unanimous No. 1 and Florida State No. 2. That marked the first time since the Associated Press poll began with the 1936 season that the top two teams in the final rankings were from the same state.

* * *

The Jimmy Johnson years at Miami came to an abrupt halt in February 1989, after he had guided UM to another Orange Bowl Classic victory and a No. 2 finish behind Notre Dame.

Johnson had never denied that his grand coaching plan included a final stop in the National Football League. And no team was more appealing to him than the Dallas Cowboys, who had been coached since Day One in 1960 by Tom Landry.

When one of Johnson's Arkansas teammates, oilman Jerry Jones, worked out an agreement to buy the Cowboys from struggling Dallas banker "Bum" Bright, Jones wanted his old friend as the coach.

Word of the impending sale and coaching change was broken by a Dallas television station two nights before the announcement was made. On the night before the news conference, Johnson and Jones were photographed together at a Dallas restaurant—which gave the appearance that these "intruders" were all but dancing on the grave of the ousted Cowboys regime.

Johnson endured a 1-15 season in which he greatly changed the shape of the team's roster. In 1990 the Cowboys were within one victory of clinching a playoff berth with two games to play, but when second-year quarterback Troy Aikman was injured, the Cowboys lost both games. Johnson then guided Dallas to the playoffs in 1991 and a first-round upset of the Chicago Bears before being ousted by the Detroit Lions.

No matter what the future holds for Johnson, there will always be the 1987 national title. And with that title will always be the question of what might have happened if Bobby Bowden had decided to kick an extra point with 42 seconds to play.

Florida State vs. Miami
So Much for No. 1

Being ranked first in the country during preseason isn't an event in itself; it happens to some team every year.

But not every preseason No. 1 team comes out with its own sound track. That's what set the 1988 Florida State Seminoles apart from the rest. Before they had even taken the first snap as the top team in the land, they appeared on a video aptly named the "Seminole Rap."

FSU's first game of the season was against the defending champion Miami Hurricanes, who went into the game ranked a relatively lowly sixth. The 'Canes, not exactly docile and pristine during their romp through the '80s, were infuriated by this display of arrogance—especially, they said, with "Neon" Deion Sanders prancing about as a lead vocal. For the Hurricanes, this was high-tech bulletin board inspiration.

❋   ❋   ❋

The 'Noles had every reason to believe their preseason ranking was justified. Florida State had annually put up some of the most impressive numbers in all of college football.

The '87 season was no exception, when only a failed two-point pass prevented them from winning the national championship. When playing against five teams that finished in the top 10 in total defense, the Seminoles averaged 25 points. Over the preceding five seasons, FSU's offense averaged 433.69 yards to trail only Brigham Young, Nebraska and Iowa.

But Bobby Bowden and his staff knew better than to discount the Hurricanes, college football's winningest program over those same five years, boasting a record of 52-9. The biggest question mark regarding the 'Canes was whether they could successfully replace 16 seniors, 11 of whom were on NFL rosters a year later.

Florida State arrived at the Orange Bowl prepared to show the Hurricanes, a boisterous crowd of 77,836 and a national television audience that it deserved to be called the best team in the country.

Junior quarterback Steve Walsh, so poised as a sophomore in the one-point victory at Tallahassee in '87, started the Hurricanes' engine at the UM 17-yard line. He calmly passed 21 yards to Cleveland Gary on the opening play, and after another first down at the 50, tailback Leonard Conley found room

Steve Walsh still had some doubters even after leading Miami to the 1987 national championship as a sophomore.
(UNIVERSITY OF MIAMI)

In Chip Ferguson's odd Florida State career, he was the Seminoles' top quarterback as a freshman, watched Danny McManus lead the way during his sophomore and junior seasons, then regained the top spot as a senior. (FLORIDA STATE UNIVERSITY)

on a trap play and raced 25 yards to FSU's 25. At that point, Florida State's defense stiffened, and Miami had to settle for a 39-yard field goal from Carlos Huerta.

The 'Noles opened their first possession with typical Bowden flare. Wide receiver Ronald Lewis carried on a reverse for 14 yards to the FSU 34. But Florida State then tried a second consecutive reverse. This time, a flubbed handoff resulted in Sammie Smith's falling on the ball for a loss of nine. An

incompletion and a 15-yard gain by Smith forced FSU to punt.

Miami pushed back into Florida State territory, but the 'Noles' Tracy Sanders knocked the ball out of the hands of Conley. Steve Gabbard fell on it for FSU at the 'Noles' 15. But Florida State couldn't capitalize when a pass by Chip Ferguson was intercepted by Bobby Harden, who returned it from the Seminoles' 37 to the 20. For the third time in as many possessions, Miami was inside the

Steve Walsh gets a pass away in the face of the Florida State rush. (UNIVERSITY OF MIAMI–RHONA WISE)

Florida State 25. The period ended with Walsh hitting Dale Douglas on a short pattern to the 11. So far, this No. 1 business was not all it was cracked up to be.

It took the Hurricanes only two plays starting the second quarter to get in the end zone. Gary scored on a two-yard run to put Florida State in a 10-0 hole. The 'Noles went nowhere on their next series, kicking the ball right back to the Hurricanes. But Miami stalled, and Jimmy Johnson elected to send in Huerta for a 59-yard field goal attempt. The gamble would probably cost Miami about 25 yards if the kick failed. It did fail, but FSU in turn failed to capitalize. Richie Andrews followed with a 47-yard field goal attempt for Florida State only to have the kick sail wide.

Something unusual happened on the following series—Miami punted. Coming with 8:03 to play in the half, this was UM's first. The

Seminoles celebrated the event by fumbling the ball back to the 'Canes near midfield. But Miami misfired on the subsequent series, and Huerta missed on a 37-yard field goal try.

With only a few minutes remaining in the half, Florida State's next punt didn't even clear out of its end of the field. The 'Canes moved down to the Seminoles' 37, where they called time out from punt formation with 1:15 left in the half. After the timeout, Johnson rushed his offense back onto the field, and Walsh passed six yards to Douglas for a first down. Three plays later, with 15 seconds remaining, tight end Rod Chudzinski caught a 19-yard pass for a touchdown. Huerta added the extra point that sent Miami to the locker room with a stunning 17-0 lead. The Hurricanes had run twice as many plays as the Seminoles (46-23) while outgaining Florida State 239 yards to 91.

With the option for the second half, Florida State predictably decided to take the ball. The 'Noles shortly gave it up again, though. Ferguson threw his second interception, this one picked off by Donald Ellis. Later in the period, Miami was fortunate to retain possession on a fumble deep in FSU territory. Walsh had passed to Randal Hill, who had the ball knocked loose by Sanders. But the ball rolled toward the FSU goal line, and UM's Douglas fell on it at the five. Conley caught a five-yard touchdown pass, giving Miami a 24-0 lead.

In the fourth quarter, both coaches decided to sub their quarterbacks—for vastly different reasons. Ferguson had been unable to generate any offense for the Seminoles and was pulled in favor of Peter Tom Willis. Walsh, on the other hand, was given a well deserved rest for his part in picking apart the Florida State defense. Walsh hit 18 of 37 passes for 228 yards and two touchdowns without an interception.

With the help of a parade of three FSU quarterbacks—Bowden even went to freshman Casey Weldon in the closing moments—throwing five interceptions, Miami was able to maintain the rare shutout of Florida State. It was the first since Bowden's second game as FSU coach in 1976, which also came against Miami, also at the Orange Bowl, by the even more lopsided score of 49-0. Doubtless, though, this one was much more painful to the Seminoles and their fans. The breakdown offensively was total, not confined to the inexperienced quarterbacks. The Florida State running game was almost nonexistent. Dayne Williams was the 'Noles' top rusher with all of 20 yards. Ronald Lewis, a wide receiver, was second with the 14 yards he gained on FSU's first play from scrimmage. Sammie Smith, touted as a Heisman Trophy candidate, carried 10 times for six yards. That was a mere 183 yards short of what he gained on the 'Canes a year earlier.

In the locker room after the game, Jimmy Johnson tried to imply that the impressive win wasn't an indication of what to expect from Miami the rest of the year: "All this talk about rankings—a year ago is history. All we've done is won one more game and nothing more. I told the team all this means is the worst we can end up is 1-10." Another thing it meant was, in one of the all-time great streaks in college football history, Miami had defeated the preseason No. 1 for the sixth consecutive season.

Given a night to reflect on the defeat, Bowden assessed the damage Sunday: "We couldn't get our skilled athletes in position to do their thing. Again, I was amazed at the speed of Miami."

Someone could have taken a page from Johnson's book and told Bowden that all the game meant was that the best FSU could finish was 11-1. He probably wouldn't have listened.

* * *

Of course, that's exactly what happened. For the second consecutive season, the Seminoles' only loss of the year came at the hands of the Hurricanes. FSU dropped to 10th in the Associated Press poll following the shutout, then inched its way back up toward the top. The 'Noles earned a Sugar Bowl berth opposite Auburn. With Deion Sanders breaking up an Auburn pass in the end zone on the final play of the game, FSU won, 13-7, to finish No. 3 in the nation.

Miami held on to the top spot through four games, until it traveled to South Bend, Indiana, to face fourth-ranked Notre Dame. The game was turned into a morality play because of the thug image that Miami had been tagged with, especially since the battle-fatigue incidents at the '87 Fiesta Bowl. T-shirts sprouted up across the Notre Dame campus proclaiming the game to be a matchup of "CATHOLICS VS. CONVICTS." In what turned out to be the game that decided the national champion, Miami failed on a two-point pass in the final minutes to lose, 31-30—the same score by which UM won the title in the '84 Orange Bowl Classic by knocking down a two-point pass by Nebraska. The 'Canes settled for No. 2 in the country after beating Nebraska in another Orange Bowl Classic.

Walsh proved himself to be the next in the great line of UM quarterbacks. He was a relative unknown coming out of St. Paul, Minnesota, with his recruiting list once featuring Montana State, Cornell and Northwestern. He eventually narrowed his list to Iowa State, Louisville (coached by Howard Schnellenberger) and Miami before choosing the 'Canes. There were some skeptics before he made his first start as a sophomore in September 1987 against Florida in the Orange Bowl. Those voices were pretty much silenced when Walsh completed 17 of 27 passes for 234 yards as the 10th-ranked Hurricanes harassed preseason Heisman Trophy candidate Kerwin Bell and the 20th-ranked Gators, 31-4, in the final game of the continuous Florida-Miami series.

Starting as a sophomore and junior, he passed for 5,369 yards and tied Vinny Testaverde's school record of 48 touchdown passes. Like Bernie Kosar, Walsh opted to go pro before completing his college eligibility. His

Miami coach Jimmy Johnson has reason to look relaxed, as his Hurricanes rough up the top-ranked Seminoles. (UNIVERSITY OF MIAMI–RHONA WISE)

destination in the NFL supplemental draft was none other than the Dallas Cowboys, where Johnson had left Miami for just a few months earlier. The move was a surprise since Dallas had made UCLA quarterback Troy Aikman its first overall pick in the regular phase of the draft. Here the Cowboys were, with a pair of million-dollar rookie quarterbacks. Walsh started some when Aikman suffered a hand injury. But Aikman was the acknowledged No. 1, and Walsh was eventually traded to New Orleans.

Recalls Johnson of that opening upset of FSU: "Off the '87 team, we had 17 players that signed professional contracts. So we went into that game with basically almost an entirely new team, and obviously an inexperienced team. I think because of the hype of Florida State being No. 1 and because we knew that we had not played well against Florida State the previous years, our guys were ready to play."

As for videos, the "Seminole Rap" did not race to the top of the charts. Bowden acknowledged that next time he would like to advise his players to wait until the season is over before recording such a novelty. Because for all intents and purposes, as midnight approached on September 3, 1988, the season had already ended for many FSU players.

*   *   *

A year later Deion Sanders was on the cover of FSU's media guide for the Sugar Bowl, in complete formal attire. In the foreground were the words "IT'S PRIME TIME IN NEW ORLEANS." Even his critics had to admit that Sanders' play had earned him such recognition. He was a two-time consensus All-American. He would win the Jim Thorpe Award as the nation's best defensive back. His average of 15.2 yards per punt return would lead the nation. He scored three touchdowns, two on interceptions and one on a punt return. His 14 career interceptions ranked second on the all-time FSU list. On top of all this, he was a top-notch base-

ball prospect who was thinking of pursuing both sports professionally.

Deion Sanders could play baseball, dash over and compete in a track and field meet, then return to the baseball game. And he did just that while at Florida State. Outrageous.

He specialized in the outrageous. Outrageous clothes. Outrageous jewelry. Outrageous comments. The spotlight was always on, it seemed, as if shielding the real Deion Sanders from the rest of the world. The Deion Sanders who grew up poor in Fort Myers. The Deion Sanders who would work himself into such an emotional frenzy as a kid that he would suffer from terrible migraine headaches. The Deion Sanders who would call home from Tallahassee and ask his mother what to do about this or that.

Playing professionally in two sports would have seemed more outrageous had Bo Jackson not recently turned the trick. Sanders began his pro baseball career in the summer of 1988—with one more FSU football season to play—at the bottom of the New York Yankees' organization, at Sarasota of the rookie league. He hit .280 in 17 games, showing off his potent speed with 11 stolen bases. He finished the year with an impressive flurry at Fort Lauderdale of the Class A Florida State League (hitting .429 in six games) and a dose of reality at Columbus of the Class AAA International League (.150 in five games).

After his Jim Thorpe-winning senior football season, Sanders headed for spring training the following February while awaiting the NFL draft in April. He spent most of the year at Columbus, hitting .276 and trying to refine his still relatively raw baseball skills. He was called up to the Yankees for a brief trial before leaving baseball in July to join the NFL team that drafted him in the first round, the Atlanta Falcons. His contract with the Falcons stipulated that football was his primary sport, that unlike Jackson, Sanders would move over to football as soon as training camp opened.

In 1990, Sanders showed more promise, hitting .321 in 22 games at Columbus. The Yankees called him up and made him a regu-

Florida State cornerback Deion Sanders became as well known for his behavior off the field as for his outstanding play on the field. (FLORIDA STATE UNIVERSITY)

lar in the outfield. But it was a long summer for "Prime Time." He hit a paltry .158 in 57 games, stealing only eight bases. Near the end of the baseball season, months after Sanders had left for the Falcons, the Yankees released him. On January 30, 1991, Sanders signed a free-agent contract with the Atlanta Braves, giving him the opportunity to play professionally with two teams in the same city. Even Bo hadn't done that. While "Prime Time" wasn't a vital cog in the

Braves' drive to their first National League pennant in 33 years, he did earn his place in professional sports history. On one memorable afternoon, he took a helicopter from the Falcons' camp northeast of Atlanta downtown to make it to Atlanta-Fulton County Stadium to appear as a pinch-runner for the Braves. He also became the first athlete to score a run in a major league baseball game and a touchdown in an NFL game in the same week.

The premature departure of Bo Jackson from professional sports—it's difficult to ever say he has retired for sure—because of the injury he suffered in the 1990-91 NFL play-offs speaks to the difficulty of playing both football and baseball. But there was no denying "Prime Time" was having a good time, being selected for the NFL's Pro Bowl team in February 1992 and tearing up the National League as one of its hottest hitters two months later.

"'Prime Time' never been one to be like nobody else," Sanders once told a magazine reporter. "'Prime Time' isn't acting out there; he's doing what he feels. I just gotta be me. Having fun. Being 'Prime Time' releases my frustrations."

Miami vs. Florida State
Loss Can't Deny Hurricanes

No rap videos were necessary to ignite combustible feelings between the Florida State Seminoles and Miami Hurricanes before their 1989 meeting. Here was Miami, rolling along with a 6-0 record, ranked second in the nation behind an unbeaten Notre Dame that was seeking its second consecutive national championship and, perchance, grabbing from Miami recognition as college football's premier program of the '80s. And then there was Florida State, possibly college football's most frustrated program of the '80s. All of those quality teams, all of those 10- and 11-win seasons, yet no title.

By the time the final weekend of October had arrived, the Seminoles had recovered from a numbing start that threatened to crumble their season. FSU, ranked sixth in the preseason, opened the campaign against Southern Mississippi in a road game that the Golden Eagles agreed to move to Jacksonville. The 'Noles got off to a 10-0 lead, only to watch Southern Miss quarterback Brett Favre rally the Eagles to a pair of fourth-quarter touchdowns to shock Florida State, 30-26. Were that not enough, the Seminoles were

beaten at home the following week by No. 10 Clemson, 34-23.

In the course of two weeks, the Seminoles had equaled their loss total for the previous two seasons. FSU had not gone through such a streak of futility since early in the 1986 season, when it lost to Nebraska, tied North Carolina and lost to Michigan. To find the most recent consecutive losses, go back to the end of the '83 season when Jeff Davis kicked Miami past the 'Noles, 17-16, and Florida followed with its 53-14 rout.

But Florida State righted its ship quickly with five consecutive victories, bringing the Seminoles back to No. 9 in the AP national rankings.

In the spring of 1989, when word leaked out that Miami's search for a new coach had reached the office of Washington State coach Dennis Erickson, the story was not greeted cheerfully across the Northwest. Erickson had been in Pullman, Washington, only two seasons, leading the Cougars to an 8-3 finish during the '88 season capped by an Aloha Bowl victory over Houston. Wins had been hard to come by over the years at Washington State, a relatively isolated school located

Dennis Erickson (left) is introduced as Miami's new football coach by athletic director Sam Jankovich. (UNIVERSITY OF MIAMI)

in the far eastern portion of the state. The nine wins equaled the school record set in 1930. Erickson's victories that season included some particularly impressive triumphs—52-24 at Tennessee, 34-30 over UCLA, 32-31 at Washington.

As speculation increased that Miami was about to pluck Washington State's future, Seattle *Times* columnist Blaine Newnhan wrote that Erickson, a native son of the West who went to college at Montana State, would be making a mistake if he chose to go coach what Newnhan called the "Miami vice squad."

Despite such well-meaning warnings, Erickson indeed accepted UM's offer and was introduced as the Hurricanes' new coach on March 5. He brought with him a reputation of being more attuned to the offense than defense; Jimmy Johnson, though proudly preserving the reputation of Quarterback U. with Kosar, Testaverde and Walsh, was more of a defensive strategist.

Dennis wasn't the only Erickson in the UM spotlight. With Walsh having left for the NFL after his junior year, junior Craig Erickson became Miami's number-one quarterback. In fact, Erickson's presence on the UM roster helped convince Purdue transfer Jeff George to continue his college at Illinois and not Miami.

With plenty of talent returning in Coral Gables and a smooth coaching transition, Miami was fourth in the preseason poll behind Michigan, Notre Dame and Nebraska. A 51-3 win over Wisconsin during the first week convinced voters to flip-flop UM with Nebraska. Two weeks later, the Hurricanes inched up to No. 2 behind Notre Dame, where they remained going into the Florida State game.

Craig Erikson was sidelined for the game against the Seminoles, out with a broken knuckle. But his replacement, freshman Gino Torretta, had thrown for 707 yards in the two previous games, including a school-record 468 against San Jose State.

* * *

Tempers were short when the teams reached their respective sidelines that night at Doak Campbell Stadium. The captains—Odell Haggins, Peter Tom Willis, Corian Freeman, Kirk Carruthers and Lawrence Dawsey of Florida State; Gino Torretta, Bernard Clark, Greg Marx and Randal Hill for Miami—walked to the center of the field for the coin toss. The captains began shoving each other, and both squads determined it was their duty to report to the middle of the field in defense of the team's honor.

Order was somewhat restored in time for Florida State's mascot, Chief Osceola, to perform his pre-kickoff ritual. The well-known tradition was for the costumed chief to ride his horse, Renegade, to the middle of the field and dramatically hurl his flaming spear into the turf. Well, the Hurricanes just weren't up for that much excitement. They refused to leave the center of the field. It took the game officials and Miami coaching staff to return the Hurricanes to their sideline. Chief Osceola went through his routine, but not without being taunted by some of the UM players.

By the way, the coin toss was won by FSU, which elected to defer to the second half. Miami ran its first play from the 22-yard line with new quarterback Gino Torretta, a redshirt freshman whose older brother, Geoff, was a backup quarterback at UM behind Testaverde. Gino's first pass was intercepted at the 37 by cornerback Leroy Butler. On Florida State's first play from scrimmage, senior tailback Dexter Carter—all of 5-foot-9 and 172 pounds—raced into the end zone for a touchdown. Twenty-three seconds had gone by, and the 'Noles already had stamped their intentions on this game.

But Toretta guided the Hurricanes to the tying score, an eight-yard rollout pass to Hill, to cap an 11-play, 80-yard drive that consumed four minutes and 40 seconds.

The 'Noles opened their next possession at their 19. Their quarterback was Willis, a senior who had served as an understudy for three years before earning the opportunity to start. He guided FSU to the go-ahead score, aided by a Miami offsides penalty on third-and-four at the UM 12. On second-and-goal at the 7, Willis was unable to hook up with tight end Dave Roberts in the end zone, but the 'Canes were whistled for roughing the passer. Fullback Edgar Bennett carried in from the one to put Florida State back ahead, 14-7, with 5:11 to play in the first quarter.

Miami started right back downfield with fullback Shannon Crowell converting a fourth-and-one gamble at the FSU 46 by hurdling over a pile of players at the line of scrimmage for the first down. UM eventually stalled at the Florida State 27, and Carlos Huerta's 44-yard field goal cut FSU's lead to 14-10 with 1:09 still left in the quarter.

The Seminoles' next possession, which carried into the second quarter, was punctuated by Miami mistakes. A 15-yard face-mask penalty and an offsides penalty that gave FSU a first down set up the 'Noles at the Miami 36. But at the UM 32, Willis was sacked by linebacker Richard Newbill and fumbled. Linebacker Maurice Crum made the recovery at the Miami 43. The Hurricanes couldn't do much, though, and punted, a sequence that was repeated on both sides for much of the period. Miami finally got the upper hand midway through the quarter and reached first-and-goal at the FSU eight. But on third down at the one, Toretta was intercepted in the end zone by linebacker Kevin Grant. Two series later, Toretta threw his third interception of the half, with freshman cornerback Terrell Buckley tipping the ball into the hands of Carruthers at the FSU 35.

Willis got into the interception derby on the first possession of the second half. Miami cornerback Roland Smith returned

Junior quarterback Craig Erickson missed the FSU game with a broken knuckle, but returned to help UM win the 1989 national title. (UNIVERSITY OF MIAMI)

the ball to the Miami 45, where the fans had to pull out their calculators to keep up with the penalties; UM was penalized 15 yards for clipping, but Florida State was hit for a pair of 15-yard personal fouls. The result of all this was Miami starting from the Florida State 40. The 'Canes moved downfield—the drive kept alive by a pass interference penalty—and reached first-and-goal at the 'Noles' two. Fullback Stephen McGuire carried for a yard on first down and was stopped for no gain on second down. On third down at the one, Crowell attempted to dive over the pile. He made it, but didn't take the ball with him. The fumble was recovered at the one by

Carruthers, his third turnover of the game. For the second time in the game, Miami had reached the Florida State one, yet had no points to show for it.

On the next play, Willis shocked Miami by dropping back in the end zone and heaving the ball to wide receiver Ronald Lewis for a 51-yard gain. That was the catalyst for the 99-yard drive that culminated with freshman running back Amp Lee's one-yard touchdown run with 2:20 to play in the third quarter. The stunning drive had given Florida State a 21-10 lead. Miami was unable to get anything going on its next drive, and the Seminoles responded—thanks to another personal foul penalty against UM—with Andrews kicking a 41-yard

Bobby Bowden, who once thought Florida State would be a stepping-stone position, turned down overtures from LSU and Alabama to commit himself to the Seminole program for the balance of his coaching career. (TALLAHASSEE DEMOCRAT–MARK WALLHEISER)

On Florida State's first play from scrimmage, Dexter Carter races around left end and runs 37 yards for a touchdown.
(FLORIDA STATE UNIVERSITY)

field goal. Two plays into the fourth quarter, the 'Noles had built a 24-10 lead.

Toretta and the Miami offense continued to struggle in the fourth quarter. The Seminoles threatened again the next time they got the ball with a drive that took more than nine minutes off the clock, stretching to the Miami 13. But Andrews' 37-yard field goal attempt was blocked by Miami freshman Darryl Williams.

The Hurricanes had the ball back but trailed by two touchdowns with only 3:32 to play. Florida State lent a helping hand by committing a defensive holding penalty on fourth-and-10 at the Miami 40. Toretta succeeded in guiding the 'Canes into scoring position, but the drive was extending into the closing minutes of the game. Even with a touchdown, the Hurricanes would be hard

pressed to have enough time to score the necessary second touchdown. Miami reached the FSU one, and on fourth-and-goal, a pass for wide receiver Dale Dawkins fell incomplete. For Miami, it was another futile trip to the Florida State one. With only 55 seconds to play, Willis—who was thrown in as a mop-up in the 'Canes' rout of FSU a year earlier—was able to run off the final plays of the game.

A Miami team that was averaging 41 points was held to 10. Miami's top-ranked defense watched Dexter Carter skip and stutter for 142 yards rushing. That more than compensated for Willis hitting only seven of 20 passes for 129 yards. Toretta's overall 208 passing yards were credible. But the four interceptions—all in the first half—along with two lost fumbles and the inability to score on three trips to the Florida State one were crushing.

"You can't turn the ball over as many times as we did and expect to beat an outstanding team like Florida State," Erickson told reporters after the game, having suffered his first defeat as UM coach. "If we scored those times we were on their one-yard line, it would have been a different game."

"You've to give our guys up front credit," Bowden said in reference to the goal line stands. "Our passing game couldn't get off the ground. Thank goodness our running game worked. Just credit the defense and the running game."

As for the theatrics before and during the game, FSU offensive tackle John Brown summed it up: "Bernard Clark said they're bringing their M-16s. Well, we brought our tanks."

*   *   *

Florida State did not lose another game, routing Nebraska in the Fiesta Bowl, 41-17, to cap the 10-game winning streak that followed the opening losses to Southern Miss and Clemson. That was good enough to put FSU at No. 3 in the final poll.

As for the Hurricanes, they rebounded with wins over East Carolina, Pittsburgh and San Diego State to hold at No. 7 in the poll going into a showdown with top-ranked Notre Dame on November 25 at the Orange Bowl. The 'Canes, motivated by the national championship they lost in '88 because of a one-point loss to the Irish and by the national championship in '89 that could still be won, dumped Notre Dame, 27-10. That moved Miami up to No. 4 in the poll, behind Colorado, Alabama and Michigan. The 'Canes eventually slid into second place behind the Buffaloes going into the bowls. Colorado was matched against No. 4 Notre Dame in the Orange Bowl Classic, while Miami was invited to the Sugar Bowl to face No. 7 Alabama, which was 10-0 before losing its regular-season finale to Auburn. If Miami could beat Alabama and Notre Dame knock off Colorado, UM would be in great position to finish No. 1.

And that's exactly what fell into place. Notre Dame beat Colorado, 21-6, while Miami held off Alabama in New Orleans, 33-25. In the final voting, Miami received 39 first-place votes and 1,474 total points to 19 and 1,452 for Notre Dame. (Florida State received the other two first-place votes.) Irish coach Lou Holtz held to his opinion that Notre Dame deserved to be No. 1. Dennis Erickson held the national championship trophy, becoming the third Miami coach to accomplish the feat—all within seven seasons.

And like Howard Schnellenberger, he did it in a season in which the No. 1 team in the country could not claim to be the best in the state. In 1983, Miami was national champ and Florida "state champ" by beating UM and Florida State. In 1989, Miami was national champ while Florida State toppled both the 'Canes and the Gators.

Miami vs. Florida State
The National Title Showdown in Tallahassee

All of the great games, the matchups involving Florida and Miami and Florida State through all of the years pale in comparison to the meeting of Miami and FSU in 1991.

Not only were two unbeaten teams squaring off at Doak Campbell Stadium, but not since the Associated Press college football poll was started out of popular demand in 1936, had two teams from the same state met while occupying the top two slots in the rankings. The Seminoles were No. 1, had been since preseason. The 'Canes were No. 2, inching their way closer to the top after opening at No. 3. And with only a few weeks remaining in the season, there was the likelihood that Miami-FSU for 1991 would ultimately decide the national championship.

Such a 1 versus 2 showdown had happened 25 other times, with the second-ranked team pulling out the victory on only five occasions. Miami had been involved in two of those games in which No. 2 beat No. 1. There was the infamous 1987 Fiesta Bowl, in which the top-ranked 'Canes were rudely bumped from the top by Penn State, 14-10. A year later, Miami was sitting at No. 2 and matched against No. 1 Oklahoma in the Orange Bowl Classic. The result was a 20-14 UM victory that vaulted the Hurricanes to their second national title.

Remember that Miami's 26-25 win at Tallahassee in 1987 made Miami the national champ and not Florida State. And the following year, FSU's only loss was a 31-0 whipping at the Orange Bowl as the Seminoles stumbled out of the gate after being picked No. 1 during the preseason. Noting the discrepancy in national titles won by both schools, Florida State coach Bobby Bowden said: "But then again, Dennis (Erickson, UM coach) ain't going to let us have one to make us feel good."

FSU, with a 16-game winning streak at home, was established as a three-point favorite. A sign in a Tallahassee business window summed up how meaningful Florida State's season to date had been: "Congratulations FSU on a perfect 10-0 preseason record."

It already had been a long, taxing season for the Seminoles. Because they figured to be one of the best—if not the best—teams in the nation and with a reputation for exciting play, the 'Noles were selected to face Brigham Young and 1990 Heisman Trophy winner Ty Detmer in the Disneyland Kickoff Classic in

Florida State fans are armed and ready for the Hurricanes. (TALLAHASSEE DEMOCRAT–MARK WALLHEISER)

Anaheim. The fans wanted offense; they got offense. Florida State wanted to avoid an ambush; it did so, with a 44-28 win in which Detmer was "held" to 229 yards and two touchdown passes.

The 'Noles' scoring machine didn't skip a beat in subsequent weeks. Tulane was disposed of, 38-11, and FSU waltzed to a 38-0 halftime lead in beating Western Michigan, 58-0. That set up what figured to be Florida State's toughest road game—at least until the season-ending trip to Gainesville. On September 28, Florida State played at No. 3 Michigan, which featured the dream matchup of FSU All-American junior cornerback Terrell Buckley and Michigan junior All-American wide receiver Desmond Howard.

On the second play from scrimmage, Buckley intercepted a pass thrown by Michigan's Elvis Grbac and returned it 40 yards for a touchdown. Dan Mowrey added the extra point, and late TV viewers soon discovered FSU was already ahead, 7-0. Howard responded with a 13-yard touchdown catch that tied the score with only five minutes played. The wild first half included two more scoring plays covering in excess of 40 yards each—tailback Amp Lee's skittering run of 44 yards and a diving catch in the end zone by Howard good for a 42-yard touchdown. The half closed with Florida State leading, 31-23.

Florida State built a 44-23 lead early in the fourth quarter and held on for a 51-31 victory that set a record for points scored by the visiting team at storied Michigan Stadium. While Howard had caught four passes for 69 yards, Buckley had scored a personal victory with two interceptions and a touchdown of his own. Collectively, Florida State appeared capable of beating any team at any venue.

The Seminoles did away with Syracuse, Virginia Tech, Middle Tennessee State, LSU, Louisville and South Carolina to reach the Miami game with a 10-0 record. There had been, though, a continuing problem when it came to the usually simple matter of kicking extra points. Troubles mounted for Dan Mowrey with eight missed PATs through six games, equaling the number that FSU had missed during the previous seven seasons. That led Bowden to choose between punter and sometimes kicker John Wimberly or sophomore walk-on Gerry Thomas to take over the PAT chores. "I can see now why the pros hate to draft kickers," Bowden joked. His solution was to use Thomas on conversions and continue with Mowrey on field goals. A few weeks later, Thomas also took over on field goals.

Miami was picked third in the preseason poll and opened by smothering Arkansas up in the hills, 31-3. That set up what was expected to be a major test for the UM defense, stopping the Houston Cougars and senior quarterback David Klingler in a special Thursday night game before a national cable TV audience. In Houston's Run-and-Shoot offense, Klingler was virtually unstoppable against Southwest Conference competition as a junior in 1990 and surprised many when he elected to return for his senior season. But the 'Canes mercilessly rushed Klingler into mistake after mistake and didn't allow Houston to score a touchdown until the closing minutes in a 40-10 rout.

From then until the journey north to Tallahassee, only Penn State presented the 'Canes a true challenge (with UM hanging on to a 26-20 victory at the Orange Bowl, highlighted by Kevin Williams' 91-yard punt return for a touchdown). In the following three victories over Long Beach State, Arizona and West Virginia, the Hurricanes held a combined scoring advantage of 111-12. That gave Miami a scoring defense for the season of 7.3 points, best in the nation. Critics, many of them dressed in garnet and gold, noted that the 'Canes' schedule was a rather under-whelming group with the exception of twice-beaten Penn State. Miami supporters countered by examining the FSU schedule, in which BYU and Michigan stood apart from the balance of opponents.

But no one was mentioning Middle Tennessee State or Long Beach State when a dazzling sun made its way over Tallahassee on the morning of November 16. As Miami coach Dennis Erickson put it, "Right now, it's the best rivalry in all of college football." The winner would be invited to play in the Orange Bowl Classic against the Big Eight Conference champ as the frontrunner to win a national title.

Would this be the year that Bowden, so often the coach of a superior team but never the best, finished on top?

＊　　＊　　＊

Bobby Bowden, coach of the West Virginia Mountaineers, was coaching in the All-American Bowl in Tampa following the 1975 season. He and his wife, Ann, were happy in Morgantown, where Bobby had coached for 10 years since being elevated from an assistant under Bill Peterson at Florida State. But Bowden, an Alabama native, had a longing in the back of his mind to return to the South, to his roots. And when FSU athletic director John Bridgers extended an invitation to come to Tallahassee to discuss the school's coaching vacancy, Bowden decided it was worth looking into. By the time the Bowdens had returned to West Virginia, FSU officials had decided to offer Bobby the job. He accepted, and a new era of Florida State football was about to begin.

As Bowden began to recruit better athletes and turn the program into a consistent winner, the coach and his program took on two traits. One was the ability to win big games on the road. Florida State was forced to play most of its so-called "big name" opponents on the road for financial reasons. Schools like Nebraska and LSU and Notre Dame simply weren't interested in signing contracts that required them to make visits to Doak Campbell Stadium. It was during Bowden's fourth season in Tallahassee that he scored what could be considered his first major road victory, a 24-19 upset at LSU during what would become an undefeated regular season.

The victory had even greater implications for the program. Longtime LSU coach Charley McClendon had announced before the season that he planned to step down following the season. Bowden, who first visited LSU's Tiger Stadium watching the Tigers play Alabama in 1945, had a soft spot in his heart for LSU. And LSU athletic director Paul Dietzel led Bowden to believe a job offer would be coming.

"There's no doubt that if LSU had beat us that day, I would have taken the head job at LSU," Bowden says. Instead, just the opposite took place. The victory convinced Bowden that he could win a national championship at Florida State, that there was no reason to make Tallahassee a stepping stone.

More startling road wins lay ahead. In 1980, it was an 18-14 triumph that quieted the red-clad crowd at Nebraska. In 1981, it was going 3-2 during the famed "Octoberfest" schedule that featured victories at Notre Dame, Ohio State and LSU. In fact, a contract that forced Florida State to play at LSU for five consecutive seasons resulted in four FSU wins. As Florida State added other impressive road wins against Michigan, Arizona State and Auburn to its collection, a new tradition was born. Following such landmark road wins, FSU players would cut out part of the host team's field—it didn't matter if the surface was grass or artificial turf—and bring it back to campus to place in the road graveyard.

The other characteristic of the Bowden teams was an unpredictable offense that made Florida State arguably the most entertaining in the country—and a natural for national TV. There were reverses and passes off fake field goals and quarterbacks becoming receivers and the famed "puntrooskie," in which a fake punt on fourth-and-four in the closing minutes of a tie game with Clemson led to the winning field goal.

While Bowden had committed himself to remaining at Florida State, he left the door open in the event that Alabama invited him to come to Tuscaloosa. It happened following the 1989 season, a fractious year at Alabama in which Bill Curry had the Tide at 10-0 and No. 2 in the country only to lose to Auburn and Miami (in the Sugar Bowl) and flee for greener pastures in Kentucky. The subsequent search led to Bowden's doorstep, where at age 60 he was forced to make one last career decision. The choice was to politely say no to Alabama, to his native state, and acknowledge that he would finish his coaching career in Tallahassee.

But as good as Florida State became under Bowden, there was a void when it came to the ultimate prize in college football. Even if Florida State had beaten Oklahoma in the 1980 Orange Bowl Classic, the unbeaten 'Noles probably would have finished behind Alabama. In 1987, only the 26-25 loss to Miami separated FSU from the national title. A year later, Florida State opened the year as the top-ranked team only to be bombed in its opener at Miami—for the only loss of the year, again costing the Seminoles a possible national title.

In 1991, for the second time in four years, Florida State was picked to win it all. And as Miami came to Tallahassee in mid-November, the grail stood only three games away.

* * *

A Florida State fan from Orlando telephoned Bobby Bowden's office, offering a lifetime supply of citrus in exchange for tickets to the Miami-FSU game. Such was the fervor surrounding this matchup, televised nationally by ABC. As had often been the case in recent years, a Doak Campbell Stadium record was set when the crowd was officially counted at 63,442. Florida State, a three-point favorite, was nevertheless burdened with a curious stigma. Miami had won on four of its last five visits to Tallahassee. Two of those trips resulted in one-point wins that propelled the Hurricanes to national championships.

This game, too, was expected to determine a national champion no matter the winner.

Miami did little in the opening drive to dispel its reputation as the giant killer, the team that had come away from seven consecutive collisions with No. 1 teams with seven consecutive victories. The 'Canes took the opening kickoff and drove 74 yards in seven plays to a 7-0 lead after junior fullback Stephen McGuire burrowed into the end zone over left guard. Only once on the drive did UM even have to resort to a third down. That came on third-and-eight at the Florida State 13-yard line, when quarterback Gino Torretta scrambled for 11 yards and the first down that set up McGuire's touchdown. It had taken Miami only 1:53 to quiet the better part of the crowd. The top scoring team in the country had its way with an FSU defense ranked third nationally in scoring defense.

Seminole fans had reason to perk up when Amp Lee broke for a 12-yard gain on Florida State's first play from scrimmage. But the Seminoles stalled quickly, quarterback Casey Weldon not even attempting a pass, and FSU punted.

The Seminoles had the ball back within a matter of minutes after Torretta was sacked for the first time by linebacker Kirk Carruthers. Vintage FSU offense was back on display on first down at the Seminoles' 41 when Weldon began the series by overthrowing wide receiver Shannon Baker down the middle. Three plays later, Baker drew a pass interference penalty from strong safety Hurlie Brown to get Florida State past midfield for the first time, to the UM 48. On second-and-15 at the FSU 47 following a sack, Weldon let fly toward the end zone for Lee. Only a desperation tackle by Brown prevented a score,

FSU quarterback Casey Weldon is downed by the Miami rush, one of five sacks by the Hurricanes.
(TALLAHASSEE DEMOCRAT–MARK WALLHEISER)

Kicker Gerry Thomas walks back to the Florida State bench after his 34-yard field goal attempt barely sailed to the right of the right upright with 25 seconds left to play. (TALLAHASSEE DEMOCRAT–MARK WALLHEISER)

Lee being dropped at the Miami two for a 51-yard gain.

But Miami's determined defense rose up to force Bowden to settle for a field goal attempt. On first down, Lee was tripped up by Brown for a six-yard loss. Bowden saw something he didn't like in the formation on second down and tried to signal someone to call a timeout—to no avail. Instead, Weldon was pressured and threw a pass into the end zone for an incompletion. Facing third-and-goal from the eight, Weldon rolled out toward the right sideline, then threw back across the field to a wide-open tight end Lonnie Johnson standing near the four-yard line. But the pass fell short of Johnson, and Gerry Thomas kicked a 25-yard field goal to cut Miami's lead to 7-3 with 5:15 to play in the first quarter.

Florida State was in threatening position again during the closing seconds of the first quarter. McGuire carried up the middle on second-and-10 at the UM 22. Seminoles defensive lineman Joe Ostaszewski spun off a block and unwittingly slapped the ball out of McGuire's hands. Ostaszewski's twin brother, Henry, made the recovery for Florida State at the Hurricanes' 24 with 51 seconds left in the quarter.

Fullback Edgar Bennett raced for 20 yards to the Miami four, and Lee struggled to add another yard on the final play of the quarter. It took three consecutive one-yard carries by backup fullback Paul Moore—the last coming on fourth-and-goal—to give Florida State a touchdown and the lead. The first touchdown scored against Miami during the first half all season put the 'Noles ahead, 10-7.

Miami's usually dangerous offense sputtered the rest of the half. UM's next three possessions ended in a punt and two interceptions. The first interception was by Terrell Buckley, coming inside the FSU 15 when Torretta overthrew junior wide receiver Lamar Thomas, part of the highly acclaimed "Ruthless Posse" of UM wideouts. The second interception also occurred deep in Seminole territory. This time, the pass intended for junior tight end Coleman Bell was tipped at the line of scrimmage by defensive back Richards Coes. Linebacker Marvin Jones alertly reacted to the UFO and made a diving grab at the FSU 13.

But hospitable Florida State gave the ball right back to Miami three plays later. With defensive lineman Rusty Medearis bearing down from his left side, Weldon hurried his pass and was intercepted by Charles Pharms at the FSU 40 with 3:49 to play in the half.

Miami's final drive of the half stalled at the FSU 27, where Carlos Huerta attempted a 41-yard field goal attempt. Florida State's Sterling Palmer broke through the line to get a hand on the ball, blocking the attempt and leaving FSU with a 10-7 halftime lead. While many fans expected a pinball-like offensive show, Florida State's defense had forced Miami into three turnovers while the Hurricanes' defense had limited the 'Noles to six first downs. At halftime, Erickson informed his players: "Boys, we're here to chew bubble gum and kick ass, and I'm all out of gum."

The second half got off to a terrible start for Florida State. Weldon was sacked by Corwin Francis from the blind side, knocking his wind out and forcing him to be replaced by understudy Brad Johnson. Johnson drew applause from the surprised crowd when he scrambled right and threw back across the field to Lee for 19 yards, then scrambled on first down for nine yards to the 50-yard line. Lee carried for four yards, then Weldon returned—and was promptly sacked for the fourth time. But three consecutive passes for first down—including one that broke FSU's 0-for-6 streak on third down—gave the Seminoles first down at the UM eight.

Lee got the call on first down but was tackled for a two-yard loss. On second down at the 10, Lonnie Johnson was called for holding, pushing Florida State back to the 22 and visibly angering Bowden on the sideline. Bennett made up eight of the lost yards, giving the Seminoles third-and-goal at the 14. Weldon dropped back and looked toward the left corner of the end zone, where Baker and Johnson were both running patterns. Weldon threw a pass that appeared intended for Baker, but Miami defensive back Ryan McNeil broke up the play. In came Thomas to kick a 31-yard field goal, and Florida State increased its lead to 13-7 on a 13-play, 58-yard drive that left only 8:29 to play in the third quarter.

Miami put together its own impressive drive, advancing from its 28 to the FSU 34. Erickson sent in Huerta for a 51-yard field goal attempt with less than four minutes left in the period. A split second before Huerta sent the ball short and to the right, Florida State called time out. Erickson then changed his mind and sent in his punt team, which caused Huerta to fling his helmet to the ground after he had trotted behind the Hurricanes' bench.

Florida State methodically marched downfield against Miami's vaunted defense, running up the middle on trap plays that frustrated UM's hard-charging rush. Here were the Seminoles again, with a first down at Miami's 10 with only seconds remaining in the third quarter.

Lee carried into the middle of the line for no gain. On second down, Weldon threw over the middle to Lonnie Johnson down to the UM 4. On third down, Bennett took the handoff to Weldon's left but found little blocking. He skipped to his left and was lucky to gain a yard to the three.

With the 'Noles leading by six, Bowden would have been silly to gamble for a touchdown. An easy field goal would give Florida State a nine-point lead and force Miami—which had not scored since the game's initial possession—to score at least twice to win.

Thomas kicked his third field goal, a 20-yarder, to put FSU ahead 16-7 with 14:22 to play.

But Miami was far from dead. Mixing Torretta's passing with McGuire's running, the Hurricanes pushed their way to the FSU 13 with a little more than 11 minutes to play. A false-start penalty and the fifth and sixth sacks of Torretta left Miami with fourth-and-24 at the Seminoles' 27. Needing a touchdown and a field goal to win, Erickson chose to get the field goal and hope the touchdown would follow. Huerta's 45-yard attempt was good, and the 'Canes had pulled within 16-10 with 9:48 to play.

It was then the Miami defense's turn to prevent Florida State from putting together its third consecutive scoring drive of the second half. The 'Canes held the Seminoles to only one first down, and FSU was forced to punt from its 32. Miami took over at its 42 with 7:20 to play.

Torretta was dropped for a five-yard loss on first down, marking the third consecutive UM play from scrimmage in which the 'Canes' quarterback was dropped for a loss. On the next play, Bell broke free down the right side and made a leaping catch over cornerback Errol McCorvey for a 22-yard gain to the FSU 41. McGuire carried around left end for eight yards, then broke free up the middle for 17 more to the Seminoles' 16.

On first down, Torretta played it safe and threw wide for Thomas on an out pattern to the right sideline when Buckley had him well covered to the inside. McGuire pushed forward for four yards on the next play, leaving the 'Canes with third-and-six at the FSU 12. Torretta looked for another out pattern, this time to running back Kevin Williams. But Williams slipped after making his cut and fell down as the pass got near him. Miami's shot at upsetting No. 1 Florida State had come down to a fourth-and-six play at the Seminoles' 12.

Torretta walked up to the line of scrimmage with tailback Darryl Spencer and wide receiver Horace Copeland split to the right. Strong safety Mack Knight lined up opposite Spencer, and Buckley lined up opposite Copeland. With the ball on the 12, Buckley chose to line up at the five and not play any kind of bump coverage.

As the ball was snapped, Buckley kept his distance from Copeland, backpedaling to the goal line. That allowed Copeland to run down past the first-down marker and turn to look for the pass from Torretta. Knight recognized the situation and abandoned his coverage of Spencer. But Buckley and Knight were both too far from Copeland to make the play. Copeland made the catch—his first of the game—and was tackled by Knight for a nine-yard gain at the FSU three.

With a little more than four minutes to play, Erickson determined Miami would be most successful attacking the right side of the Florida State defense. McGuire followed the left side of the UM front for a one-yard gain and did the same thing on second down at the two. On third down at the one, tight end Joe Moore and fullback Jason Marucci lined up in the backfield to the left of Torretta, with freshman fullback Larry Jones behind the quarterback. Torretta took the snap and handed off to Jones, who followed his blocking and burrowed into the end zone. With 3:01 to play, the score was tied, 16-16, pending Huerta's PAT attempt.

What should have been an automatic situation took on unusual drama because Miami's regular PAT snapper, Tom Patterson, had been sidelined earlier in the game with a strained knee. Defensive lineman Rusty Medearis trotted onto the field to snap for a PAT that could pave the way for Miami's fourth national championship in nine seasons.

Medearis' snap was fine. Huerta's kick faded to the right but was never in danger of missing the goalposts. The score was Miami 17, Florida State 16—the same score by which UM won at Doak Campbell Stadium eight years earlier to earn an Orange Bowl Classic berth opposite No. 1 Nebraska.

The subsequent kickoff landed deep in the end zone, forcing Florida State to settle for starting the all-important possession at its 20. The Seminoles had two timeouts left, having used one on defense late in the third quarter. On ABC's national telecast, Keith Jackson noted: "All they need is three. Their history in place kicking has not been pronounced."

Weldon passed nine yards to Kez McCorvey on first down, and Lee followed with a four-yard run that gave the 'Noles a first down at the FSU 33. Weldon then hit Eric Turral on an out pattern to the right sideline

left. Bennett ran outside to the left for a six-yard gain to the FSU 47 with two minutes to go. Weldon floated a pass over the middle to Bennett, but he was stopped a yard short of the first-down marker. Florida State called its final timeout with 1:15 to play, facing fourth-and-one at Miami's 47.

Both Mowrey and Thomas were limbering their kicking legs on the Florida State sideline as Bowden sent in the play needed to produce a yard—or the Seminoles' stay at No. 1 would

Marcus Carey's sign declares the 'Canes as state champs, which in 1991 meant national champs.
(TALLAHASSEE DEMOCRAT–MIKE EWEN)

to gain 11 yards to the 44 and stop the clock with 2:27 to play.

Defensive tackle Eric Miller then broke through Florida State's offensive line to sack Weldon for a three-yard loss back to the Seminoles' 41. That forced Florida State to use its second timeout, stopping the clock with 2:18

be coming to an end. If there was ever a time when you might have expected the usually flamboyant Bowden to be conservative, it was at this time. Weldon handed off to Bennett, who slid off tacklers and skirted around right end for a seven-yard gain that kept the 'Noles' championship dreams alive. An injury to

Medearis even managed to stop the clock with 1:10 to play.

At the UM 40, Weldon rolled right but was unable to find anyone open downfield. He was, though, able to spot Bennett free near the left sideline and threw a pass across the field. Bennett made the catch and got out of bounds with 1:04 left after gaining seven yards to the Miami 33. On second-and-three, Weldon threw incomplete to Johnson. On third down, he went for it all, throwing for Turral in the end zone. Turral turned back to face the ball and got position on defensive back Ryan McNeil. With Turral leaping toward the ball, McNeil was forced to push Turral for a 15-yard pass interference penalty. That gave Florida State the ball at the Miami 18 with 53 seconds to play.

At that point, the Seminoles would be looking at a 35-yard field goal attempt if they didn't gain another yard. Thomas's longest field goal of the season was 40 yards in the cold of Louisville. On first down, Lee couldn't find any running room in the middle and was stopped for a one-yard gain. Complicating matters for Florida State, which was working without any timeouts, was the fact that Weldon lost his shoe. The clock ran down, and Weldon simply took the snap and grounded the ball to stop the clock. That left the Seminoles with third-and-nine at the UM 19 with 29 seconds to play.

Bowden decided running another play from scrimmage would most likely result in disaster rather than celebration. If Weldon were sacked—as he had been five times—Florida State would face a long field goal attempt with the clock running. So Bowden decided to send in Thomas and the field goal team to get the game-winning three points on third down.

Thomas received some encouraging words from a student manager before he headed out toward midfield. On the way, he exchanged a subdued hand slap with Kevin Mancini. Thomas marked off the distance, and holder Brad Johnson set up to receive the snap at the 24.

*   *   *

The story of this latest edition of college football's Game of the Century actually dates back to the previous summer, when the NCAA Football Rules Committee altered the width of the goalposts from 23 feet, four inches to 18 feet, six inches. By narrowing the width of its goalposts by four feet, 10 inches, the committee intended to cut down on the number of attempted field goals. NCAA research indicated too many coaches were content to seek the easy three points from middle distances.

*   *   *

The kick sailed toward the south end zone, toward the right upright. On the east sideline, Miami's Stephen McGuire couldn't bear to watch; he instead chose to close his eyes and face the ground, to depend on the crowd reaction to inform him of the kick's fate. What he heard was an FSU crowd that thought the ball was going to pass between the uprights and began to celebrate. Brad Johnson thought the ball was headed through the posts and raised his arms to signal three points. Thomas, standing a few feet behind Johnson, made no such gesture. He could tell from the time he kicked the ball that it was drifting ever so slightly to the right.

The ball didn't pass through the posts. It sailed to the right of the goalposts by a matter of inches. Bobby Bowden was confused; the officials were signaling that the kick was no good while many of the fans and some of the players indicated it was good. Bowden threw off his headset and carried a dazed look on his face as he ran downfield toward the end zone. "What's goin' on?" the stunned Bowden said to no one in particular. "I thought it was good."

A few moments after the kick, ABC's Keith Jackson noted: "You know what just ran through my mind—and (ABC staffer) Todd Berry reminded me of it—last year, that kick is good."

Coaches Dennis Erickson of Miami and Bobby Bowden of Florida State meet after UM's thrilling 17-16 victory at Doak Campbell Stadium. (MIAMI HERALD–BILL FRAKES)

The following figures likely would not console Thomas or any of the Seminoles, but statistics compiled after the season showed that the goalpost change yielded the desired effect. Field goals made from between 20 and 29 yards decreased by 15.5 percent. From 30 to 39 yards, they were down by 19.4 percent. From 40 or 49 yards, down 20.5 percent. And from 50 yards and beyond, down 22.4 percent.

For the fourth time since 1980, Miami had beaten Florida State by a single point; twice those victories were parlayed into national titles. The Miami sideline broke into delirium, Dennis Erickson embracing any and all within reach. The Hurricanes were penalized for excessive celebration, a penalty that was delightfully accepted. Some of the Hurricanes turned toward the FSU fans and provided a mock rendition of the tomahawk chop. Gerry Thomas may have been tempted to crawl into a hole and hide. What he did instead was stand right there on the Florida State sideline, where kickers are rarely seen under such circumstances. Miami ran one play, and the game was over. Bobby Bowden walked to midfield sporting a disgusted smirk that made him look like Lou Costello, just having been duped one more time by Bud Abbott.

In the Florida State dressing room, Gerry Thomas politely answered all inquiries and volunteered to accept blame for defeat. "I didn't do my job," he said, his eyes red and swollen. Kirk Carruthers was more general and damning in his postgame appraisal: "We knew in the fourth quarter we were the better team, and Miami knew in the fourth quarter they were going to win."

Statistics didn't ease Florida State's pain any. The Seminoles had outgained Miami in total offense 365 yards to 310. FSU had sacked Torretta six times, one more time than Miami got to Weldon. The most revealing stat—and the most damning to the 'Noles—was one-for-10 production on third downs.

"It was the greatest win I've ever been involved with," Erickson said. With it, of course, would come an official invitation to play in the Orange Bowl Classic. The only difference, which UM players had learned to live with, was moving over to the visitors' locker room since the Big Eight champ is technically recognized as the bowl's host team. Florida State tried to put on the happy face for going to Dallas, where it would play a Texas A&M team only blemished by a one-point loss at Tulsa in September. Before then, though, there was the matter of finishing the regular season at Florida.

Virtually all of the reporters had left the FSU locker room when Casey Weldon, national championship dreams having been dashed, sat alone on a stool in the showers. But Tallahassee *Democrat* sports editor Bill McGrotha was around to hear Weldon's crying bounce around the porcelain walls. The lamentation was interrupted only by the repeating of a one-word question.

"Why?"

Bobby Bowden presided over his postgame news conference as someone would at a relative's funeral. It would take the fall of an incredible sequence of dominoes for Florida State to get back in the national championship race. It wasn't even worth considering. Bowden had gone through five seasons in which one loss cost his Seminoles a national championship (three times the loss coming against the 'Canes). Then came 1991 and a preseason No. 1 ranking that had been defended week after week—until this.

"We had too many things going for us here," he said. "It's just like '87. We just needed one more play."

Florida State vs. Florida

Florida State Tries to Survive "Rocky II"

Frankly, it probably was a game the Florida State Seminoles would rather not have played. Having watched their national-championship season crumble beneath the weight of the Miami Hurricanes, FSU had to sit through an agonizing off week before traveling to Gainesville. There waiting for them was a band of Gators savoring its first official Southeastern Conference championship.

But for Florida, there was also the matter of ending its streak of futility against FSU. The 'Noles had run up a string of four consecutive victories in the series, equalling their best streak ever. This included FSU's best offensive days in the series, a 52-17 win at Doak Campbell Stadium in 1988 and a 45-30 drubbing again at Tallahassee in 1990. The latter was Steve Spurrier's "introduction" to the rivalry—at least in terms of coaching the Gators.

While the Noles had spent the bulk of the season atop the Associated Press rankings, the Gators enjoyed a lower profile not far from No. 1. They were picked fifth in the preseason poll (third in the state, with FSU at No. 1 and Miami No. 3). They easily disposed of San Jose State in the opener as expected, 59-21, but turned many heads with their dominance

of Alabama next time out, 35-0. But just when it appeared Florida State, Miami and Florida might monopolize the top three spots in the poll, the Gators were surprised by Syracuse, 38-21, in a trip to the Carrier Dome.

That would be UF's last loss of the regular season. With national-championship thoughts put on hold, Florida now aimed to make good on the predictions that the Gators would indeed win the SEC title. Wins over Mississippi State and LSU set up an anticipated showdown with Tennessee, which had humiliated the Gators a year earlier in Knoxville, 45-3. This time, it was Florida that put on a show. The Gators' 35-18 win cleared a major hurdle. Down the stretch in the SEC, Florida had easy times with a pair of longtime nemeses. The Gators dominated the second half to defeat Auburn, 31-10, then blasted Georgia, 45-13. The latter marked the first time since 1962-63 that the Gators had scored consecutive victories in their oft-frustrating series with the Bulldogs.

On the same afternoon in which Miami pulled the top-ranked rug from beneath Florida State, the Gators were busy claiming their first conference championship trophy by out-

Was Florida State coach Bobby Bowden (right) telling Florida coach Steve Spurrier that the Gators should also experience the thrill of playing Miami? (UF INFORMATION SERVICES–BUDDY LONG)

lasting a stubborn Kentucky team, 35-28. That clinched a berth in the USF&G Sugar Bowl against Notre Dame. It was the Gators' first appearance in one of the so-called "major" bowl games since playing in New Orleans on New Year's Eve in 1974. Rated fifth in the nation going into the FSU game, could UF possibly finish No. 1?

The catalyst for Florida was the offense that Spurrier installed after coming in from Duke before the 1990 season to replace interim coach Gary Darnell. Spurrier had developed into one of the country's brightest young offensive coaches since retiring from pro football. As an assistant coach at Florida, Georgia Tech and Duke, and as a head coach with Duke and the United States Football League's Tampa Bay Bandits, Spurrier settled on an offensive agenda that featured multiple formations, flooded zones with wide receivers and—

the bottom line—plenty of scoring. It made it possible for UF quarterback Shane Matthews to be named the SEC's Player of the Year as a sophomore in 1990. In 1991, Matthews was backed by the running of sophomore Errict Rhett and seniors Willie McClendon and Dexter McNabb. On defense, the Gators were led by senior linebacker Ephesians Bartley and senior tackle Brad Culpepper.

"Steve knows exactly what he's doing offensively," FSU coach Bobby Bowden said of Spurrier before the game. "Great confidence. I don't know anybody who has more confidence than Steve does, and I think his players pick right up on that."

Looking for some impressive pregame stats? Try Matthews ranking third in the nation in total offense, Weldon fifth in passing efficiency. Try Florida ranking fourth in passing, Florida State fourth in scoring. Bowden came to Gainesville owning a 4-3 record at Florida Field while Spurrier had never lost a game at Florida Field as a coach.

But would Florida State have enough left, especially after a defensive effort against Miami that registered six sacks and forced three turnovers? The 'Noles and their fans were hoping this would be a sequel that didn't disappoint.

"As I've been saying, Rocky II," Bowden said.

✳ ✳ ✳

As has often been the case when Florida and Florida State meet, a record crowd had gathered. This one numbered 85,461 beneath a sunny sky at Florida Field. The Seminoles marked this special occasion by leaving their standard gold uniform pants home in favor of the special white outfits.

Florida forced a turnover on the Seminoles' opening possession to take over at the FSU 35. Weldon was trying to move up in the pocket when the ball was knocked loose from behind by defensive end Darren Mickell. Tim Paulk made the recovery for the Gators.

An apparent touchdown pass to Tre Everett was called back because of a false start. On the next play, FSU All-America cornerback Terrell Buckley made Florida pay for that mistake with an interception at the Seminoles' 25 on another pass intended for Everett. That gave Buckley—a high school teammate of UF's Matthews in Pascagoula, Mississippi—11 for the season (best in the nation) and 20 for his career.

In the closing minutes of the first quarter Florida pushed downfield on the strength of a 41-yard pass from Matthews to Aubrey Hill, to the FSU 23. A sack by Kirk Carruthers on third down forced Spurrier to send in kicker

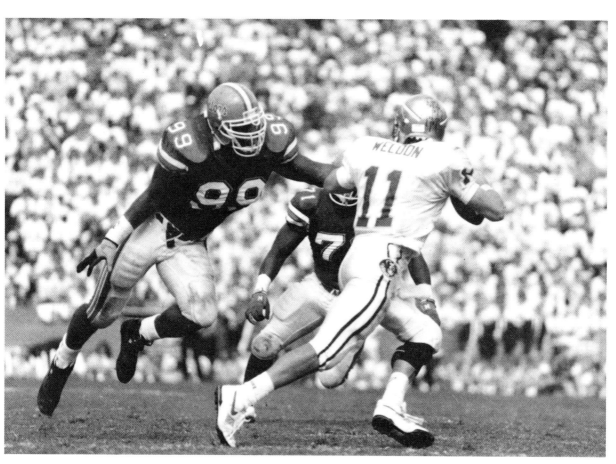

200   *Florida's Tim Paulk (99) gives chase to Florida State quarterback Casey Weldon.* (UF INFORMATION SERVICES–BUDDY LONG)

Arden Czyzewski to attempt a 47-yard field goal on the first play of the second quarter. The kick fell short and to the left. Florida had nothing to show for a first quarter in which it ran 23 plays to Florida State's 12 and gained 112 yards to the Seminoles' 18.

reach over the goal line for the score, but the play was negated because FSU wide receiver Lonnie Johnson moved too soon. With second-and-goal at the six, Amp Lee gained back to the two. Weldon tried to loft a pass into the far side of the end zone to McCorvey but

Florida's Aubrey Hill (82) eludes a Seminole defender on a pass play that gained 41 yards.
(UF INFORMATION SERVICES–GENE BEDNAREK)

The missed field goal gave FSU possession at the 'Noles' 31. FSU reached the Florida 27, where Bowden decided to go for the first down on fourth-and-eight. Weldon dropped back and found sophomore Matt Frier alone on a slant pattern over the middle for a 12-yard gain and the first down. A diving catch by Kez McCorvey on a third-down pass gave the 'Noles first down at the Florida one.

Fullback Edgar Bennett carried up the middle on first down but only got back to the line of scrimmage. Next, Bennett tried to

cornerback Del Speer didn't allow McCorvey to get inside him. On fourth down, FSU's Gerry Thomas kicked a 19-yard field goal.

Florida, still with no points, began its seventh possession of the game at its 23. Ironically, it was the oft-ignored Gator running game that proved effective—against a defense that went into the game ranked third nationally in rushing defense. In fact, Spurrier went downright radical (for him), lining up with two tight ends—bringing Mickell over temporarily from the defense—on the play that resulted in Rhett's three-yard touchdown run with 3:11 to play in the half. That gave Rhett 96 yards rushing for the half.

Weldon brought the Seminoles back downfield before facing a fourth-and-seven at the UF 37 with 1:16 left in the half. He found Frier over the middle for a completion, but Frier fell a yard short of the first down. The Seminoles had made up ground in total yards—trailing by 186 to 128—but had rushed for only 27.

Midway through the third period, Florida struck suddenly after forcing an FSU punt. On first down at the Gators' 28, Spurrier decided to go deep. But Aubrey Hill couldn't get position on Buckley and nearly committed offensive pass interference as the ball fell incomplete. On second down, Matthews was flushed out of the pocket and scrambled to his right. With pursuit from the FSU line and cornerback Buckley barreling in on him, Matthews spotted receiver Harrison Houston breaking toward the end zone while covered by outside linebacker Reggie Freeman. Awkwardly trying to knock the pass down while backpedaling, Freeman stumbled and fell, allowing Houston to make the easy catch just inside the FSU 45 and race in untouched for the touchdown and a 14-3 lead.

The 'Noles headed for the Florida end zone again on the following possession. On third-and-three at the Florida 16, Sean Jackson caught a pass near the right sideline along the line of scrimmage, then danced and dove into the end zone. But the play was brought back because Florida State had let the 25-second clock run out. Weldon still managed to pass to McCorvey for a first down at the 11.

On first down, Frier was interfered with by Speer on a slant over the middle of the end zone. That gave Florida State first-and-goal at the UF two with 3:17 to play in the third quarter. Sound familiar? Sean Jackson tried to skirt around right end on first down but lost a yard. On second down, Weldon overthrew Shannon Baker. On third down, Weldon was sacked by Harvey Thomas and fumbled. After a handful of players had a shot at the ball,

FSU made the recovery at their 34. Bowden had to send in Gerry Thomas for a 44-yard field goal attempt, but the kick drifted to the right of the uprights. Two trips inside Florida's three had resulted in only three points for the usually explosive Seminoles.

Florida State stopped UF easily on the following series to end the third quarter, but Weldon tried to loft a pass over the middle to McCorvey at the Florida 10 despite double coverage. The result was an interception by defensive back Lawrence Hatch. The Gators appeared primed to put the Seminoles away midway through the fourth quarter when they moved to FSU's six, but Florida State safety Lavon Brown intercepted a pass intended for wideout Willie Jackson on the right side of the end zone to give the 'Noles new life. Weldon immediately guided FSU in the other direction. At the Florida 25, he passed to Amp Lee at the 20, who sprinted around UF defenders for a touchdown with 5:24 to play. The 80-yard drive was accomplished in six plays (all passes) taking only 2:09 off the clock. Weldon, who had been knocked around all afternoon, was pulled in favor of Brad Johnson when Bowden decided to go for two points. Johnson passed, but the ball was knocked down by the Florida line. That left the Seminoles needing another touchdown to win.

The Gators failed to gain a first down on their next series and were forced to punt from their 43 with 4:23 to play. Spurrier called a timeout before the punt. Before the ball was snapped, Florida raced its regular offense back out onto the field. That forced Florida State to use the first of its three second-half timeouts to be certain the Gators weren't just faking going for the first down. If nothing else, Spurrier had prompted FSU to burn a timeout that could be valuable later on. When time was whistled back in, UF repeated the stunt. This time, Florida State brought its defense up, held its ground and dared Matthews to snap the ball. He didn't. Florida took the five-yard penalty for delay of game and sent in Shayne Edge to punt from the Florida 38. Buckley fielded the twisting punt at the FSU

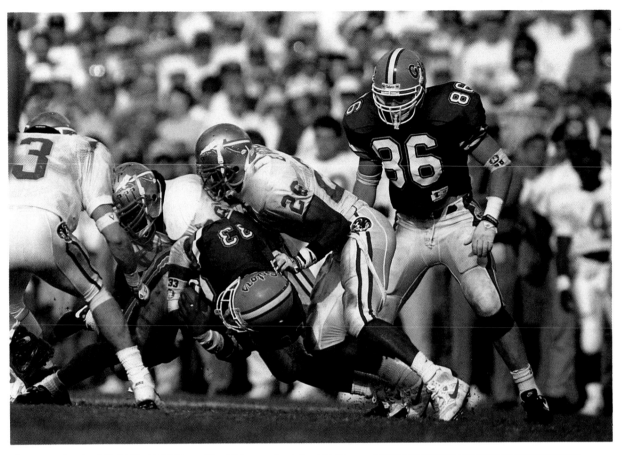

Gator running back Errict Rhett (33) is met by FSU cornerback Errol McCorvey. (UF INFORMATION SERVICES–GENE BEDNAREK)

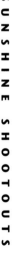

23, got protection down the right sideline and returned the kick to the Noles' 49 with 4:09 left.

Weldon reentered the game. He passed 19 yards to Amp Lee on second down, moving the ball to the Florida 32 as the clock moved inside four minutes. A missed tackle resulted in a 17-yard hookup with McCorvey to the 15. The Seminoles were penalized five yards for illegal motion on first down, moving the ball back to the 20. Weldon then passed underneath coverage to Lonnie Johnson at the 14. On second-and-nine, Weldon rolled right and tried to hit Kevin Knox in the right corner of the end zone. But the pass hung in the air long enough for Will White to get position and leap up along with Knox. As they battled for the ball, it fell incomplete. On third-and-nine, the play clock nearly expired on FSU and Weldon was forced to use the Noles' second timeout of the second half with 2:19 to play. Weldon dropped back to pass and had McCorvey slanting over from the left side. Weldon threw behind him, incomplete.

That left Florida State with fourth-and-nine at the 14. And again, much to the Seminoles' chagrin, Weldon had to use the final timeout to avoid a five-yard delay-of-game penalty. Weldon rolled right and stepped back up toward the 15 before throwing for the end zone toward a crowd of two Seminoles and four Gators. It appeared Weldon—who might have been able to run for the first down—was trying to get the ball to McCorvey, who was coming across from the left side of the field. But the pass was knocked down by Will White, giving the ball back to Florida with 2:03 to play.

203

With no timeouts left, Florida State was helpless to stop the clock as the Gators ran off a couple of plays to end the game. The 'Noles actually finished with more total yards (342-325), and Weldon finished with 305 yards passing compared to 208—with three interceptions—for Matthews.

The leading rushers for the 'Noles were Lee with 24 yards and Jackson with 22. Conversely, Rhett topped UF with 109 yards, though 99 of those came in the first half. And there was no forgetting FSU coming away with only one touchdown for four trips inside Florida's 20. And only the field goal to show for first-and-goals at the one and the two.

"I never thought I would ever in my life win a game 14-9," Spurrier admitted after the game.

Florida State, first in the nation less than a fortnight earlier, was now last in its home state.

"All losses are disappointing to me," Bowden told reporters after the game. "I can't stand 'em. After you lose that one (to Miami), can anything be more painful?

"Except losing two like that?"

❊   ❊   ❊

January 1, 1992, marked the first time in college football's long and storied history that the three Florida schools competed in New Year's Day bowls. And even with the glut of games moved to that day in the name of ratings and dollars, all three were playing in the so-called "major" bowls.

No. 1 Miami was matched against No. 11 Nebraska in the Federal Express Orange Bowl, hoping to claim its fourth national title in nine seasons. No. 3 Florida met No. 18 Notre Dame in the Sugar Bowl, holding out hopes that a victory—coupled with losses by Miami and by No. 2 Washington, playing No. 4 Michigan in the Rose Bowl—might propel the Gators to the top. And No. 5 Florida State, left as a spectator in the national-title hunt, wanted to finish on a positive note against No. 9 Texas A&M in the Cotton Bowl.

Were it not for an impressive second-half comeback by the Irish, the three Sunshine State schools would have set another mark by all winning on New Year's Day.

The 'Noles began the day by staving off A&M, 10-2, in a game that featured more turnovers than points. When Washington beat Michigan in the Rose Bowl, 34-14, it meant that Florida was eliminated from the title hunt and that Miami would need to beat Nebraska to retain consideration for finishing No. 1. The Hurricanes had no trouble holding up their end of the bargain, routing the Cornhuskers, 22-0. In New Orleans, however, Notre Dame came back from a 16-7 halftime deficit to whip UF, 39-28. Irish fullback Jerome Bettis scored three touchdowns within a 2:44 span of the fourth quarter.

The final Associated Press poll of the 1991 season ranked Miami first, Florida State fourth and Florida seventh. Another first—never had three teams from the same state been ranked in the final top seven.

Series Statistics

Florida vs. Miami

overall: Gators lead, 25-24
at Gainesville: Hurricanes lead, 11-8
at Miami: Gators lead, 14-12
elsewhere: Gators lead, 3-1

YEAR	SITE	WINNER	SCORE	YEAR	SITE	WINNER	SCORE
1938	Gainesville	Miami	19-7	1964	Gainesville	Florida	12-10
1939	Miami	Florida	13-0	1965	Miami	Miami	16-13
1940	Miami	Florida	46-6	1966	Gainesville	Miami	21-16
1941	Miami	Florida	14-0	1967	Miami	Miami	20-13
1942	Miami	Miami	12-0	1968	Gainesville	Florida	14-10
1944	Miami	Florida	13-0	1969	Miami	Florida	35-16
1945	Miami	Miami	7-6	1970	Gainesville	Miami	14-13
1946	Gainesville	Miami	20-13	1971	Miami	Florida	45-16
1947	Miami	Florida	7-6	1972	Gainesville	Florida	17-6
1948	Gainesville	Florida	27-13	1973	Miami	Florida	14-7
1949	Miami	Miami	28-13	1974	Gainesville	Florida	31-7
1950	Gainesville	Miami	20-14	1975	Miami	Florida	15-11
1951	Miami	Miami	21-6	1976	Orlando	Florida	19-10
1952	Gainesville	Florida	43-6	1977	Miami	Florida	31-14
1953	Miami	Miami	14-10	1978	Gainesville	Miami	22-21
1954	Gainesville	Miami	14-0	1979	Miami	Miami	30-24
1955	Miami	Miami	7-6	1980	Gainesville	Miami	31-7
1956	Gainesville	Miami	20-7	1981	Miami	Miami	21-20
1957	Miami	Florida	14-0	1982	Gainesville	Florida	17-14
1958	Jacksonville	Florida	12-9	1983	Gainesville	Florida	28-3
1959	Jacksonville	Florida	23-14	1984	Tampa	Miami	32-20
1960	Miami	Florida	18-0	1985	Miami	Florida	35-23
1961	Gainesville	Miami	15-6	1986	Gainesville	Miami	23-15
1962	Miami	Miami	17-15	1987	Miami	Miami	31-4
1963	Miami	Florida	27-21				

SUNSHINE SHOOTOUTS

Miami vs. Florida State

overall: Hurricanes lead, 21-14
at Miami: Hurricanes lead, 13-12
at Tallahassee: Hurricanes lead, 9-2

YEAR	SITE	WINNER	SCORE	YEAR	SITE	WINNER	SCORE
1951	Miami	Miami	35-13	1975	Tallahassee	Miami	24-22
1953	Miami	Miami	27-0	1976	Miami	Miami	47-0
1955	Miami	Miami	34-0	1977	Tallahassee	Miami	23-17
1956	Miami	Miami	20-7	1978	Miami	Florida State	31-21
1957	Tallahassee	Miami	40-13	1979	Tallahassee	Florida State	40-23
1958	Miami	Florida State	17-6	1980	Miami	Miami	10-9
1959	Tallahassee	Miami	7-6	1981	Tallahassee	Miami	27-19
1960	Miami	Miami	25-7	1982	Miami	Florida State	24-7
1962	Miami	Miami	7-6	1983	Tallahassee	Miami	17-16
1963	Miami	Florida State	24-0	1984	Miami	Florida State	38-3
1964	Miami	Florida State	14-0	1985	Tallahassee	Miami	35-27
1966	Miami	Florida State	23-20	1986	Miami	Miami	41-23
1969	Miami	Florida State	16-14	1987	Tallahassee	Miami	26-25
1970	Miami	Florida State	27-3	1988	Miami	Miami	31-0
1971	Miami	Florida State	20-17	1989	Tallahassee	Florida State	24-10
1972	Miami	Florida State	37-14	1990	Miami	Miami	31-22
1973	Tallahassee	Miami	14-10	1991	Tallahassee	Miami	17-16
1974	Miami	Florida State	21-14				

Florida vs. Florida State

overall: Gators lead, 23-10-1
at Gainesville: Gators lead, 14-5-1
at Tallahassee: Gators lead, 9-5

YEAR	SITE	WINNER	SCORE	YEAR	SITE	WINNER	SCORE
1958	Gainesville	Florida	21-7	1975	Gainesville	Florida	34-8
1959	Gainesville	Florida	18-8	1976	Tallahassee	Florida	33-26
1960	Gainesville	Florida	3-0	1977	Gainesville	Florida State	37-9
1961	Gainesville	tie	3-3	1978	Tallahassee	Florida State	38-21
1962	Gainesville	Florida	20-7	1979	Gainesville	Florida State	27-16
1963	Gainesville	Florida	7-0	1980	Tallahassee	Florida State	17-13
1964	Tallahassee	Florida State	16-7	1981	Gainesville	Florida	35-3
1965	Gainesville	Florida	30-17	1982	Tallahassee	Florida	13-10
1966	Tallahassee	Florida	22-19	1983	Gainesville	Florida	53-14
1967	Gainesville	Florida State	21-16	1984	Tallahassee	Florida	27-17
1968	Tallahassee	Florida	9-3	1985	Gainesville	Florida	38-14
1969	Gainesville	Florida	21-6	1986	Tallahassee	Florida	17-13
1970	Tallahassee	Florida	38-27	1987	Gainesville	Florida State	28-14
1971	Gainesville	Florida	17-15	1988	Tallahassee	Florida State	52-17
1972	Tallahassee	Florida	42-13	1989	Gainesville	Florida State	24-17
1973	Gainesville	Florida	49-0	1990	Tallahassee	Florida State	45-30
1974	Tallahassee	Florida	24-14	1991	Gainesville	Florida	14-9

Florida Coaches vs.

	MIAMI	FSU	TOTAL
Josh Cody	1-1	0-0	1-1
Thomas Lieb	3-2	0-0	3-2
Raymond Wolf	2-2	0-0	2-2
Bob Woodruff	4-6	2-0	6-6
Ray Graves	5-5	7-2-1	12-7-1
Doug Dickey	7-2	7-2	14-4
Charley Pell	2-4	3-2	5-6
Galen Hall	1-2	3-2	4-4
Gary Darnell	0-0	0-1	0-1
Steve Spurrier	0-0	1-1	1-1

Miami Coaches vs.

	FLORIDA	FSU	TOTAL
Jack Harding	4-4	0-0	4-4
Eddie Dunn	1-0	0-0	1-0
Andy Gustafson	9-7	8-2	17-9
Charlie Tate	3-3	0-3	6-3
Walt Kichefski	1-0	0-1	1-1
Fran Curci	0-2	0-2	0-4
Pete Elliott	0-2	1-1	1-3
Carl Selmer	0-2	2-0	2-2
Lou Saban	1-1	1-1	2-2
Howard Schnellenberger	3-2	3-2	6-4
Jimmy Johnson	3-1	4-1	7-2
Dennis Erickson	0-0	2-1	2-1

Florida State Coaches vs.

	MIAMI	FLORIDA	TOTAL
Don Veller	0-1	0-0	0-1
Tom Nugent	1-5	0-1	1-6
Perry Moss	0-1	0-1	0-2
Bill Peterson	5-2	2-8-1	7-10-1
Larry Jones	1-2	0-3	1-5
Darrell Mudra	1-1	0-2	1-3
Bobby Bowden	5-11	8-8	13-19

Game Summaries

FLORIDA 43, MIAMI 6:
Nov. 22, 1952 at Gainesville　　　(35,000)

	1st	2nd	3rd	4th	Total
Miami	0	0	0	6	6
Florida	6	10	14	13	43

First Quarter
Florida: Dickey 1-yard run (kick failed)

Second Quarter
Florida: J. Hall 6-yard run (Casares kick)
Florida: FG 27 Casares

Third Quarter
Florida: Long 5-yard run (Casares kick)
Florida: Casares 5-yard run (Casares kick)

Fourth Quarter
Florida: Long 13-yard run (kick failed)
Miami: McDonald 7-yard pass from James (kick failed)
Florida: Oosterhoudt 4-yard run (Hurse kick)

	UM	UF
First downs	7	20
Rushing yardage	17	255
Passing yardage	103	35
Comp-Att-Int	10-15-1	2-7-1
Fumbles lost	4	1

FLORIDA STATE 17, MIAMI 6:
Nov. 7, 1958 at Miami　　　(31,879)

	1st	2nd	3rd	4th	Total
Florida State	6	0	0	0	6
Miami	7	7	0	3	17

First Quarter
Florida State: Majors 45-yard interception return (Sheppard kick)
Miami: Plevel 1-yard run (kick failed)

Second Quarter
Florida State: Pickard 8-yard pass from Prinzi (Sheppard kick)

Third Quarter
none

Fourth Quarter
Florida State: Sheppard 22-yard field goal

	FSU	UM
First downs	9	20
Rushing yardage	133	192
Passing yardage	44	117
Comp-Att-Int	5-10-1	8-23-3
Fumbles lost	2	3

FLORIDA 21, FLORIDA STATE 7:
Nov. 22, 1958 at Gainesville　　　(43,000)

	1st	2nd	3rd	4th	Total
Florida State	7	0	0	0	7
Florida	7	14	0	0	21

First Quarter
Florida State: Pickard 1-yard run (Sheppard kick)
Florida: Hudson 4-yard run (kick failed)

Second Quarter
Florida: Dunn 9-yard run (Booker kick)
Florida: Dunn 12-yard run (Booker kick)

Third Quarter
none

Fourth Quarter
none

	FSU	UF
First downs	15	14
Rushing yardage	97	219
Passing yardage	189	19
Comp-Att-Int	14-30-1	2-5-2
Fumbles lost	3	1

MIAMI 7, FLORIDA STATE 6:
Oct. 3, 1959 at Tallahassee　　　(18,600)

	1st	2nd	3rd	4th	Total
Miami	0	7	0	0	7
Florida State	0	0	0	6	6

First Quarter
none

Second Quarter
Miami: Rosbaugh 9-yard pass from Curci (Dangel kick)

Third Quarter
none

Fourth Quarter
Florida State: Pickard 8-yard run (kick failed)

	UM	FSU
First downs	10	3
Rushing yardage	178	56
Passing yardage	54	92
Comp-Att-Int	6-15-1	9-19-0
Fumbles lost	1	1

FLORIDA 23, MIAMI 14:

Nov. 28, 1959 at Jacksonville   (25,000)

	1st	2nd	3rd	4th	Total
Miami	0	0	14	0	14
Florida	7	0	6	10	23

First Quarter
Florida: Allen 3-yard run (Allen kick)

Second Quarter
none

Third Quarter
Miami: Bouffard 1-yard run (Dangel kick)
Miami: Markowski 1-yard run (Dangel kick)
Florida: Deal 53-yard pass from Allen
(kick failed)

Fourth Quarter
Florida: Allen 30-yard field goal
Florida: Hudson 9-yard pass (Allen kick)

	UM	UF
First downs	17	12
Rushing yardage	192	56
Passing yardage	152	220
Comp-Att-Int	12-23-5	10-29-0
Fumbles lost	0	0

FLORIDA 3, FLORIDA STATE 0:

Sept. 24, 1960 at Gainesville   (38,000)

	1st	2nd	3rd	4th	Total
Florida State	0	0	0	0	0
Florida	0	3	0	0	3

First Quarter
none

Second Quarter
Florida: Cash 25-yard field goal

Third Quarter
none

Fourth Quarter
none

	FSU	UF
First downs	14	16
Rushing yardage	100	272
Passing yardage	99	18
Comp-Att-Int	11-26-0	3-10-2
Fumbles lost	0	1

FLORIDA STATE 3, FLORIDA 3:

Sept. 30, 1961 at Gainesville   (44,000)

	1st	2nd	3rd	4th	Total
Florida State	3	0	0	0	3
Florida	0	3	0	0	3

First Quarter
Florida State: Harilee 29-yard field goal

Second Quarter
Florida: Cash 28-yard field goal

Third Quarter
none

Fourth Quarter
none

	FSU	UF
First downs	5	15
Rushing yardage	30	196
Passing yardage	28	95
Comp-Att-Int	4-15-2	6-15-1
Fumbles lost	3	0

MIAMI 15, FLORIDA 6:

Dec. 2, 1961 at Gainesville

	1st	2nd	3rd	4th	Total
Miami	0	6	6	3	15
Florida	0	6	0	0	6

First Quarter
none

Second Quarter
Florida: Goodman 1-yard run (kick failed)
Miami: Bahen 93-yard kickoff return (kick failed)

Third Quarter
Miami: Spinelli 7-yard pass from Mira (kick failed)

Fourth Quarter
Miami: Wilson 19-yard field goal

	UM	UF
First downs	12	14
Rushing yardage	155	99
Passing yardage	112	146
Comp-Att-Int	8-18-1	9-21-0
Fumbles lost	1	1

FLORIDA STATE 16, FLORIDA 7:
Nov. 21, 1964 at Tallahassee   (43,000)

	1st	2nd	3rd	4th	Total
Florida State	0	7	3	6	16
Florida	0	0	0	7	7

First Quarter
none

Second Quarter
Florida State: Biletnikoff 55-yard pass from Tensi (Murdock kick)

Third Quarter
Florida State: Murdock 24-yard field goal

Fourth Quarter
Florida State: Murdock 34-yard field goal
Florida State: Murdock 40-yard field goal
Florida: Harper 6-yard run (Hall kick)

	UF	FSU
First downs	9	15
Rushing yardage	57	142
Passing yardage	178	190
Comp-Att-Int	12-24-2	11-22-2
Fumbles lost	4	2

MIAMI 16, FLORIDA 13:
Nov. 20, 1965 at Miami   (67,762)

	1st	2nd	3rd	4th	Total
Florida	7	6	0	0	13
Miami	6	0	7	3	16

First Quarter
Florida: Casey 34-yard pass from Harper (Barfield kick)
Miami: Banaszak 1-yard run (kick failed)

Second Quarter
Florida: Barfield 24-yard field goal
Florida: Barfield 30-yard field goal

Third Quarter
Miami: Miller 8-yard run (Curtright kick)

Fourth Quarter
Miami: Curtright 24-yard field goal

	UF	UM
First downs	17	15
Rushing yardage	170	155
Passing yardage	113	45
Comp-Att-Int	9-23-2	6-12-0
Fumbles lost	2	0

FLORIDA 22, FLORIDA STATE 19:
Oct. 8, 1966 at Tallahassee   (46,798)

	1st	2nd	3rd	4th	Total
Florida	7	7	0	8	22
Florida State	7	3	9	0	19

First Quarter
Florida:Trapp 35-yard pass from Spurrier (Barfield kick)
Florida State: Mankins 1-yard run (Roberts kick)

Second Quarter
Florida State: Roberts 26-yard field goal
Florida: Trapp 6-yard pass from Spurrier (Barfield kick)

Third Quarter
Florida State: Mankins 1-yard run (kick failed)
Florida State: Roberts 37-yard field goal

Fourth Quarter
Florida: Smith 41-yard pass from Spurrier (Trapp pass from Spurrier)

	UF	FSU
First downs	15	21
Rushing yardage	98	106
Passing yardage	219	230
Comp-Att-Int	14-24-0	20-34-2
Fumbles lost	2	0

FLORIDA 35, MIAMI 16:
Nov. 29, 1969 at Miami   (70,934)

	1st	2nd	3rd	4th	Total
Florida	2	13	7	13	35
Miami	0	7	3	6	16

First Quarter
Florida: Ghesquire tackled Cochran in end zone

Second Quarter
Florida: Durrance 3-yard run (Franco kick)
Florida: Alvarez 12-yard pass from Reaves (kick failed)
Miami: Sullivan 32-yard run (Huff kick)

Third Quarter
Miami: Huff 33-yard field goal
Florida: Durrance 4-yard run (Franco kick)

Fourth Quarter
Miami: Griffin 25-yard pass from Cochran (pass failed)
Florida: Durrance 62-yard run (Franco kick)
Florida: Alvarez 33-yard pass from Reaves (kick failed)

	UF	UM
First downs	22	17
Rushing yardage	121	105
Passing yardage	349	223
Comp-Att-Int	31-44-2	20-45-2
Fumbles lost	1	0

MIAMI 14, FLORIDA 13:

Nov. 28, 1970 at Gainesville   (50,149)

	1st	2nd	3rd	4th	Total
Miami	7	0	7	0	14
Florida	0	0	7	6	13

First Quarter
Miami: Sullivan 1-yard run (Cummins kick)

Second Quarter
none

Third Quarter
Miami: Mundrick 2-yard run (Cummins kick)
Florida: Clifford 80-yard interception return (Getzen kick)

Fourth Quarter
Florida: Ash 41-yard pass from Reaves (kick failed)

	UM	UF
First downs	18	20
Rushing yardage	160	55
Passing yardage	89	241
Comp-Att-Int	11-27-2	19-37-0
Fumbles lost	0	3

FLORIDA 17, FLORIDA STATE 15:

Oct. 16, 1971 at Gainesville   (65,109)

	1st	2nd	3rd	4th	Total
Florida State	0	0	0	15	15
Florida	0	14	0	3	17

First Quarter
none

Second Quarter
Florida: Rich 1-yard run (kick failed)
Florida: Barr 26-yard fumble recovery (Durrance pass from Reaves)

Third Quarter
none

Fourth Quarter
Florida State: Magalski 3-yard run (Fontes kick)
Florida: Franco 42-yard field goal
Florida State: Dawson 6-yard pass from Huff (Dawson pass from Huff)

	FSU	UF
First downs	19	12
Rushing yardage	170	152
Passing yardage	184	44
Comp-Att-Int	22-40-1	4-11-0
Fumbles lost	4	0

FLORIDA 45, MIAMI 16:

Nov. 27, 1971 at Miami   (37,710)

	1st	2nd	3rd	4th	Total
Florida	7	10	14	14	45
Miami	0	0	8	8	16

First Quarter
Florida: Durrance 10-yard pass from Reaves (Franco kick)

Second Quarter
Florida: Durrance 9-yard pass from Reaves (Franco kick)
Florida: Franco 47-yard field goal

Third Quarter
Florida: Durrance 12-yard pass from Reaves (Franco kick)
Florida: Reaves 17-yard pass from Durrance (Franco kick)
Miami: Foreman 1-yard run (Beckman pass from Hornibrook)

Fourth Quarter
Florida: Kendrick 1-yard pass from Reaves (Franco kick)
Florida: Clark 82-yard punt return (Franco kick)
Miami: Hornibrook 8-yard run (Perkins pass from Hornibrook)

	UF	UM
First downs	24	14
Rushing yardage	66	191
Passing yardage	365	19
Comp-Att-Int	34-52-3	1-14-2
Fumbles lost	2	1

FLORIDA STATE 21, MIAMI 14:

Nov. 8, 1974 at Miami (17,985)

	1st	2nd	3rd	4th	Total
Florida State	7	7	0	7	21
Miami	0	0	0	14	14

First Quarter
Florida State: Bright 14-yard run (Askin kick)

Second Quarter
Florida State: Goldsmith 48-yard pass from Mathieson (Askin kick)

Third Quarter
none

Fourth Quarter
Miami: Beckman 77-yard pass from Glover (Dennis kick)
Florida State: Leggett 1-yard run (Askin kick)
Miami: August 80-yard pass from Marcantonio (Dennis kick)

	FSU	UM
First downs	18	15
Rushing yardage	232	130
Passing yardage	172	240
Comp-Att-Int	12-22-2	11-23-2
Fumbles lost	0	1

FLORIDA STATE 37, FLORIDA 9:

Dec. 3, 1977 at Gainesville (63,563)

	1st	2nd	3rd	4th	Total
Florida State	10	7	7	13	37
Florida	0	9	0	0	9

First Quarter
Florida State: Unglaub 35-yard pass from Woodham (Cappelen kick)
Florida State: Cappelen 47-yard field goal

Second Quarter
Florida: Yepremian 32-yard field goal
Florida State: Overby 4-yard pass from Jordan (Cappelen kick)
Florida: Yepremian 50-yard field goal
Florida: Yepremian 41-yard field goal

Third Quarter
Florida State: Overby 20-yard pass from Jordan (Cappelen kick)

Fourth Quarter
Florida State: Lyles 1-yard run (Cappelen kick)
Florida State: Overby 20-yard pass from Jordan (Cappelen kick)

	FSU	UF
First downs	27	10
Rushing yardage	234	141
Passing yardage	344	59
Comp-Att-Int	20-31-1	6-19-0
Fumbles lost	1	1

MIAMI 22, FLORIDA 21:

Dec. 2, 1978 at Gainesville (47,815)

	1st	2nd	3rd	4th	Total
Miami	0	3	13	6	22
Florida	14	7	0	0	21

First Quarter
Florida: Collinsworth 11-yard pass fromn Groves (Yepremian kick)
Florida: Stephens 37-yard pass from Groves (Yepremian kick)

Second Quarter
Miami: Miller 21-yard field goal
Florida: Collinsworth 9-yard pass from Groves (Yepremian kick)

Third Quarter
Miami: Anderson 3-yard pass from McMillian (Miller kick)
Miami: Miller 37-yard field goal
Miami: Miller 43-yard field goal
Miami: Anderson 8-yard run (pass failed)

	UM	UF
First downs	14	16
Rushing yardage	178	128
Passing yardage	39	133
Comp-Att-Int	7-21-3	8-30-7
Fumbles lost	0	3

MIAMI 10, FLORIDA STATE 9:

Sept. 27, 1980 at Miami (50,008)

	1st	2nd	3rd	4th	Total
Florida State	0	0	3	6	9
Miami	0	7	3	0	10

First Quarter
none

Second Quarter
Miami: Kelly 1-yard run (Miller kick)

Third Quarter
Florida State: Capece 26-yard field goal
Miami: Miller 22-yard field goal

Fourth Quarter
Florida State: Childers 11-yard pass from Stockstill (pass failed)

	FSU	UM
First downs	10	15
Rushing yardage	25	109
Passing yardage	182	182
Comp-Att-Int	19-30-0	14-26-1
Fumbles lost	2	2

MIAMI 31, FLORIDA 7:
Nov. 29, 1980 at Gainesville   (56,437)

	1st	2nd	3rd	4th	Total
Miami	10	12	0	9	31
Florida	7	0	0	0	7

First Quarter
Florida: Young 15-yard pass from Peace (Clark kick)
Miami: Joiner 19-yard pass from Kelly (Miller kick)
Miami: Miller 32-yard field goal

Second Quarter
Miami: Rush 1-yard run (kick failed)
Miami: Walker 16-yard pass from Kelly (pass failed)

Third Quarter
none

Fourth Quarter
Miami: Roan 5-yard run (kick failed)
Miami: Miller 35-yard field goal

	UM	UF
First downs	23	20
Rushing yardage	194	70
·Passing yardage	191	239
Comp-Att-Int	13-21-1	19-41-3
Fumbles lost	1	1

MIAMI 17, FLORIDA STATE 16:
Nov. 11, 1983 at Tallahassee   (57,333)

	1st	2nd	3rd	4th	Total
Miami	7	0	7	3	17
Florida State	2	7	7	0	16

First Quarter
Miami: Bentley 1-yard run (Davis kick)
Florida State: safety; Ponder blocked punt out of end zone

Second Quarter
Florida State:Greg Allen 3-yard run (Hall kick)

Third Quarter
Florida State: Davis 1-yard run (Hall kick)
Miami: Eddie Brown 37-yard pass from Kosar (Davis kick)

Fourth Quarter
Miami:Davis 19-yard field goal

	UM	FSU
First downs	19	22
Rushing yardage	66	282
Passing yardage	243	146
Comp-Att-Int	21-35-1	14-24-0
Fumbles lost	0	0

FLORIDA 17, FLORIDA STATE 13:
Nov. 29, 1986 at Tallahassee   (62,307)

	1st	2nd	3rd	4th	Total
Florida	7	3	0	7	17
Florida State	3	7	3	0	13

First Quarter
Florida: Gould 8-yard run (Dawson kick)
Florida State:Schmidt 36-yard field goal

Second Quarter
Florida:Dawson 19-yard field goal
Florida State: Smith 1-yard run (Schmidt kick)

Third Quarter
Florida State: Schmidt 21-yard field goal

Fourth Quarter
Florida: Nattiel 18-yard pass from Bell (Dawson kick)

	UF	FSU
First downs	14	14
Rushing yardage	136	200
Passing yardage	65	48
Comp-Att-Int	8-17-1	5-16-1
Fumbles lost	0	0

MIAMI 26, FLORIDA STATE 25:
Oct. 3, 1987 at Tallahassee   (62,561)

	1st	2nd	3rd	4th	Total
Miami	3	0	8	15	26
Florida State	0	10	9	6	25

First Quarter
Miami:Cox 29-yard field goal

Second Quarter
Florida State: D. Williams 1-yard run (Schmidt kick)
Florida State: Schmidt 36-yard field goal

Third Quarter
Florida State: A. Williams 5-yard blocked punt return (kick failed)
Florida State:S chmidt 25-yard field goal
Miami:B ratton 49-yard pass from Walsh (B. Blades pass from Walsh)

Fourth Quarter
Miami:Irvin 26-yard pass from Walsh (W. Williams pass from Walsh)
Miami: Irvin 73-yard pass from Walsh (Cox kick)
Florida State:Lewis 18-yard pass from McManus (pass failed)

	UM	FSU
First downs	11	25
Rushing yardage	52	225
Passing yardage	254	201
Comp-Att-Int	13-29-0	16-24-1
Fumbles lost	0	1

MIAMI 31, FLORIDA STATE 0:
Sept. 3, 1988 at Miami   (77,836)

	1st	2nd	3rd	4th	Total
Florida State	0	0	0	0	0
Miami	3	14	7	7	31

First Quarter
Miami: Huerta 39-yard field goal
Second Quarter
Miami: Gary 2-yard run (Huerta kick)
Miami: Chudzinski 19-yard pass from Walsh
(Huerta kick)
Third Quarter
Miami: Conley 5-yard pass from Walsh
(Huerta kick)
Fourth Quarter
Miami:P. Smith 17-yard pass from Erickson
(Huerta kick)

	FSU	UM
First downs	12	25
Rushing yardage	42	184
Passing yardage	200	266
Comp-Att-Int	18-36-5	22-41-0
Fumbles lost	1	1

FLORIDA STATE 24, MIAMI 10:
Oct. 28, 1989 at Tallahassee

	1st	2nd	3rd	4th	Total
Miami	10	0	0	0	10
Florida State	14	0	7	3	24

First Quarter
Florida State: Carter 37-yard run (Andrews kick)
Miami: Hill 8-yard run (Huerta kick)
Florida State: Bennett 1-yard run (Andrews kick)
Miami: Huerta 44-yard field goal
Second Quarter
none
Third Quarter
Florida State: Lee 1-yard run (Andrews kick)
Fourth Quarter
Florida State: Andrews 41-yard field goal

	UM	FSU
First downs	26	23
Rushing yardage	129	220
Passing yardage	208	134
Comp-Att-Int	23-48-4	8-21-1
Fumbles lost	2	1

MIAMI 17, FLORIDA STATE 16:
Nov. 16, 1991 at Tallahassee   (63,442)

	1st	2nd	3rd	4th	Total
Miami	7	0	0	10	17
Florida State	3	7	3	3	16

First Quarter
Miami: McGuire 2-yard run (Huerta kick)
Florida State: Thomas 25-yard field goal
Second Quarter
Florida State: Moore 1-yard run (Huerta kick)
Third Quarter
Florida State: Thomas 31-yard field goal
Fourth Quarter
Florida State: Thomas 20-yard field goal
Miami: Huerta 45-yard field goal
Miami: Jones 1-yard run (Huerta kick)

	UM	FSU
First downs	21	21
Rushing yardage	165	137
Passing yardage	145	228
Comp-Att-Int	14-27-2	18-27-1
Fumbles lost	1	0

FLORIDA 14, FLORIDA STATE 9:
Nov. 30, 1991 at Gainesville   (85,461)

	1st	2nd	3rd	4th	Total
Florida State	0	3	0	6	9
Florida	0	7	7	0	14

First Quarter
none
Second Quarter
Florida State: Thomas 19-yard field goal
Florida: Rhett 3-yard run (Czyzewski kick)
Third Quarter
Florida: Houston 72-yard pass from Matthews
(Czyzewski kick)
Fourth Quarter
Florida State:Lee 25-yard pass from Weldon
(pass failed)

	FSU	UF
First downs	20	16
Rushing yardage	37	117
Passing yardage	305	208
Comp-Att-Int	24-51-1	13-30-3
Fumbles lost	1	0

SUNSHINE SHOOTOUTS

218